Winning with Data

For many years, sports rights owners have had an 'if you build it, they will come' attitude, suggesting they take their fans for granted. Combined with advances in broadcasting quality, digital marketing, and social media, this has resulted in diminishing attendances and participation levels. The use of CRM (Customer Relationship Management), BI (Business Intelligence) and Data Analytics has therefore become integral to doing business in sports, emulating the approach used by brands such as Amazon, Netflix, and Spotify. Technology has made the world a smaller place; clubs and teams can now connect with their fans anywhere in the world, allowing them to grow their marketplace, but they operate in an 'attention economy' where there's too much choice and engagement is key.

This book sets out to share the processes and principles the sports industry uses to capitalise on the natural loyalty it creates. Case studies and commentary from around the world are used to demonstrate some of the practices implemented by the world's leading sports brands including clubs Arsenal and the San Antonio Spurs, the governing bodies of UEFA and Special Olympics International, and the MLS and NHL.

With a focus on our unique challenges coupled with the opportunities the use of data creates, this book is essential reading for professionals within the sports industry.

Fiona Green has worked in the sports industry for 30 years, representing rights owners across sponsorship, TV rights, and merchandise. Fiona moved into the field of CRM and BI over seven years ago and now runs a specialist sports consultancy, Winners, based in Manchester.

Winning with Data

CRM and Analytics for the Business of Sports

Fiona Green

Routledge
Taylor & Francis Group

LONDON AND NEW YORK

First published 2019
by Routledge
2 Park Square, Milton Park, Abingdon, Oxon OX14 4RN

and by Routledge
711 Third Avenue, New York, NY 10017

Routledge is an imprint of the Taylor & Francis Group, an informa business

British Library Cataloguing-in-Publication Data
A catalogue record for this book is available from the British Library

Library of Congress Cataloging-in-Publication Data
A catalog record has been requested for this book

ISBN: 978-1-138-09063-7 (hbk)
ISBN: 978-1-315-10853-7 (ebk)

Typeset in Bembo
by Swales & Willis Ltd, Exeter, Devon, UK
Printed by CPI Group (UK) Ltd, Croydon CR0 4YY

Contents

Figures

Foreword

I love sports. I have not only been a sports fan for over 60 years – diehard New York Yankees, NY Giants, NY Knicks, NY Rangers – but I've been interested in the culture, the literature and the business of sports. In fact, the fascination I've had with not only the games themselves but the business led me, due to a fortuitous set of circumstances, to become the only non-sports business professional on the Global Board of Advisors of the largest, and I might add the best, sports business professionals organization – The SEAT Community (Sports Entertainment Alliance in Technology).

That's where I met Fiona Green. She called me out on the stage of one of SEAT's annual conferences, we met, and I have been impressed ever since. You'll see why in a minute.

There is no question in my mind that someone – she – needed to write a book on CRM for the sports world. Sports has one unique trait that no other industry has, and every other industry would kill for. They have fans from the get go. I've been active in the CRM world for two plus decades and if someone asks me (as they often have) what would be the optimal customer strategy, I would tell them – aim at creating advocates, settle for loyal customers and know that, if done well, it will leave satisfied customers in its wake. But sports franchises don't have to create advocates – they have the most passionate advocates in the world – their fans. These are people who root for teams out of nostalgia, civic pride, heritage, reasons known only to them, which could range from that they were enthralled by a player when they were little on a particular team who wasn't in their hometown and thus rooted for that team their whole life, to perhaps that they went to a stadium and just met their future spouse there. Who knows? The beauty of sports is that, whatever the reason, the fans love, love, love their teams – and as often as not are students of their particular sport.

But, we often forget that sports are a business – and there are few franchises that are truly all that big. Sure, there is Real Madrid, Manchester United, Dallas Cowboys and (of course) the New York Yankees that meet what I would call in the business world an enterprise standard, but beyond that the vast majority of teams are mid-sized businesses with revenues to match. So, for example, the largest three sports franchises in the world, according to the 2017 Forbes annual ranking are:

1   Dallas Cowboys ($4.2 billion)
2   New York Yankees ($3.7 billion)
3   Manchester United ($3.69 billion)

The average value of a sports team by league according to Forbes in April 2017 is the following:

4   NFL $2,390,000,000
5   MLB $1,540,000,000
6   Soccer $1,470,000,000
7   NBA $1,360,000,000
8   NHL $520,000,000

This isn't change, but it is small by comparison with what fans think that these franchises are worth. A lot of that comes due to the outsized money that the teams give to their athletes, salaries that are beyond the imagination of even well-paid workers in a normal professional environment. Part of the inflated expectations that fans have is due to their own passion and commitment to the team, and in an age where social validation and communication and conversation about this passion is commonplace on social media, the fans' expectations for the teams are far greater than the teams can deliver.

If you get past the athletes and look at the business staff of any given team, large or small, you find a small number of employees devoted to large areas of the teams' business. So, for example, a typical team in a professional league in the US has perhaps three–five people at the most devoted to marketing. Not a lot given the public visibility of any professional franchise and the need to be competitively visible.

Yet we live in a digital age, and we live in an era of economic uncertainty, and sports is not a required spend for our hard-earned dollars (or whatever currency you might use). It is discretionary and competes with not only other teams in our city but movies, dinners out, concerts and even staying at home and doing nothing.

So, here's the dilemma of professional and, in a different way, collegiate sports. You have companies that, when it comes to revenues, are mid-market sized. You have fans who are so passionate about the clubs that they have what I would call enterprise-level expectations of what the team needs to provide, and you have small business-sized staffs devoted to the business and operations side of the house. And the teams are competing with all discretionary income spending, including none at all. So, enterprise customer expectations, mid-sized company revenues, small-business sized staff and insane competition for revenue. Not the most effective combinations when you are competing to keep your almost entitled fans happy.

This is where CRM comes in – and I say this without hesitation. The value of CRM, whatever your definition of it, is as an enabler of capabilities that make your business operations and your interactions with fans not only work more effectively, but at the same time allow for timely communications with the fan base. Not only does that mean happier fans because you are showing them some active love, but happy employees (and management) because you have a way of organizing those interactions and transactions individually via storing them in an accessible customer record. Having that information allows sports teams to tailor what they offer those fans, e.g., their season ticket packages or merchandise (depending on the league), and to provide the kinds of automated processes and enabled systems that give the sales people a leg up on who to focus on so they don't waste their energy on long shots, the marketing people a reach that allows targeted campaigns to millions of people potentially that are in specific communications formats – email, social media, websites, that resonate with those same fans and customer service – meaning solving problems or dealing with real-time issues that show up – usually on social media. Customer relationship management gives you as a team or league or other kind of franchise the means to handle all that efficiently and effectively.

But, because sports is a different creature than most other industries using CRM, Fiona Green is the one who needed to be writing this book. She has the experience, the insights and the writing chops to make sure that you not only understand CRM per se but understand how it applies to the world of sports in the way that it is supposed to do. A generic book on CRM (I wrote that one) won't do. What Fiona Green does here will. Pay attention to her because, while we know that winning teams bring in the cash from the fans, that doesn't happen every year and yet you have to be playing on the field and running your business every year. Fiona tells you not just how to think about it but what to do. Then it will be up to you to do it. But if you do, then you'll understand why a book on CRM in sports needed to be written – and was by someone insanely well qualified to write it – and you will be grateful.

Ciao.
Paul Greenberg
Managing Principal, The 56 Group, LLC
Author, *CRM at the Speed of Light* (4th Edition)

Preface

In 2011, when I first entered the world of CRM in sports, I struggled to understand the different terminology I heard and read, and the different systems and processes being used. I would constantly Google 'CRM' in the hope that the next result would somehow shed some light on what was a mystery to me at that time. Instead, I found myself trying to determine the difference between software like Microsoft Dynamics and SAP, Salesforce and Sage, and wondering why I kept reading that CRM projects fail and email marketing is dead.

My usual sense of logic was challenged when I started working with data, and I even battled with the prolific use of acronyms so common in the world of CRM. I should have been used to them. At that time I'd already been in the sports industry for 24 years and, boy, have we got our fair share of them.

These memories are what inspired me to write this book. I decided that if I could help just a few of you who are new to this game get to a position of understanding quicker than I did, then the long days and sleepless nights would have been worth it. And if, in the process of tending to the uninitiated, my words also help the more experienced of you move further along in your development, then I'll consider that a bonus. If any CRM veterans can say I validated a thought for them, or provided additional insight, I'll feel like I've scored a hat trick. For England!

This book does not set out to tell you everything you need to know about CRM. You'd need quite a few books, each with a different focus, to achieve that. Instead this book aims to:

1   Dispel a common myth about the use of CRM. This is not the first time you'll hear me say that it's not just about technology. Nor is it just about the data. Having a strategy, systematic processes and the right culture are just as important to be successful.
2   Provide a helicopter view of the way the sports industry uses data to make decisions and engage with fans, customers and participants. This is different to how we use data for performance. There are many great books out there that cover that subject – this one is strictly for off-the-field.

3   Provide real-world examples that put the theory into perspective. Thanks
    to the generosity of UEFA, Mic Conetta of Arsenal FC, MLS, Special
    Olympics International, to name just a few, you'll learn how these rights
    owners approach the unique challenges in their organisation or sport,
    applying the different principles discussed in this book.

Both as an individual and with Winners, the CRM, Business Intelligence and
Data Analytics consultancy I set up to service sports' rights owners, I'm passionate about sharing knowledge with anyone and everyone – our clients,
students, fellow professionals, even our competitors. You'll often see us out at
conferences and other speaking events, recording podcasts, and writing blog
posts for both our own website and others.

   This isn't just a philanthropic leaning – it's a nod to all the people who have
shared their knowledge with me along the way. I've been in the sports industry
for over 30 years and have been fortunate enough to be mentored or helped
along by some amazing and generous people. From Paul Fletcher, the scorer
of what many believe was Burnley FC's best ever goal, himself a published
author of several sports management books who never fails to motivate and
inspire, through to Tony Stephens, the revered football agent who over 20
years ago first said to me, 'don't chase the money and it will come'. Along the
way there's also been Alan Pascoe MBE, Olympic medallist and former owner
of several highly successful sports agencies, who has always been generous with
his time when I've requested it. There's Ilika Copeland, a business professional
who has been consistent in her willingness to offer me any and all types of
advice, at any time of the day. More recently, Christine Stoffel, one of the first
female CIOs in US sports and owner of SEAT, the must-attend technology,
CRM and digital conference for rights owners, who enabled me to network
with some of the most advanced thinkers in the use of data in sports. And,
of course, Paul Greenberg who so generously provided the foreword for this
book, an undisputed thought leader of CRM, best-selling author of the 'bible'
of our industry *CRM at the Speed of Light*, and owner of the highly anticipated
annual award, CRM Watchlist.

   One final influencer who is sadly no longer with us, not only set me on
the path that led me to where I am today but did the same for several of my
competitors. More than that, he was the visionary that first established a business to introduce the UK sports industry to CRM but, unfortunately, he passed
away before he could fully make his impact. Stuart Dalrymple, founder of The
Goodform Group, I salute you.

   I've been a member of a team all my life, so it seems natural that in setting
the scene for this book I'd highlight those that have given me immeasur-
able support over the years. Continuing on that theme, I'd also like to thank
Winners' amazing clients for selecting us to work with them, the founding
partners that helped me set the business up, our incredible team of passionate,

loyal and brilliant staff, my professional network, always there to brainstorm, help, challenge and debate, and of course my family and friends who have had my back every step of the way.

Let's turn the page and start talking CRM.

Fiona Green
16 February 2018

Chapter 1

CRM for the digital age

CRM: an introduction

In this digital world people happily tell us what they're doing through their online activity and social media. We can see what they're doing through behavioural analytics and when we analyse all the data available to us, we've got the closest thing we're ever going to get to a crystal ball.

Seventy years ago, when George Orwell first wrote his immortal words 'Big Brother is Watching You', he was referring to the authorities of a fictional totalitarian state in his acclaimed novel *1984*. Back then, his readers must have scoffed at the thought of anyone being able to watch them constantly but fast forward to 2018 and anyone can watch anyone else. In fact, not only do we know what people are doing, we can predict what they may want to do next.

That's the theme of this book – that we can now engage with people at a very deep and personal level, giving us the ability to tell them what they want to hear at a time when they need to hear it. This in turn increases the chances that these people – our customers, fans or other stakeholders – will then do what we want them to, whether it's to spend, review, participate or interact.

To quote the late Peter Drucker, an industry great, 'for 50 years, Information Technology has focused on the T in IT . . . The new information revolution focuses on the I' (Drucker, 2001). Drucker was an oft-quoted international management consultant described by *Forbes* as the founder of modern management, so when he said that Information, rather than Technology, will be the new focus of the IT industries, we knew we should sit up and pay attention.

This is a great starting point for any book about CRM (Customer Relationship Management), BI (Business Intelligence) or BA (Business Analytics). It perfectly demonstrates how we've moved from an era of technological focus to one of data and insight. Drucker died in 2005, but the use of data for business is still largely in its infancy in many sports organisations. That tells us plainly how far behind we are in this area. Back in 2012, *Harvard Business Review* published an article famously titled 'Data scientist: the sexiest job of the 21st century' (Davenport and Patil, 2012), but, despite this, we are still catching up. Today the need for professionals who understand data in the sports industry is rapidly growing.

When discussing this issue with Adrian Wells, Marketing and Communications Director for the Cricket World Cup 2019, in a phone call on 24 November 2017, he confirmed he expects the importance of data to be critical to the success of the tournament and will be looking for appropriately skilled people:

> Data will underpin the Marketing, Communications and Ticketing department to ensure we are laser focused on our fans and driving engagement and ultimately purchase. When recruiting the team to deliver the plans, a detailed understanding of CRM and leveraging data is a core skill set I look for in every team member. I believe this will be a common approach across the sports industry in the future.
>
> (Wells, 2017, 24 November)

As we look to bring CRM into the sports industry, how can we learn from the mistakes and the successes of the many businesses that have gone before us in their quest to become data-driven organisations? Let's start by looking at what CRM means and, more importantly, what it means for sports rights owners.

Gartner, the leading IT research and advisory firm, define CRM as:

> A business strategy that optimises revenue and profitability while promoting customer satisfaction and loyalty. CRM technologies enable strategy, and identify and manage customer relationships, in person or virtually. CRM software provides functionality to companies in four segments: sales, marketing, customer service and digital commerce.
>
> (Gartner, 2017)

I like this definition for two key reasons:

1   It uses the word strategy at the start. Too often we come across sports organisations that don't have a strategy or, if the management has defined a strategy, it hasn't filtered down to the operational teams.
2   It emphasises technology as an enabler not a driver. For too long, business decisions have been driven by technology when it should be the other way around.

Ed Thompson, a Gartner analyst, discussed the definition of CRM with me via email on 15 December 2017. He advised that I shouldn't worry so much about the accepted definition of CRM and, instead, focus on coming up with my own. At Winners, the company I founded over five years ago to support the sports industry in this area, we simply define CRM as 'getting the right message, to the right person, at the right time'.

We don't claim ownership of that now ubiquitous phrase. I've tried to trace the origins and have identified three points of reference. In 2004 the deceased mathematician Benoit Mandlebrot, when interviewed for the book *Candid Science IV: Conversations with Famous Physicists*, said 'scientific creation presupposed three elements – "the right person, the right place and the right time"' (Hargittai and Hargittai, 2004). The November 2005 edition of the *Harvard Business Review* led the marketing section with an article titled 'The perfect message at the perfect moment' (Kalyanam and Zweben, 2005), and then Jerry Della Femina, the American advertising executive, observed in a *Financial Times* article in 2013 that it's now possible to target adverts 'to the right person at the right time in the right place' (Femina, 2013).

It's also not the shortest definition of CRM. That honour goes to Don Peppers, globally recognised as a leading authority on marketing and business competition, who refers to the 'accurate but concise *treating different customers differently*' (Peppers, 2014). This book builds on these ideas and will chart how you can get the right message to the right person at the right time, with the aim of achieving your business objectives.

But what about the right platform? In a world where the term omni-channel is universally used and disliked in equal measure, we don't feel the need to refer to channels or platforms individually because the world is now channel-blind. We switch from email to Facebook, Twitter to Snapchat, Instagram to Pinterest, and mobile app to desktop without a second's thought. We don't care about the channel; we just want the message, content, or inter-action. It's implicit that we know what channel to use.

So, we've got the right message, the right person, the right time and the right platform. It is now left for us to make sure these messages work to achieve our business objectives. Unlike many other industries, sports organisations are not all about selling. The original meaning of CRM, coined back in the early 1990s, was about B2B (Business to Business) software; they were programmes that helped sales reps stay on top of their leads as they moved through the sales process, from initial contact to contract signed. This has led to CRM strategies and processes focussing on sales; selling larger quantities, cross-selling, selling more efficiently, and predicting how sales can increase.

Operating in the sports industry however, we're acutely aware that the pri-mary business objective isn't always to sell. Sometimes the focus is on increas-ing participation, demonstrating governance and improving reputations. While we know each of these will indirectly bring financial reward, the approach you take to upgrade a fan who has bought a ticket, or one who might spend more for a VIP experience, can seem very different to how you would encourage a retired player to become a coach, or a parent to become a volunteer. But, despite the different end goals, these objectives utilise similar CRM processes that promote engagement in all its forms, and it is this that leads to the desired end result.

There's no doubt that the principle of a sales funnel, the concept of nur-turing a prospect to a sale and minimising attrition while maximising repeat purchases, are all valid but, where we previously might have focussed purely on CRM to optimise ROI (Return on Investment), we now hear more about ROO (Return on Opportunity) and ROE (Return on Experience).

While working with one of Winners' clients, a major rights owner sponsored by Adidas, Colin Rattigan, VP of Consumer Engagement, told me that his KPIs (Key Performance Indicators) are not based on $s or €s, but based on engagement metrics and data. When engagement is the objective, revenue is the result.

Intelligent customer engagement

In May 2016 at the CRM Evolution Conference in Washington DC, I was fortunate enough to speak about the use of the term CRM with Jujhar Singh, former General Manager for Microsoft Dynamics, North America. I questioned the relevance of the three-letter acronym in the digital age and he agreed that it was outdated, adding that 'we don't call it CRM in our office – we call it intelligent customer engagement' (Singh, 2016, 24 May). Shortly afterwards, when Dynamics 365 launched in November 2016, those three letters, CRM, had been dropped from the product name.

So, the term CRM is no longer just about the software that an organisation uses to manage its customers and sales processes. It's become more of a collective that describes an entire business approach, driven by access to unlimited data, multiple digital engagement channels and, most crucially, the age of the savvy consumer.

I'll discuss this more later but, for now, consider that while sports rights owners may aspire to Amazon, Netflix and Spotify levels of engagement, we don't do it with an exclusive focus on the sales funnel. We have to think of engagement as a primary focus that will then lead to the successful achievement of our business goals and objectives.

Why now?

The sports marketing industry has been around for many years. While the 1984 Los Angeles Olympics holds claim to being the first US event to generate broadcasting fees, the to-the-death arena fights of ancient Rome could also be considered a foundation to what's now a multi-billion-dollar global business. Regardless of whether you believe the catalyst was our first formalised approach to commercialising an event, or wealthy aristocrats sponsoring gladiators, why has CRM become so important to the sports world that it now deserves its own book?

The sports industry is facing a lot of challenges:

1   **We're not turning out**. MLB (Major League Baseball), NFL (National Football League), Test Cricket, French Rugby, NASCAR, the BNP Paribas Open, to name but a few, are all suffering declining audiences (Koba, 2013).

2   **Our attention spans are shortening**. According to a 2015 study by Microsoft, the average person's attention span, thanks to our growing dependence on technology and social media, is now just eight seconds — less than that of a goldfish, and less than the 12 seconds it was at the start of the millennium (Watson, 2016).

3   **We're participating less**. In the UK, the number of people playing sport or exercising has decreased since the London 2012 Olympics and, across the Atlantic, the Sports and Fitness Industry Association reports that inactivity among children has nearly doubled since 2015 (SFIA, 2016).

4   **Customers want more**. Thanks to the amount of information that's available to us on any one of our connected devices, we have multiple options, so when we select one we expect it to meet our expectations.

Whether you have 2,000 or 200,000 fans, they're all individuals with different wants and needs. They expect you to know them. According to global CRM software brand Salesforce, 63% of millennials will share their data in return for personalised offers and discounts (McGinnis, 2016). They expect tailored recommendations and offers.

But, despite these challenges, there are also many opportunities. This is where I see CRM playing a huge role in shoring up our business models, helping us secure financial sustainability and ensuring we don't have to rely on our performance on the field to ensure performance off it.

We have passion. Lots of it. Sports can move fans to tears of joy or sadness. While global consumer brands from Coca-Cola to Visa have to pay for media attention, conjuring up storylines when launching a new product, a club can announce a new signing, an athlete can produce a personal best and their fans on the other side of the world will be discussing it before a web page has time to load.

We have natural loyalty. While any one of the individual companies in the FTSE 100 could purchase all the football clubs in the English Premier League, they can't buy what Arsenal, Chelsea and Everton have in abundance — loyalty. Of course, it's not just elite football. Worcester Warriors, Glamorgan Cricket, Team GB, the All Blacks, the Wildcats (to name just a few), all have fans that would go without food before they would go without their season ticket. Barclays and Bank of America, Marks & Spencer and Home Depot, Tesco and BestBuy, Vodafone and Sprint can only dream of that kind of allegiance.

We don't have to buy column inches, likes, retweets and follows. Whatever your frame of reference, when a club announces a new midfielder, quarterback, pitcher or bowler, the media have dissected the decision before the athlete's chosen their locker.

We have an abundance of content. We don't need to hire PR teams and ad agencies to conjure up stories and creative narratives. We create images that are shared at the speed of light and memories that truly last a lifetime.

The use of CRM has proven to be so powerful in building custo for companies who don't have half of what the sport industry has natu we believe when we truly embrace the use of data the impact will be significant. We'll win back our audiences, get more people on the field and remain our fans' number one choice when it comes to their focus, attention and share of disposable income, because we'll be giving them what they want.

Amazon's approach to CRM

When I talk about aspirational CRM, I often refer to Amazon. Even though at Winners we work with clients that range from global organisations representing our biggest sports, to niche rights owners that have less than a dozen back-office staff, we talk about a business approach that's the same for everybody. It's just the scale and focus that's different.

With 304 million customers at the end of 2015 (Statista, 2017), Amazon makes it easy for you to say 'yes', no matter what the question. When you visit their website you see a simple easy-to-use interface with one-click ordering and single sign-on across their merchant base. They make product recommendations based on your previous browsing and order history. When you purchase a product, you receive a series of notifications that inform you about the status of your order. You know when they've received your request, processed the order, dispatched your package, what day you're going to receive it and, finally, what time you can expect it to arrive. They even tell you when a new product has arrived that you will really want, even before you knew it existed.

This approach is enabled by Amazon's CRM ecosystem that captures and analyses customer data and uses it to instantly personalise a user's digital experience. Their system deals with most customer queries before the need for human intervention, providing access to order history and an automated returns process that supports an incredible level of customer service. But, crucially, it's not just the software that drives Amazon's approach. It's their culture. It's their data-driven DNA. And it's their focus on the customer.

Jeff Bezos, Founder and CEO of Amazon, in a letter written in 2016 to the company's shareholders, called out the biggest advantage to taking a customer-centric approach by stating:

> Customers are always beautifully, wonderfully dissatisfied, even when they report being happy and business is great. Even when they don't yet know it, customers want something better, and your desire to delight customers will drive you to invent on their behalf.
>
> (Bezos, 2017)

He calls their approach a 'True Customer Obsession'. Does this sound familiar? Does a reference to wonderfully dissatisfied customers wanting something better sound at all familiar when it comes to the sports industry? In a telephone interview on 10 October 2017 with Mark Bradley of the

Fan Experience Company, I asked him how far the sports industry is from delighting our customers and rewarding them for their passion and loyalty:

> Many sports fans feel that they are held at an arm's length from the object of their love. Talk to any long-term fan of any sports team and while they all might not use the same words, they will all be able to articulate what their club STANDS for – what its values are. And here's the problem. Fans may know what their teams' values are, but how many owners do? Fans want their sports teams to honour the shield or respect the badge, but most sports teams just want to fill the stadium.
>
> There's only one question that matters: "Does my club/league/sport/ governing body consistently act in ways that show that it has the best interests of its fans at its heart?"
>
> (Bradley, 2017)

Bradley's sentiment is the underlying theme of this book. The use of CRM, business intelligence and data analytics is how we'll answer his question. He goes on to add:

> Other progressive growing businesses in other sectors do that because customer engagement is so important in a world where 80%+ businesses are now in the service sector. They can only prosper if the customer feels valued.
>
> When the customer feels valued – usually when adherence to core values ensures that their experiences continually convince them that their service provider has their best interests at heart – then their resulting emotional loyalty is so strong it TRANSCENDS financial incentives, like loyalty points and "money off".
>
> They trust. They forgive. They defend you. They may not say it (but they quietly love you). OK, so in these days of social media sniping and faceless message board terrorists, it might not be possible to get EVERYONE on board, but wouldn't we all appreciate the opportunities a positively engaged (majority) fan community would offer?
>
> In customer-driven organisations leaders talk about it all the time. Decisions are filtered through their brand values. There are customer value KPIs. Employees matter too and there is continuous open transparent dialogue between the service provider and its customers. Employees are recruited based on their values fit and rewarded when they live those values.
>
> The irony (or possibly even the explanation) is that by nature of our love for our teams, we already have the strongest levels of emotional loyalty and so maybe deep inside we genuinely feel there's no need to build it any further.
>
> Isn't it ironic then that the thing non-sports businesses envy us for the most, we simply take for granted. But the rewards for the sports business that genuinely embraces the values-driven approach will be immeasurable.
>
> (Ibid.)

The role of CRM in sponsorship

I've touched on the role of CRM to increase ticket sales and attendance, engagement and participation through rights owners communicating one-to-one with individuals, but there's another key focus area within every single sports organisation whether you're a member association, team, club, league, event or governing body: sponsorship.

Prior to moving into the CRM and BI space seven years ago, I worked primarily with rights owners, representing their sponsorship and media rights. When I discovered CRM, it was like a light bulb flashing on. I've said it 100 times before, and will continue to say it another 100 times, that if I'd known then what I know now I'd have made a lot more commission and it would have come a lot easier. True, 20 years ago we didn't have access to the data and technology that now enables our CRM processes, but it represents how strongly I feel about the significant impact this area will have (or for some rights owners, already has) on their ability to sell and leverage their sponsorships with greater effect. Sponsorship is one of the areas where I truly believe we'll see the biggest opportunities.

CRM in other industries

The global CRM software market is expected to reach $81.9 billion by 2025, up from $26.3 billion in 2015 (*Cision PR Newswire*, 2017). When you factor in the industry rule of thumb that you should expect to spend $1 on consulting related to implementation for every $1 in annual subscription costs, then you're looking at a lot of money to keep customers happy. But is it worth it? Let's take a quick look at some success stories in other industries.

Financial services

Asset management company Aegon, who manage approximately €816 billion in assets globally, is dependent on intelligent analytics to enhance sales performance and excellence. Aegon's global sales increased by more than 15% to €12 billion in 2016. According to Duncan Jarret, the UK Retail Managing Director at Aegon:

> Everyone has personalised dashboards powered by our CRM software, so they can see what business they are bringing in and how it relates to our overall goals. We can have more informed conversations about the dynamics we are seeing not only in our business but also in their businesses. This gives us a real competitive edge and helps us serve our end customers better.
>
> (Aegon, 2014)

Customer relationship management software underpins the entire opportunity process for Aegon's distribution operation – from forecasting and pipeline management to bid coordination and lead conversion. More than 3,500 new opportunities are logged every month. They've been using CRM software since 2008, and it's become fundamental to how they operate and grow their business (Aegon, 2014).

Retail

Customer relationship management has been growing as a business discipline at John Lewis, currently the UK's fifth largest retailer based on 2015/16 sales data (Wiggenraad, 2017). According to Chris Bates, Head of Customer Marketing, it's now used as the primary vehicle for new product launches.

Bates gives the example of when their Stratford store opened in 2011; 'above-the-line' was the predominant way to announce the launch, using mass media that included conventional advertising format. But just four years later in Birmingham they used a different approach with a focus on their loyalty scheme, *my John Lewis*, launched in 2013, targeting members within the area. Direct marketing was used to spread the word, with an exclusive preview for their members two days before the store opening. This resulted in a turnout that Bates says was 'phenomenal' (Fisher, 2015).

Now with close to 2 million members, the *my John Lewis* programme includes an innovative app that removes the need to carry a plastic card and includes the opportunity to store receipts and product guarantees digitally; a service that was identified as a problem-solver for their customers.

The UK's sixth largest retailer, Marks and Spencer, recently posted a 2.3% rise in clothing and homewares sales for the first time in two years (Wiggenraad, 2017). It's no coincidence that when their new CEO, Steve Rowe, started in 2016 he placed a lot of emphasis on analysing data to understand their customers better.

Nathan Anstell, Global Director of Loyalty, Customer Insight and Analytics at Marks and Spencer, is responsible for making sure his colleagues have access to the right customer data to enable them to make decisions, citing the importance of being able to demonstrate a direct link between 'a brilliant customer experience and delivery of results' (Tesseras, 2017).

Now accountable for their *Sparks* loyalty card, Anstell is able to produce data on how often people visit their stores, the merchandise they're interested in and, of course, what they're buying. Going further in his belief in the value of data, Anstell says:

> Good marketers in the future will need to have a really thorough understanding of different data sources and how to use them in their roles – it's a critical part of a marketer's tool kit. If I were to give someone who is coming into marketing advice, I would say understanding data and analytics right from the beginning of your career will hold you in really good stead.
>
> (Ibid.)

Telecommunications

The company EE (Everything Everywhere) went on record in 2014 publicising a 400% increase in mobile phone sales after implementing CRM with the rollout of new software to 11,000 customer agents in telesales and retail stores. They credit the initiative with helping to both triple the value of its customers and win new ones citing 4% less churn, an incremental £4 spend per customer and a 300% increase in the value of retained customers thanks to an integration between their retail and telephone sales channels. Furthermore, EE proposed that the CRM roll out helped improve customer engagement, reduced the use of more expensive outbound channels and improved customer satisfaction (Goodwin, 2014).

Suzanne Woolley, EE's Head of Customer Base Management, said:

> Ninety per cent of offers we sell in our service transactions are from our top three recommendations. We know our decision making is right. We are picking the right offers, picking relevant offers, and offers our customers are interested in.
>
> . . .
>
> Not only are we retaining the right customers, and we are retaining more of them, we are growing their value. And that is really important, and that is key to success of the system, and it's key to the acceptance of the tool we have had internally.
>
> (Ibid.)

Customer relationship management software takes into account a wide range of factors, including how customers use their phone, their lifestyle and their strategic value to EE, to automatically generate three recommended deals personalised to that customer. This allows EE to assess the contribution of a customer, their risk of leaving, and cost to service to create tailored budget and handset recommendations for each customer.

> As conversations progress and we learn more about the customer, we go through the loop and we talk to the customer about their needs, we refine that personal recommendation. We can connect that conversation across all of those channels. So regardless of which channel you go in, your browsing history is there, the offers you have had presented to you that you are thinking about are there for any other agent to pick up.
>
> (Ibid.)

Top industries that use software

Based on research undertaken in 2015 by Capterra, the retail industry is the biggest user of CRM, focussing on the ability to track purchase behaviour, cross-sell and up-sell, and offer loyalty programmes that provide customer rewards.

The next four biggest industries using CRM all operate in an environment where the purchase process is very complex. Business services, technology, financial services and manufacturing, with B2C (Business to Consumer) companies representing 60% of all research respondents, demonstrating the need for all businesses to understand their individual relationships. While there is a preconception that implementing CRM is a cost-heavy process, 52% of Capterra's respondents worked at organisations with less than $10 million in annual revenue (Hollar, 2015).

There are many preconceptions, but a major one is the amount of time CRM implementations take. At Winners we see this a lot with our clients. They usually underestimate, with six months being the most commonly proposed timeframe. However, according to 80% of Capterra's respondents, it took them up to 18 months to be up and running (ibid.). I'll look at this in more detail in a later chapter to discover why organisations' expectations rarely align with reality.

The most interesting element of Capterra's research for me involves the respondents' attitudes to social media functionality. One quarter of all respondents wanted more (ibid.). I'm a huge fan of social media (who wouldn't be?) but, as a CRM practitioner, until we can get more of the rich data generated by social media channels like Facebook, YouTube and Pinterest into our clients' CRM databases, it will continue to represent a silo to me. I talk more about this later (look for the introduction of a Data Management Platform, or DMP), but at the rate social media is developing, I expect my words will be out of date by the time you get there.

Case study: UEFA

The fundamentals of CRM in the digital age can sound relatively simple: getting the right message to the right person at the right time. But for sports organisations in particular, the media revolution that has enabled a vast and rapid extension of their visibility, popularity and reach, has also made that task an increasingly challenging one to accomplish.

With membership spanning 55 countries, a database of 21 million fans and an ambition to continue accelerating its current trajectory of commercial growth, European football's governing body UEFA is a prime example, not just of the complexities that sports organisations face in building one-to-one relationships with their supporters, but also of the processes they need to adopt in order to succeed.

This case study demonstrates some of the thought processes that UEFA had to go through when adopting their own approach to CRM.

Stakeholder relationships: CRM is not just about the fans

UEFA has had a clear vision for its CRM goals since it started developing its capabilities in the field in 2014. It faces on-going challenges in having to align its objectives with the interests of three important stakeholder groups:

members, sponsors and media partners. I interviewed Peter Willems, Head of Marketing Activities and Sponsorship in UEFA's Marketing Division on 12 October 2017 at UEFA's Nyon headquarters.

> Our digital vision is quite straightforward – we want to engage with football fans everywhere. This means building lasting and valuable relationships built on authentic two-way communication with both our current fans around the world and with those we don't yet have – fans of other sports, or other interests. We need to know where they are, what they're interested in and how we can connect with them in a way that makes it easy for them to connect with us.
>
>   . . .
>
> When you look at our relationship with our members – the 55 national associations – we also have a role there to support them in everything they do for the sport, whether it's the way they engage with their fans or the responsibility they have to grow the sport. We deliver this through a programme called UEFA GROW and CRM sits at the very heart of that.
>
> Secondly, our sponsors are absolutely crucial to our work here and while they still value our events for the traditional opportunities we provide – brand exposure, access to tickets, exclusive experiences – they want access to our fans on a one-to-one basis. This will be achieved through our digital channels and the unique relationship we have with our fans driven by what we know about them and that two-way communication we talked about.

The pace of change in digital technology however, means Willems is also happy to admit that UEFA does not yet have all the answers as far as media objectives for CRM are concerned. An open mind is essential to being able to react and adapt as new opportunities emerge due to the sport industries' recent adoption of data-driven practices.

> We haven't yet figured out how we use CRM with our media partners – the broadcasters that have helped us grow the European Championships, Champions League and Europa League into the biggest football properties in the world – but we're talking to them and trialling various approaches. What is clear is that OTT ('over-the-top' media broadcasting) is not just a buzzword – whether it's direct-to-consumer from UEFA, or via our trusted network of broadcasters – fans will be taking more control of what footage they see and when, and we have to be able to support their decisions and therefore help our broadcast partners with theirs.

Know your fans, and be able to reach them

Delivering the right message to the right person at the right time is primarily an issue of knowledge. It is only by understanding the customer, their habits and preferences, that the organisation can determine what sort of offers a customer will best respond to and identify the moment at which they will be most receptive to them.

To achieve the necessary level of customer knowledge, Willems talks about how UEFA has placed a strong emphasis on the quality of its database and the number of data points it can track.

> We certainly know more about our fans than we did before we adopted CRM. We've still got a long way to go but, of the 21 million fans we have in our database, we know the age and gender of nearly half of them, the location and language of over two thirds, and we even know the favourite teams of over a quarter of them.
>
> So, a clean and centralised database is definitely an achievement we can be proud of – making sure our individual data sources have standards that are aligned took some work but now we have that in place, the work needed to maintain the central source is minimised. Our next step will be to build out our Single Customer View, increase the level of automation, and potentially include unknown data with our known records.

Customer knowledge is of little value without the means to act on it, meaning an effective communication platform is essential to ensure the right message is actually delivered to the right person at the right time. For UEFA, this has meant prioritising email marketing.

> The engagement level we achieve through our email marketing programme is well above industry average, thanks to not just an increase in our activity, but a different approach – we don't blast emails out, we use segments that enable a targeted and personalised communication.
>
> Now we need to build on the success we've had with our email marketing programme – we even won a database marketing award for innovation in insight-driven emails – and roll-out the approach through our other digital channels. Our website is already optimised with a user log-in that holds valuable information to improve our fans' experience, so we're going to focus on more dynamic content and, as with any CRM approach, we'll look to maintain the customer journey across our other platforms, specifically our mobile apps.

Expect the unexpected

The American author and entrepreneur Seth Godin famously said that it takes six years of hard work to become an overnight success (Godin, 2008). UEFA is now moving into year four of its CRM journey and beginning to see the sort of results that can look like a sudden breakthrough. Here, Willems sheds light on the quantity of work that went on below the public radar to get the programme to this point.

When I think back to our first sessions discussing this subject, I'm sure none of us expected to be where we are now. Some of us might have expected a slower pace. We can't move the same way our corporate sponsors or partners do, as we're a governing body, run by its members and fully accountable to them. Others may have preferred quicker results but, on balance, I think the approach has been absolutely right for UEFA, our members, our partners and of course our staff.

. . .

When I think about the challenges we've had, I'd say that organisational change is definitely one of them. It's no secret that people are naturally averse to change, they fear the implications for themselves, so getting the buy-in of our colleagues has been tough.

The majority of activity has focused on my department, marketing, so of course we've experienced the biggest shift, and for us the biggest process change has been in the way we've operated with our legal team to implement the former EU Data Protection Directive and now the GDPR (General Data Protection Regulations). Before we started this CRM approach, we were collecting data – asking our fans if they wanted to hear from us, looking at our Google Analytics, tracking behaviour across our digital channels – but it's safe to say that while I'm sure we were compliant with regulations, they didn't come first. Now, we place as much emphasis on the way we do things as the result we're looking for. We work with our legal team at the start to understand the framework of our approach before we talk to ICT about the way we do it. As a governing body, UEFA operates under strict corporate governance, so ensuring that approach is rolled out to the way we use, collect and store data, particularly that of our fans, is absolutely paramount.

The other major challenge UEFA has consistently faced is that of the unknown, derived from the way that fans' behaviours and preferences will change to the unpredictability of football itself.

Of course, like all sports businesses, whatever plans we might make, whatever key dates we put in our diaries, when our major events hit us, we focus 100 per cent on those and other business issues have to take a back seat. The 2016 European Championships were a huge success for us and, while we managed to maintain our CRM focus throughout, our pro-active development had to take a back seat for a while. Anyone involved in the event side of sports will understand what I mean here. They take over your focus, time and every spare amount of resource you have.

The other unknown that Willems has become accustomed to is pinpointing exactly where his organisation sits on the CRM roadmap.

It's impossible to say because we don't know what the end looks like. Does anybody? Just as we think we have a plan, some new technology is developed that we didn't imagine, or a new social channel has taken over East Asia and we have to reconfigure our approach to accommodate it. But we're a lot further along than we were one year ago, and when I think back to 2014 when we started, we can see some great achievements.

As for what the future holds? It's difficult to say with any certainty. We've no idea what changes will be thrust upon us from external forces: changes in technology, the demands of our fans and our partners, the economic environment, etc. But we know some of the key outcomes we're looking for.

While new communication and engagement channels may emerge and consumer behaviours will inevitably evolve, the building blocks of UEFA's CRM strategy will remain the same with a focus on data, content and channels.

For Willems, these three elements create a circle in which channel access to compelling content yields data insights that can improve and be repeated (almost) ad infinitum.

To achieve our vision, we have to ensure we're where our fans want us to be and we have to demonstrate we're listening to them. We want to be able to pick up our conversation with them regardless of what channel they're using and when they last talked to us. We have to know their intent and predict their actions so we can make the journey as easy for them as possible: we want them

(continued)

(continued)

to come to UEFA because we can give them exactly what they want when it comes to European football. We want to ensure they think of us before anyone else, including their own team.

A centralised database that powers this is absolutely crucial. It needs to house the information we need to deliver this experience for our fans, but that's the engine that powers the rest of it. We need the right digital platforms: a highly personalised website experience, a mobile app that integrates with our website, social channels that don't operate in silos, and as many forms of push messaging as are necessary to ensure we meet the needs of the European football family.

But, of course, most crucial to all of this is the content. We have to have the right content for our fans to want to engage with us but, as you can imagine, as owners of two of the biggest football properties in the world, we don't struggle a lot in that area. It's knowing what within our gigabytes, terabytes and petabytes of content we need for which fan, and that's where our centralised database comes in.

Lessons for the long term

UEFA's experience in developing CRM for the digital age highlights four important lessons for other organisations taking the same path:

1   be clear on objectives
2   obtain senior buy-in
3   draw on the experience of others
4   be in it for the long term.

Be absolutely clear about why you're doing this – get your objectives written down and ensure you can demonstrate the progress you're making within each of these objectives. And you also need senior level approval for this – unless your top management know and support what you're doing, you'll never get the right amount of resource to take it forward.

Just as there is a difference between quality and quantity in the data side of CRM, the experience of UEFA leads Willems to advise drawing a similar distinction when it comes to building strategy. Learn the right thing, not everything.

> Make sure you have the right people working with you. There's so much information about what you should or shouldn't be doing, you need to work with people who understand your business. And don't be afraid to ask for help – don't think you know all the answers because you probably don't. Even the most advanced CRM practitioners in the world are still learning every day.

As Seth Godin observed, achieving success will also take longer than most people think, and Willems couldn't agree more.

> You should also double or triple whatever timeframe you have identified for whatever data-related task you have coming up next. It rarely goes so smoothly that you get it right first time, and you usually underestimate what dependencies you have before that task completes.

(Source: Willems, 2017, 12 October.)

Key chapter ideas

1   CRM is no longer just about software – data and insight have become the drivers of successful use of CRM but you also need to have a strategy and Business Change programme in place.
2   The sports industry is adopting CRM at a fast pace – if this isn't yet on your radar, start to investigate what you need to know.
3   CRM is not just an implementation – it's a way of doing business: it needs time and commitment but it produces results.
4   We need to put our fans and other stakeholders at the centre of the way we operate – we need to emulate Amazon's approach to customer service but frame it for the size of our opportunities.

References

Aegon (2014). *Aegon's 2014 Review: Creating and Sharing Value* [online]. The Hague: Aegon. Available at: www.aegon.com/siteassets/sitewide/reports-and-other-publications/annual-reviews/2014/aegon-2014-review-en.pdf.

Bezos, J. (2017). *About Amazon – 2016 Letter to Shareholders* [online]. Available at: www.amazon.com/p/feature/z6o9g6sysxur57t.

Bradley, M. (2017, 10 October). Email correspondence.

Cision PR Newswire (2017). Customer Relationship Management (CRM) market is expected to reach 81.9 billion USD by 2025 [online]. *Cision PR Newswire*. Available at: www.prnewswire.com/news-releases/customer-relationship-management-crm-market-is-expected-to-reach-819-billion-usd-by-2025-300461786.html.

Davenport, T. and Patil, D. (2012). Data scientist: the sexiest job of the 21st century [online]. *Harvard Business Review*. Available at: https://hbr.org/2012/10/data-scientist-the-sexiest-job-of-the-21st-century.

Drucker, P. (2001). *Management Challenges for the 21st Century*. New York: Harper Business.

Femina, J. (2013). A glimpse into the second golden age of advertising [online]. *The Financial Times*. Available at: www.ft.com/content/4877d0e4-f911-11e2-a6ef-00144feabdc0.

Fisher, L. (2015). How CRM is becoming the 'new advertising' [online]. *Marketing Week*. Available at: www.marketingweek.com/2015/11/09/how-crm-is-becoming-the-new-advertising.

Gartner (2017). *Customer Relationship Management (CRM)* [online]. Available at: www.gartner.com/it-glossary/customer-relationship-management-crm [accessed 25 September 2017].

Godin, S. (2008). What Dave just did [online]. *Seth's Blog*. Available at: http://sethgodin.typepad.com/seths_blog/2008/06/what-dave-just.html.

Goodwin, B. (2014). EE drives mobile phone deals with CRM software implementation [online]. *Computer Weekly*. Available at: www.computerweekly.com/news/2240222345/EE-drives-mobile-phone-deals-with-CRM-software-implementation.

Hargittai, I. and Hargittai, M. (2004). *Candid Science IV: Conversations with Famous Physicists*. London: Imperial College Press, p. 505.

Hollar, K. (2015). *CRM Industry User Research Report* [online]. Capterra. Available at: www.capterra.com/customer-relationship-management-software/user-research.

Kalyanam, K. and Zweben, M. (2005). The perfect message at the perfect moment [online]. *Harvard Business Review*. Available at: https://hbr.org/2005/11/the-perfect-message-at-the-perfect-moment.

Koba, M. (2013). Keeping fans in the stands is getting harder to do [online]. *CNBC*. Available at: www.cnbc.com/id/100886843.

McGinnis, D. (2016). Please take my data: why consumers want more personalized marketing [online]. *Salesforce Blog*. Available at: www.salesforce.com/blog/2016/12/consumers-want-more-personalized-marketing.html.

Peppers, D. (2014). *Treating Different Customers Differently* [online]. LinkedIn. Available at: www.linkedin.com/pulse/20140909180730-17102372-treating-different-customers-differently.

SFIA (2016). *Shocking Youth Participation Data: NEARLY 35 MILLION KIDS NOT ACTIVE TO HEALTHY LEVELS* [online]. Available at: www.sfia.org/press/812_Shocking-Youth-Participation-Data%3A-NEARLY-35-MILLION-KIDS-NOT-ACTIVE-TO-HEALTHY-LEVELS-.

Singh, J. (2016, 24 May). Personal interview.

Statista (2017). Number of Amazon customers/users 2015 [online]. *Statista*. Available at: www.statista.com/statistics/237810/number-of-active-amazon-customer-accounts-worldwide [accessed 25 September 2017].

Tesseras, L. (2017). M&S's Nathan Ansell on proving the value of customer experience [online]. *Marketing Week*. Available at: www.marketingweek.com/2017/02/10/ms-proving-value-customer-experience.

Watson, L. (2016). Humans have shorter attention span than goldfish, thanks to smart-phones [online]. *Telegraph*. Available at: www.telegraph.co.uk/science/2016/03/12/humans-have-shorter-attention-span-than-goldfish-thanks-to-smart.

Wells, A. (2017, 24 November). Phone interview.

Wiggenraad, P. (2017). Data: top 50 retailers by sales during 2015/16 financial year [online]. *Retail Week*. Available at: www.retail-week.com/data/data-top-50-retailers-by-sales-during-2015/16-financial-year/7018511.article.

Willems, P. (2017, 12 October). Personal interview.

Chapter 2

The principles of CRM

I've worked in the sports industry for over 30 years, starting when my approach to CRM consisted of a landline, a Rolodex and a desk diary. The closest I could get to the 'right message to the right person at the right time' back then was asking my match sponsor if he wanted to support the next leg in the Littlewoods Challenge Cup and taking a punt that the combination of a 2–0 win and an afternoon of executive box hospitality would create the right mix for him to say yes. Fast forward to 2018 and things are quite different, and I don't just mean that it's now called The Carabao Cup.

In Chapter 1 we addressed why the sports industry needs to use CRM as a way of doing business. Now we'll start to look at how we go about it, breaking down what we, at Winners, consider the different elements to implementing a CRM approach. It's not just about technology. I'll look at the perfect circle, the CRM pyramid, Single Customer View and then end with a glimpse at customer personas.

CRM's perfect circle

Winners' approach to CRM is based on the principle of the perfect circle. This principle consists of five key elements, all five weighted with equal importance. If you place less emphasis on one element over another, the circle collapses.

Ironically, there's a suggestion that outside the world of pure mathematics there's no such thing as a 'perfect circle' (Lamb, 2014), and I'm quite happy to accept this as truth. While we use the term quite liberally among our rights owner clients, we also know how incredibly hard it is to achieve and, when Google throws up over 99 million search results, most of them suggesting that CRM is just about software, it's easy to understand why there's such a challenge in our industry.

One of the purposes of this book is to dispel that software myth and redress the balance. Sports organisations looking to start their own CRM journey, or those who are already making headway, need to understand that software isn't a magic bullet. Indeed, when you go into developing your own approach to CRM believing that buying the right software will make sure it happens, you can be confident yours will be one of the 60% of projects that reportedly fail (Gould, 2015).

So, let's look at these five key elements of the CRM perfect circle and understand what they mean in the real world of our day-to-day business.

Strategy

We all need to have a strategy for the way we work, to make sense of our operational delivery and ensure that across the organisation we're all heading in the same direction. With the implementation of CRM as a business approach it's no different. We need to know what we want to achieve (our goals), align them with our business objectives, determine what resources we have to achieve them, and put a timeline against it so we know by when we want to have achieved them.

I've already referred to the 'CRM journey', and will reiterate it here. The implementation of CRM is not a destination that you arrive at, nor a project that you complete. It's a journey. Customer relationship management is a way of doing business and, once it's embedded, its role within an organisation continues to evolve. As we use CRM to make decisions and deliver results, driven by the continuing development of our digital world and the masses of data it produces, we'll continue to progress, because technology, the quantity of data we have access to, and our drive for success are also progressing. Once we've successfully moved from A to B, we'll then want to move to C and, once we've started moving in the direction of C, you can bet your life someone's thinking about how you start moving to D.

When it comes to your strategy, it doesn't have to be a long document supported with dozens of spreadsheets. It can be easily summarised in one page. As with so many concepts, it really is about quality over quantity. I have a simple belief that a CRM strategy can be created in just three steps:

1   **Identify your main goals**, such as increased revenue, participation and insight, and understand why you want to achieve them. What difference will they make to your business? How will they support the overall business objectives?

2   **Understand your current situation**, for example, the extent of your customer data, tools and other available resources. Audit your staff capabilities so you know what gaps you have when it comes to operational delivery and review your customer journeys. What experience do your fans have when they engage with you?

3   **Roadmap the journey** or the milestones that will help you to get from where you are now to where you want to be. Itemise the steps that will get you there. Within this, I always recommend that you identify a leader or sponsor, ideally at the highest level of management possible, who will champion what you're trying to achieve. For example, selling your approach to the board, lobbying for more support or managing the messaging when things have gone slightly off plan.

What's really key to your CRM strategy is that you support it with quick wins. We're looking for marginal gains that keep your management and team members motivated and excited as you push forward with your delivery. So, make sure you've included a few of these aims in your roadmap. They should be ones that show an increase in revenue, engagement or any other KPI that's been identified as important to your business.

Data

We must have data, but it's not any old data, and it's definitely not 'big data'. According to the International Data Corporation's report, *The Digital Universe*, there will be 5,200 gigabytes of data for every man, woman and child in 2020, with the digital universe doubling every two years (Gantz and Reinsel, 2012). That's way too much data for the majority of rights owners to handle.

Big data gives us huge amounts of information but by its very nature it can be overwhelming. So, what we need instead of data quantity is data that's relevant to our strategy; the data that will help us achieve our business objectives. Data can help us do two things. It can provide us with the foundation on which we make decisions, and enable the use of personalised and highly targeted communication, whether marketing-specific or content-related.

Most crucially, it's not just about the quantity but also about the quality. As we think about our utopian scenario in CRM (the Single Customer View, single version of truth, golden record or any other term you use for all the information you have about your stakeholders in one place), we must remember that we need all our databases to merge into one. This task is made immeasurably easier when we use consistency in our approach to gathering that data (we will look at data normalisation and standardisation later in the book).

On top of that, it's about the way we use data within our CRM approach, how we collect, store, manage and protect it. This becomes even more important with the impending EU GDPR (General Data Protection Regulation), which imposes a standard set of data protection laws across many countries in Europe. I will also examine this oh-so-dry but oh-so-crucial area later.

Finally, we need to think about the way we maintain our data, how we keep it clean, continually improving and enhancing it, and how we ensure our data will continue to deliver our objectives that in turn ensure we support our overall strategy.

Technology

The role of technology is to act as an enabler in the use of CRM. I'll delve into this in more detail later, but there are two main points here:

1   We don't start with technology and the technology department doesn't lead on CRM. For those rights owners without an IT department this will

be a relief because it is the CEOs and Marketing Directors who should be the drivers of your CRM implementation. We lead with business needs, not technology.

2   At Winners we don't talk about CRM systems. We refer to CRM ecosystems. There isn't one piece of software, technology or platform that can deliver everything you need to get the right message to the right person. We use several of them, each playing its own role within its niche sector or perhaps multiple roles to bring together a few tasks and disciplines. But, all these individual components are interacting and interconnected.

While it is undeniable that the right software and hardware can make things work more efficiently, the best technology in the world is unable to deliver CRM in isolation. It's one of the five principles. Consequently, a technology-led CRM approach could lead to you being one of those failing 60% we discussed earlier and, most importantly, cost you both time and money: something that most rights owners have in short supply.

This is a great place for one of my favourite Bill Gates' quotes – 36 words that perfectly sum up this point:

> The first rule of any technology used in a business is that automation applied to an efficient operation will magnify the efficiency. The second is that automation applied to an inefficient operation will magnify the inefficiency.
>
> (Gates, 1996)

When Gates wrote those words over 20 years ago, the world didn't have the technology we have today. Moore's Law states that technology will 'dramatically increase in power and decrease in relative cost, at an exponential pace' (*Futurism*, 2018). If so, then technology will be just as disruptive in the next two decades as it has been in the past two. As Baroness Martha Lane Fox put it, when speaking at the CIPD Annual Conference and Exhibition in Manchester on 9 November 2017, 'today technology is developing at the slowest rate it will ever develop in the future' (Fox, 2017). I had to think about that one for a while before realising the absolute truth in it.

Process

The definition of process is 'a series of actions or steps taken in order to achieve a particular end' according to Oxford English Dictionaries online (2017). While that definitely applies here, I'd like to expand just a little. In our world, where 'data is the new oil' (Humby, 2006), we should be taking the data output from previous processes and analysing it before we apply the next process, using that data to inform appropriate decisions. A further key aspect of our processes is that we must repeat them, do them consistently and with the same approach as before and, where appropriate, add improvements along the way.

I'll be looking at some of these processes later; areas such as data collection, digital campaign management and campaign reporting. These are the day-to-day things that we do; the tasks and actions that make up our working day in a data-driven organisation. When you apply best-practice CRM you're given the opportunity to streamline these processes across your organisation's different departments, with workflows or automation that will increase efficiencies, effectiveness and speed up manual tasks.

Jeff Bezos, Founder and CEO of Amazon, warned in his 2016 letter to shareholders of the danger that processes can do the opposite of what was originally intended. They can lead to downfalls, not improvements:

> A common example is process as proxy. Good process serves you, so you can serve customers. But if you're not watchful, the process can become the thing. This can happen very easily in large organisations. The process becomes the proxy for the result you want. You stop looking at outcomes and just make sure you're doing the process right. It's not that rare to hear a junior leader defend a bad outcome with something like, 'well, we followed the process'.
>
> (Bezos, 2017)

So, the tempered message is that while we need processes (and we need to be constantly improving them), we must also be aware that we don't do things by rote; that while following processes, we must continue to learn.

Culture

Perhaps the element that is most likely to hold up progress in the development of any CRM strategy is culture or, more importantly, cultural silos. Cultural silos are natural divides that occur within organisations and minimise collaboration.

Even if every element of the perfect circle is in place and running smoothly, if your business is unable to function as a cohesive whole, all forward momentum can stall at this point. Having the right business culture can be the most difficult part in the implementation of any new strategy. It requires inter-departmental trust and teamwork to be managed effectively. But natural silos, or department-centric attitude, aren't unique to implementing CRM. These silos have been in the workplace long before we were introduced to databases. So, why do we see so many rights owners specifically struggling in this area?

While silos may indeed have existed, they haven't caused many issues up to this point because very few business functions are cross-organisational. Finance and IT often work together, after all, no one puts up a barrier when it comes to being paid or getting their laptops fixed. Yet when it comes to the sharing of data, production of content, and agreement of priorities, there can be a clear

Figure 2.1 The CRM perfect circle. (Source: Winners FDD Ltd.)

lack of cooperation, intentional or otherwise. I will talk more about this later. Look out for the chapter on Business Change.

Gartner's eight building blocks

This is a perfect moment to introduce readers to what Gartner, one of the world's leading information technology research and advisory companies, proposes as the eight building blocks for the successful implementation of CRM. They align with my use of the perfect circle, but were first introduced in 1996 before intelligent customer engagement was a concept. The building blocks are updated every three years:

1   **Vision**: The board must take leadership in creating a CRM vision for the enterprise. The CRM vision should be used as the guide to the creation of a CRM strategy.
2   **Strategy**: The CRM strategy is all about how to build and develop a valuable asset: the customer base. It must set objectives and metrics for attaining that goal. It directs the objectives of other operational strategies and the CRM implementation strategy.
3   **Customer experience**: The customer experience must be designed in line with the CRM vision and must be constantly refined, based on actively sought customer feedback.
4   **Organisational collaboration**: Changes to organisational structures, processes, metrics, incentives, skills and even the enterprise culture must be made to deliver the required external customer experience. Ongoing change management will be key.

5   **Process**: Successful customer process reengineering should create processes that not only meet customers' expectations and support the customer value proposal, but also provide competitive differentiation and contribute to a designed customer experience.

6   **Information**: Successful CRM demands the creation of a customer-information blood supply that flows around the organisation, as well as tight integration between operational and analytical systems.

7   **Technology**: CRM technologies form a fundamental part of any enterprise's application portfolio and architecture. The CRM application needs should be considered as the provision of integrated functionality that supports seamless customer-centric processes across all areas of the enterprise and its partners.

8   **Metrics**: Enterprises must set measurable CRM objectives and monitor all levels of CRM indicators to turn customers into assets. Without performance management, a CRM implementation will fail (Britt, 2003).

Gartner's approach emphasises the importance of breaking down CRM in this manner. Whether it's five principles or eight building blocks, the key message is that CRM is not just about technology. I urge you to follow either outline, devise your own, or even research others.

The CRM pyramid

Another foundation that we build on at Winners is what we refer to as the CRM pyramid. For any reader who has worked in sales, this is the equivalent of a sales funnel but turned on its head, building from the base up as opposed to the top down.

At the base of the pyramid we have our passive fans; those who have a passing interest in a team or a particular sport but with whom there's no engagement. They're unknown to us. They may perhaps class themselves as fans but with none of the engagement or communication that would typically come with the term.

In the next step up you have the digitally engaged. They follow you on social media, they watch what's happening on Facebook, you feature in their Twitter feed but they don't actually interact with you. At this stage they're still anonymous because they use your website without leaving their details. However, they could be identified through their IP address, Facebook ID or Twitter handle.

Next we have casual fans; they'll come for a match maybe once or twice a season, buy from your online store at Christmas and watch the occasional TV broadcast. You'll have their details because they interacted with you directly and, thanks to your data collection processes, you secured enough information to identify them as individuals.

Moving up the pyramid we have frequent fans. They do the same thing as casual fans, but more often.

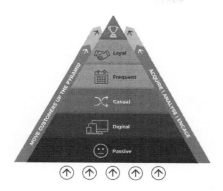

Figure 2.2 The CRM pyramid. (Source: Winners FDD Ltd.)

Then, at the top of the pyramid, you have loyal fans. This is our objective – to get as many loyal fans as possible. We aim to move our fans from their passive status to digitally engaged, from casually involved to frequently involved, and then, ultimately, to loyal at the tip of the pyramid. The way we do that is by acquiring data about them, analysing that data and then engaging in a way that's relevant, all while aiming to increase the size of our pyramid, getting more fans into the base.

The Single Customer View

According to Forrester's CustomerThink survey of 2015, a key challenge for 47% of organisations implementing CRM is the creation of an SCV (Single Customer View). Your ticket buyers, your fan club members, your corporate clients, your online store buyers, players, referees and volunteers, all have to be housed together in a single database (Leggett, 2015).

But it's not *all* the data we have about these individuals that we're after, it's just the data that supports your CRM strategy, the information that you need to support your targeted marketing campaigns and help you make decisions.

Generally, the data in your SCV includes:

- **Individual contact details**: name, full postal address, email address, mobile number and, if available, any social handles or IDs that they use. More advanced digital marketers may also have IP addresses and other digital channel identifiers such as application user IDs.
- **Demographic data**: the identifiers that are common to us all, such as age, gender, education, income level, occupation, and marital and family status. While not all of us have all this information and some of us may never go on to secure it, there are some key data fields that are important to all sports rights owners, so we'll look into this in greater detail.

- **Behavioural data**: the information that tells us how our stakeholders interact with us, both online and offline. Do they attend our events? Do they volunteer or compete? Do they visit our website (and, if so, which content areas?), use our apps, open our emails and follow us on Facebook?
- **Transactional information**: this isn't just financial, but could also include date or event-related data.
- **Lifestyle data**: within lifestyle data we include those elements that are generally of more interest to our sponsors, enabling us to create segments for targeted marketing on behalf of official partners.

In addition to these five areas we also need our SCV to hold our opt-ins from our customers and fans: the indicator that shows our fans are giving us express permission to communicate with them directly and to profile their information. This will enable us to build segments and personas that support our data-driven approach.

From an SCV to DMP and CDP

We touched on an SCV, but we also have two further database definitions to introduce at this point: DMP (Data Management Platform) and CDP (Customer Data Platform). So, what are the key differences?

As we discussed above, your SCV deals with the information you have about an individual that includes their contact data. This means you know who they are and, subject to their opt-in status, you can communicate with them directly. They're known to you.

A DMP manages the data of your customers who are a little lower in the CRM pyramid, your fans who engage with you digitally, who can be targeted on an individual basis but using non-personally identifiable information. In other words, you can identify them but they're anonymous to you. This includes IP address, mobile identifiers and cookie IDs.

Finally, a CDP is commonly used to refer to the database environment that allows you to bring both sets of data together, known and anonymous. This approach ensures that you retain the rich behavioural history of your anonymous fans (and you will have many of them) so that when they do become known to you (once they buy a ticket, register to use your site, or subscribe to a newsletter), you can link all the relevant information you have into one single record.

Admittedly, at the point of writing, I'm not aware of many sports rights owners who've yet progressed to needing a CDP, and only a few who are considering a DMP (you'll read about one of those in the case study at the end of this chapter) but there are many that are still challenged by the notion of an SCV. This book has a chapter dedicated to technology stacks so you can read more about this area.

Customer personas

Having looked at the five elements of CRM, the CRM pyramid and the SCV, we now come to what, for me, is the natural conclusion or rationale for these precursors: creating customer personas. This is the cosmetic manufacturing of your ideal customers based on the data you have in your SCV, DMP or CDP.

While the creation of personas is not yet common practice within the sports industry, it is incredibly important to your CRM evolution. Personas enable you to determine where to focus your time and how to use your budget. They can be used cross-organisationally for ease of reference and help you track and measure your key business metrics, including ROI.

In the words of Tony Zambito, the founder and authority in personas:

> Buyer personas are research-based archetypal (modeled) representations of who buyers are, what they are trying to accomplish, what goals drive their behavior, how they think, how they buy, and why they make buying decisions.
>
> (Zambito, 2013)

Customer personas are specific to you and your organisation. You create them based on the data you hold, the goals you set, and the approaches you have to develop your business. They'll be different from those of your competitors and even your peers. That's a point that evaded Ron Johnson, a formerly acclaimed retail maverick who famously pioneered Apple's high street stores and Genius bars. Unfortunately, he went on to acute failure at JC Penney, one of America's oldest stores, when he implemented a complete rebrand in 2012 that cost the company $1 billion in lost sales. Johnson admits that his failure at JC Penney was down to three factors: he didn't know what his customers wanted, he didn't know who they were and he didn't test his ideas on them. In short, he didn't use customer personas (Tuttle, 2013).

Case study: Major League Soccer

Major League Soccer (MLS) represents the sport at the highest level in both the United States and Canada. It was founded in 1993 as part of a successful bid to host the 1994 FIFA World Cup and, despite a rocky start, it has grown to include 23 teams, to oversee the construction of 12 soccer-specific stadiums and has secured a number of lucrative sponsorship and broadcast deals.

Charlie Shin is the Vice President of CRM and Analytics at MLS. He is the business lead when it comes to cross-organisational adoption of CRM, responsible for devising the strategy and implementation across the whole league, not just within MLS offices. In a telephone interview on 30 November 2017, Charlie Shin shared with me that their long-term business plan has data at its core, and that it has built something that no other league in any sport has.

Major League Soccer's comprehensive approach to CRM is considered unique among rights owners. While others may emulate the centralised approach, it's not at the same level of integration and governance. This can, in part, be attributed to the relatively recent formation of the League.

> Our ownership has been very supportive – they had the foresight to appreciate the importance of CRM and made an investment at a very early stage, also recognising that if we do this at an individual club level, we're never going to get the best results. It's been a journey in building this out, but now we're finally seeing the value of this in many areas.

MLS's unique business structure

Major League Soccer has a unique business structure that makes league-wide implementation logical: each club 'owner' is in fact an investor in the league as a whole. It holds teams and contracts centrally, and revenues are shared across the board. Each investor-operator therefore has a stake in the profitability of the whole organisation.

> What the club owners get is the operational rights to manage one of the clubs in their market. They'll have their own P&L [profit and loss] and then revenue share from tickets, sponsorship and media rights. So, there are two revenue opportunities for our owners: revenue that can be generated from their local operation then another at the League level as part of their ownership of Major League Soccer.

The clubs are individual legal entities, but are essentially operating on behalf of MLS for their individual markets.

MLS's strategy

Major League Soccer has two main objectives: to grow their sport's fan base and drive value for its enterprise. To achieve this, Shin hopes to unify its data across the whole league, which he expects will help to optimise business decisions at a strategic and operational level.

> Our data strategy is an enabler for the overall enterprise strategy. It aligns with what we're trying to do as a company. We have a five-year plan that we developed and are executing at the league level, and the data strategy is a reflection of that. It's important that we're building the right infrastructure as well as thinking about collecting the right data to be fully able to execute our overall enterprise strategy.

Echoing the Amazon approach, MLS is constantly thinking about how it can become a more fan-centric organisation. It's not just data-for-data's sake but to support the way MLS engages with and services its fans. The more data the organisation gets, the more it understands the fans and what drives them. Fans are at the centre of all its business goals, and the right data can help it to build better fan relationships, which in turn enables it to achieve these goals.

One of the cornerstones of the MLS approach to technology is to have a centralised database. In addition to being cost effective, it also reveals a full view of fan engagement and transactions across the board.

> MLS is a single entity, so I think the structure of the organisation made it much easier for us to centralise a lot of the infrastructure. The biggest benefit of having the data centralised, as well as the technology that supports the data infrastructure is really the efficiency, as well as ensuring that we are collecting and have visibility into the data. not just at the league level, but also across all our clubs, which will give us a full, holistic view of all our customers.

The CRM vision for MLS has always been about establishing an internal capability that would serve the fans in the best way possible.

> What we realised was our fans are fans of the clubs and not the league. Therefore, the areas that we needed to focus on weren't really at the League's consumer touch point: we needed to look at an infrastructure that could support our clubs who should then establish those engagements in each of their local markets.

As a result, MLS divided its strategy into three key areas: data, customer analytics and D2C (Direct to Customer). In this respect, MLS treats CRM as a B2B2C (Business to Business to Customer) strategy: from the League to the clubs to the fans.

Use of data

Major League Soccer uses its existing data to understand how fans are actively engaging and so can choose the best channels to communicate certain messages. At the moment it uses emails and push notifications, with a great deal of digital retargeting using its existing data. It is also looking to invest in technologies that will take its data to the next level of efficiency, help get the most out of paid media advertising and get more creative in targeting new audiences based on additional insights.

The MLS's data warehouse is central to all of this. Here different technologies allow for different processes, as well as custom data models provided by third-party partners. All of the data, no matter which technology has collected it, is connected to the data warehouse, ranging from ticketing, merchandising, digital subscriptions, website registrations and even international event ticket sales. On top of this, MLS has implemented an analytics solution that offers a visual dashboard, allowing the entire organisation to easily see and conceptualise the data.

While each club is able to use its own marketing tools, the central administration of MLS enables the use of CRM, analytics and marketing tools across the board to provide a standardised approach. To support its direct-to-fan strategy, MLS has given the clubs autonomy to decide on the right technology and the right structure to engage with their fans.

Centralisation in action

Major League Soccer supports the clubs centrally by designing and managing the technology infrastructure and processes relevant to the role of data from collection, cleansing and normalising through to storing, interrogating and transferring to the clubs for their local market use. This approach provides the clubs with everything they need to support fact-based decision-making and data-driven marketing.

However, instead of mandating the use of certain tools across the league, MLS has instead opted to show value in the tools it recommends. The ultimate decision rests with the clubs. With a structure that has every club owner personally invested in the profitability of the league, it was Shin's job to ensure they all understood the benefit of a uniform set of marketing and CRM tools. By taking this approach, Shin found that the utilisation was much better than if MLS had simply forced all league members to come on board.

The resources MLS offers are the same for all their clubs. They include marketing software for email, SMS, web advertising, and social media tools. However, as an acknowledgement that the League has a very different relationship with soccer fans than that of the clubs, its Contact Management Solutions are chosen individually based on the club's needs and resources, along with any extra technology it uses to enhance ticket sales performance. According to Shin, this approach enables the clubs to take advantage of the

knowledge they have of their own markets and their own fans, and to optimise the vital direct engagement data to which the league would otherwise
not have access.

> [The clubs] are really at the frontline where the rubber meets the road, and
> our clubs understand their market and their fans the best. We didn't want to
> dictate how sales prospects should be managed or even standardise how that
> engagement should be with our local clubs and their local markets. So that's
> where the local clubs have made investments on how they acquire fans and
> how they engage. And, what we try to do from the back is to provide the
> necessary data and analytic support that's really going to help them enhance
> that relationship.

Major League Soccer has a number of centralised revenue streams from ticketing and sponsorship through to broadcasting and media rights. Clubs are able
to exploit data to drive and increase the value that derives from ticket sales, but
there's a huge opportunity in that data for increased sponsorship and media value.
By consolidating the data, MLS has an in-depth understanding of its fans and
how they engage with the sport. This in turn supports its sponsorship strategy.

> It's been very helpful to leverage and analyse [our fan data] to provide insight
> to our sponsors and deliver additional value that could help increase the over-
> all value of our property. We can even use it to develop engagement for our
> sponsor's customers through our customer database. We're also consider-
> ing additional technology that allows us to identify some of those anonymous
> customers that are engaging in our digital ecosystems, allowing us to create audi-
> ences that we could potentially offer to our sponsors to reach their customers.

I've just discussed how MLS's business structure allowed for the building of
this centralised resource, and how it's being used to support individual clubs to
drive their fandom and build relationships with fans to grow the customer base.
Now let's look at the technology behind this centralised approach.

The MLS technology stack

Central to MLS's technology stack is a data warehouse that stores league and
club-level data, operating as an SCV and built in SQL. Shin expanded on how
MLS uses this resource.

> The SQL data warehouse is the centre of everything but there's different technology that goes into it. We use SAS [software] for our ETL [extract, transfer, load] process with a custom data model. It houses all our data – ticketing, merchandise, digital subscriptions such as fantasy, website registration and international event data. We also get data from our strategic partnership with EA Sports of their customers who play with our affiliated clubs. Our third-party data [from an external provider] is also integrated into the data warehouse.
>
> We then use an identity management solution within SAS to create our golden ID (unique identifier) by applying different logic, using the names, email address, birthday, zip code and phone number and other information that can help us identify that multiple records belong to the same person.

As well as the central data warehouse, Shin explains that MLS has also built a central resource bank, which saves individual clubs having to make costly investments on analytics. This allows Shin to build data models that can be implemented in one or two clubs as a pilot before scaling it out across all clubs because they use the same data set.

> Our analytics solution sits on top of our data warehouse, which is SAS again. We use their visual analytics module, which is more of a BI dashboard and is very easy to use, and then we use our enterprise data mining tools for more of the advanced analytics that we work on. We also have Tableau [data visualisation software] that we use to visualise a lot of the third-party aggregated data.

I asked Shin about the different roles played by SAS's visual analytics and their Tableau dashboard and it came down to individual data versus aggregate data: SAS is used at an individual record level, with Tableau used for Google Analytics and social data, replacing the way PowerPoint was previously used to present graphs and charts.

Moving away from demographics

Major League Soccer has developed a unique approach to customer segmenting. Instead of using the more traditional approach of fan demographics, it is now focusing on fans' needs and what they hope to get out of MLS.

> What we're seeing is there's a change in the landscape. We tended to look at demographics in the past, but we're moving away from looking at our fans from a demographic standpoint. We're more looking at them for their needs and the reason behind why they're consuming soccer.

Considering that the use of demographics is still considered a core component for creating customer personas, I asked Shin to expand on this different approach.

> We've done a huge segmentation project recently that has helped us identify some of those segments based on the data. And that's really helped us better understand our fans. Demographic data is so limited in terms of how you segment and navigate. You could be looking at different demographics but still see the same needs or reason for why you're consuming certain brands or certain products. For this reason we've kind of gone beyond using demographics and are looking at more of a need base to understand our fans.

Based on the needs it's seen, MLS has been able to identify two key segments and now aligns its strategy with improving and delivering on the needs of those segments.

So what are these segments?

1   **Soccer Enthusiasts**: Fans that consider soccer to be their primary sport and who have a positive perception of MLS.
2   **Sports Fans**: They consume soccer as one of a mix of sports, but not as their primary sport. They also have a positive perception of MLS, but tend to have a positive perception of many different leagues.

When MLS looks at these two segments, there are certain characteristics that are unique to each. Soccer Enthusiasts are interested in on-field performance and team rivalries, whereas Sports Fans are more interested in the atmosphere of the stadium experience and the social aspect of watching a game. These needs transcend demographics, so MLS will now focus on trying to pinpoint opportunities in those segments in order to increase its share of the market.

What's next for MLS?

Moving on to the next technological development for MLS, Shin was very clear about where its focus will be.

A DMP (data management platform) will be introduced in 2018. That's really exciting and that will be our 2.0 data strategy as we move on from focusing just on our known customers within our digital ecosystem. This is the next evolution of expanding our customers from known to unknown as well as extending our ecosystems to a much broader digital space.

Legal compliance is another major topic on the horizon, especially with the EU's GDPR coming into force from May 2018. Shin and MLS are taking a very pragmatic approach and preparing for a time when US and EU legislation are more closely aligned.

We don't market to, or target fans outside of the US. There could be people in our database that are coming from the EU, but we are not pro-actively targeting people in the UK for instance, so we're OK from that perspective. But the way I'm viewing this is as a trend that we're going to see down the line across the world. We saw it last year with Canada and how they've improved their policy [PIPEDA, their federal data protection law], and now we're seeing it with the EU. It's just going to be a matter of time when the US kind of takes on some of these strict policies. I'd rather be more conservative and be prepared by referencing the work that is being done in other countries so that, when the time comes, we are more buttoned-up than other entities.

Other plans include more personalisation and multivariant testing on the MLS website. Not only will this collect valuable data and fan insight, but it will also help build new initiatives to increase engagement and value in the future.

The main focus of our data strategy for 2018 and beyond is really about identifying the user, the unknown fans, and tying them back to the known fans. But segmenting is going to be all about personalisation. How do we improve the journey of our customers by using this data to provide better and more relevant information to our fans? So, whether that's content, or whether that's an offering, that's going to be the key. It's really about extracting value from all the investments that we've made in CRM to deliver value back to our fans.

(Source: Shin, 2017, 30 November.)

Key chapter ideas

1   Strategy, data, technology, process and culture all play an equal role in the implementation of CRM – each area must be given focus and consideration to enable a data-driven environment.
2   A CRM pyramid represents your most passive fans at the base and your most loyal fans at the top – the objective of CRM is to move these stakeholders up the pyramid, constantly adding more into the base. This is achieved through acquiring data about those in the pyramid, analysing that data, then using that analysis to determine how to engage with those stakeholders.
3   The holy grail of CRM is the creation of a centralised database that holds all the data you have about your stakeholders – known and unknown – who they are, how they behave, their interests and their needs.
4   Once you have your centralised database you can create customer personas. These are manufactured representations of the different groups of stakeholders based on the information you have in your database. Personas help you plan, market, and communicate more effectively and efficiently and are tailored specifically to your organisation.

References

Bezos, J. (2017). *About Amazon – 2016 Letter to Shareholders* [online]. Amazon.com. Available at: www.amazon.com/p/feature/z6o9g6sysxur57t.

Britt, P. (2003). *Eight Building Blocks for CRM Success* [online]. Destination CRM. Available at: www.destinationcrm.com/Articles/Columns-Departments/Insight/Eight-Building-Blocks-for-CRM-Success-48266.aspx.

Fox, M. (2017). Keynote: *Creating a Fair and Inclusive Digital World That Works for Everyone*. CIPD Annual Conference and Exhibition, Manchester Central, Manchester, 8–9 November.

Futurism (2018). Moore's Law [online]. *Futurism*. Available at: https://futurism.com/glossary/moores-law.

Gantz, J. and Reinsel, D. (2012). *THE DIGITAL UNIVERSE IN 2020: Big Data, Bigger Digital Shadows, and Biggest Growth in the Far East* [ebook]. Farmingham, MA: IDC. Available at: www.emc.com/collateral/analyst-reports/idc-the-digital-universe-in-2020.pdf.

Gates, B. (1996). *The Road Ahead*. Rockland, MA: Wheeler Pub.

Gould, L. (2015). *Characteristics of a Failing CRM Project* [online]. C5 Insight. Available at: www.c5insight.com/Resources/Blog/tabid/88/entryid/605/characteristics-of-a-failing-crm-project.aspx.

Humby, C. (2006). *Data Is the New Oil*. ANA Senior Marketer's Summit, Kellogg School of Management, Northwestern University.

Lamb, R. (2014). *Do Perfect Circles Exist in Our Universe?* [online blog]. Stuff to Blow Your Mind. Available at: www.stufftoblowyourmind.com/blogs/do-perfect-circles-exist-in-our-universe.htm.

Leggett, K. (2015). *CRM Success Is Simple if You Avoid These Common Pitfalls* [online]. Customer Think. Available at: http://customerthink.com/crm-success-is-simple-if-you-avoid-these-common-pitfalls.

Oxford English Dictionaries (2017). Process [definition, online]. Available at: https://en.oxforddictionaries.com/definition/process.

Shin, C. (2017, 30 November). Personal interview.

Tuttle, B. (2013). The 5 big mistakes that led to Ron Johnson's ouster at JC Penney [online]. *TIME*. Available at: http://business.time.com/2013/04/09/the-5-big-mistakes-that-led-to-ron-johnsons-ouster-at-jc-penney.

Zambito, T. (2013). *What Is a Buyer Persona? Why the Original Definition Still Matters to B2B* [online]. Available at: http://tonyzambito.com/buyer-persona-original-definition-matters.

Chapter 3

The importance of data

Previously I quoted Clive Humby's proclamation that 'data is the new oil' (Humby, 2006), but in this chapter I look a little deeper at the role of data and quote an even more ambitious sentiment: that data is the new soil (McCandless, 2010).

Within the sports industry we have an incredible amount of data at our disposal, and digitisation is producing even more. Rights owners that want to stay ahead are now becoming data-driven businesses. We use data to derive insight that informs decisions and ensures we know who our current and future customers are, where and how they live, what they like, what they don't like, what they want from us and, most importantly, what they'll do for us.

Where we used to go on gut instinct and intuition, we now use data, actionable insights extracted from analyses and modelling, to ensure we make fact-based decisions. And we're not the only industry sector doing this. Retailers combine data on their customers and the weather to predict sales, banks use predictive analytics to determine if they should approve consumer loans and which of their customers are most likely to repay them, and who can forget Barack Obama's 2012 rise to the White House being touted as 'The first big data election' (Helweg, 2012).

However, it's important to accept that while data has immense power, we must also combine this with what we already know about our fans and the way they behave. In a telephone interview on 11 January 2018 I asked Amie Becton Ray, the NHL's (National Hockey League) Director of Database Marketing & Strategy, her view of the way we use data:

> The thing about sports is it's a very emotional business. Our fans are passionate about their team; they really care about them so if their team is doing well then everything is great, the website works wonderfully, the emails they receive are fabulous. But if their team loses, then there's less satisfaction with the brand as a whole. So while I agree that data is extremely important in decision making, we still always have to factor in emotion.
>
> A great example is our All-Star Fan Vote. Every year we step back and look at the programme's analytics and metrics and think about how to

improve the experience and engage fans. One year we allowed fans to vote 30 times a day, but the data showed us most people voted once. So the next year we implemented a 10-vote limit (seeing that 30 was unobtainable, and knowing that our fans do like to vote repeatedly for their team's players); that year, most people voted 10 times each day they voted.

It is important to use a combination of what we know about our fans and what we are continually learning from the data in order to formulate the programmes that make the most sense, that we think will be the most effective. And then we test and learn, and tweak things as we go.

(Ray, 2018, 11 January)

I can't imagine there are many rights owners out there who still need convincing that data is important to their future. In reality, data is really just another word for information, and undervaluing the need for information in a business would be reminiscent of the film companies who underestimated the threat from digital photography, and the video rental companies who initially ignored growing interest in online streaming services. However, I suspect there are many that still haven't taken charge of their data, so this chapter is dedicated to you in an attempt to simplify the subject, help you understand some of the key areas of focus, and provide a way to navigate the many points of consideration.

Data as a corporate asset

The data that you have about your customers is almost as important to a rights owner as the sport or event itself and should be treated as a valuable asset. Just like your logos, images and media rights, it should be nurtured, protected and maximised.

I was first asked about the value of a rights owner's database in 2012 by a contact who often found himself advising buyers and, in this case, sellers, of English football clubs. He posed the question of how much a fan database adds to the asset value of a club. We discussed the types of analyses that would provide him with the answer; Customer Lifetime Value (CLTV) and propensity modelling being the most relevant and easy to formulate. I'll talk more about these in the next chapter.

When calculating the value of your database you can model your fans' spending power by analysing historic transactional data. A further question that needs to be answered to provide an accurate evaluation is how many fans it takes to generate *a specific value* in sales for the sponsor. Modelling that and applying it to your database will add a further dimension to your CLTV, increasing its asset value. Imagine if we could do that with media rights?

Data-driven decisions in sports performance

This book isn't about the use of data in sports performance, that is, the winning or losing of a game, performing a personal best or winning a championship.

It's about the impact data has on the business of sports, to support targeted marketing and decision-making to increase revenue, participation and engagement. But it's impossible to write a chapter on the importance of data in sports without making some sort of reference to *Moneyball*, the 2003 book about the Oakland Athletics baseball team and their approach to using data to become the 2002 league champions. Billy Beane, the Oakland A's manager at the time, used data to assess a player's value during the recruitment process, taking on a failing team and operating with a limited budget. Despite these odds, Beane's team went on to secure a record of 20 consecutive wins (Lewis, 2003).

I have another favourite example of the use of data to inform sports performance: Lewis Hamilton's debut F1 title win for McLaren in 2008. At the Brazilian Grand Prix, Hamilton needed to finish in the top five and was sitting pretty with a few laps to go. But he had a challenger behind him, Sebastian Vettel, who, desperate to pass, could have put them on a collision course had Hamilton decided to fight for his position. McLaren's CEO instructed Hamilton to let Vettel pass rather than risk a crash because the data predicted Hamilton would take fifth place at some point during the last lap. The data was right. He did, but not until the very last corner.

To me, these examples are equivalent to using predictive analytics when trying to sell a product, for example, a new VIP hospitality package, season ticket or even a piece of merchandise. If the data tells you how much your customers might pay for a product, how many of them could afford to do so, over what period of time and with what frequency, you'll have all the information you need to launch it with confidence. Scale this approach up and, as an example, rights owners could more accurately predict how many seats their new stadium should have, as opposed to constructing something that's over-sized or, conversely, not providing enough capacity for growth. Apply this to the way our development teams grow our sports and we can fight the negative trend of sports participation we highlighted in Chapter 1.

Data management strategy

As you sit and consider how to become a data-driven organisation, you need to think about your data management strategy; that is, all the processes you put in place to manage the data you use in your organisation – how you acquire, manage, store, use and improve it.

Below are your key considerations and questions you should ask when creating your data management strategy. As you read through, see how many answers you already have. You might be surprised to discover you could already be half way there:

1   **What data do you need to achieve your business objectives?** For example, when considering the data from your ticketing systems, do you need credit card numbers and expiry dates or do you just need to know who bought what, when, for how much and how often? If you're working

with your registered athlete database, do you need their height, weight and medical status or just the date they registered, the last time they played and their performance record?

2   **Where are you getting your data?** What source system, what database, is hosting that information and how can you get it? Continuing the example above, you may be using a third-party ticketing provider, so you need to get your data from their system to yours. Conversely, your athlete registration database may be housed by your sports development team, although this may again be supported by a third party or could be internally managed.

3   **Is your data accurate?** You need to understand how accurate your information is and how you can improve on that level of accuracy. It stands to reason that if your data isn't accurate then, whatever you do with it – whether you're making decisions or setting up targeted campaigns – won't be accurate either. If you address a casual ticket buyer as though they're a season ticket holder or a referee as though they're a coach, your message will lose its impact and won't achieve its objective. If you're analysing ticket buying behaviour to assist with a pricing or loyalty strategy, your plans will be flawed if your ticketing data isn't accurate. Inevitably this will lead to less-than-predicted success in your offering.

4   **Within your data management strategy, do you have a set of rules and processes that collectively make up your data governance?** It's common, and indeed recommended, to set up a data governance body or committee that takes responsibility for the implementation of these rules and processes, is accountable for the progress and ensures the approach is maintained. With a sports rights owner, this committee might be made up of representatives from your commercial/sales team, marketing, ICT and legal departments, ensuring that all key areas of the business are represented. If you're a national governing body or international federation with responsibility to grow the sport, you would also include your sports or development department within this committee.

5   **Does your data management strategy include your KPIs and metrics?** What does success look like for you? Clearly defining this will enable you to ensure your data management strategy stays on track. You'll know when you need to make adjustments and you'll stay abreast of your timing. Examples of this could be:

- Reduction in your email marketing bounce rate, demonstrating that your customers' email addresses are being used before they've had a chance to decay and that they're updated.
- The amount of time your data governance committee meetings take and the frequency of these. You can imagine that at the start of your data management strategy you'll have several issues that need to be discussed regularly and take up more time, so taking less time in these discussions can be considered a success metric.

- Percentage completion of data attributes: the amount of information you have about your customers in your database. You may have set a goal of understanding their favourite players in your team, adding their date of birth or gender, knowing their favourite channel for engaging with you, etc.
- Reduction in the number of incidences where data issues have been identified, for example, incorrect format of data fields that are supposed to merge.

Once you have documented your data management strategy in an easy-to-use format – perhaps a one-page summary for your management backed up by a more comprehensive document – it's important to maintain its relevance. Your approach to data management is not a one-off project but an ongoing set of initiatives that support both long-term goals and short-term wins. Hence your strategy will need to undergo constant review and measurement as your business objectives change and evolve, year-to-year, season-to-season.

Data to focus on

The data you should focus on is that which aligns with your business objectives, enables you to make decisions quickly and will help you achieve your goals. It's not 'big data' or data for data's sake. Going back to the first consideration of your data management strategy above, when I talk with clients about the type of data they ought to be collecting, I refer to six key categories:

1 **Contact information** – With your likely CRM objective being getting the right message to the right person at the right time, then securing email addresses of your customers is highly recommended. Email marketing remains one of the most cost-effective and measurable methods of keeping your customers informed. Adding mobile phone numbers to your customer records will allow you to use SMS marketing, another channel for fast, efficient and targeted delivery of your messages. This approach is particularly useful for in-stadium promotions where there is no Wi-Fi and for last-minute sales messages. However, while SMS marketing can play a valuable role in your CRM strategy, the costs are significantly higher than those of email marketing, so it is only recommended for highly targeted marketing. We discuss this further in Chapter 6 on data-driven marketing.

2 **Demographics** – the data points that are common for all of us. Gender, age, marital and family status, household income, location, education level and employment status can all be considered within this category.

3 **Fan engagement** – the way your customer digitally interacts with you: their usage pattern on your websites, mobile applications, online games and even how they respond to your email campaigns and text messages.

I also like to include the way they interact with your sport. Do they play, referee or coach? Do they attend your live matches or only watch on TV?

4   **Transactional** – your purchase data from ticketing, corporate hospitality, merchandise and even content is of significant value as it's usually the most accurate and richest of all your data categories. For example, asking someone for their postcode because you want to know where they live could result in false information, but asking for it so you can send them something they've purchased significantly increases the chances of you receiving something accurate.

5   **Lifestyle** – within this category we consider anything related to what your customers are interested in or engage in away from their relationship with you. This could include the other sports they follow, their favourite newspaper, the type of car they drive, their holiday choice and hobbies.

6   **Needs** – a final category of data that has significant value to a sports rights owner, indeed any organisation, is its data on customer needs. If we know what our customers need from us then we can more easily deliver it, ensuring their attention, loyalty and revenue.

Data sources and collection

Inevitably you will get your customer data from a variety of places. Your ticketing system secures transactional data, your athlete management system will secure your participation data, the various other forms that you produce will collect demographic data, and through the use of surveys you can supplement any data you already have with additional information. When I talk about the way we collect that data, I refer to three main methods:

1   **Ask for it**. You can ask for data through the use of registration or purchase forms, data collection landing pages (perhaps for competitions or a newsletter sign up) or the use of surveys. Asking someone directly to give you their information will result in the most accurate data. But, don't forget, it's a value exchange. Some of your fans will just give it to you, but some will need to know why. They'll want the hook (e.g., they can use your website or enter your competition and you'll send them news and information), and some will want an incentive such as the chance to win a competition or receive a discount code for your online store.

    On this point, creating an online registration form and inviting new customers to give you their details in return for receiving news and updates from you is an efficient and cost-effective method of increasing the size of your database. Once the form has been created, you can use your website, social channels and other modes of communication to encourage fans or followers of your sport to sign up. Most importantly, the form does not have to be dynamically integrated into your centralised database or SCV. You can manually export and import your customer data with whatever frequency you decide.

2   **Look out for it**. This is specifically true of behavioural data in the digital space. Tracking the content areas of your website that your fans visit and the links they click in your email campaigns helps you know more about their areas of interest, what they like about your sport, their favourite athlete, if they're considering attending a match or are a potential volunteer.

3   **Buy it**. You can buy data from aggregators, and while I would never advise a rights owner client to buy contact data like email addresses or mobile phone numbers, I do consider the act of enhancing your existing records in this manner a reasonable proposition. For example, you could buy demographic and lifestyle data. However, it's important to use a company with a good reputation, as you do risk the information being inaccurate, old and perhaps unethically sourced.

Different data types

There are currently three different data types. I say currently because with the pace at which this field is developing there will undoubtedly be more discovered before long. The current types are as follows:

1   **First-party data**. This is *your* data. The data that you collected and own and, as we discussed earlier in this chapter, that is one of your most valuable assets, even if you don't know it yet. In a 2015 survey by Econsultancy, almost three-quarters of marketers surveyed said first-party data provides the greatest insight into their customers (Econsultancy, 2015).

2   **Second-party data**. This is especially prevalent in the sports industry, although this term can be confusing, given the source of this data. It traditionally comes from customers of your partners – such as sponsors, ticketing and merchandise agents – who have ticked the 'third-party opt-in' box. It's the first-party data of your ticketing agents or your sponsors whose customers have said their data can be shared with you.

3   **Third-party data**. This is the data that you can buy from companies specialising in data collection and aggregation. As noted above, these data sets can be purchased 'off the shelf' so, by definition, they're not unique and their quality can vary widely.

While your first-party data is of the most value and your second-party data from a credible source can add quantity, third-party data can often get you to your desired state far quicker than the others. This is because the source of this data is usually one of the global data aggregators such as Experian or Acxiom.

One of the forms of third-party data that I particularly enjoy using is consumer marketing classifications created by socio-economic and geo-demographic profiles of neighbourhoods. This level of data enhancement is usually at a postcode or postal address level so, to that extent, the data can be classed as anonymous when passed to the data analyst. The marketing classification can then be added to each individual customer record.

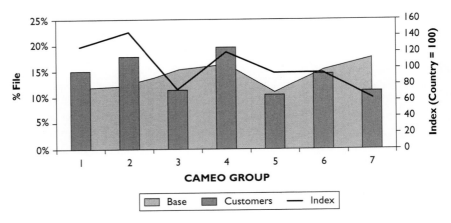

Figure 3.1 Third party data – consumer marketing profiles. (Source: Winners FDD Ltd., using CAMEO Classifications – www.cameo-online.com.)

In 2015 I demonstrated the power of this third-party data to a client, but his response wasn't quite what I expected. I demonstrated that his database contained a higher index of affluent singles and couples than the country average and that his sport had a much lower propensity to attract former council tenants and poorer singles. I added that this suggested his fan base might have a higher disposable income, enabling him to approach TAG Heuer or Mercedes for sponsorship, and possibly to even consider increasing his ticket prices (see Figure 3.1).

I thought this would be great news for my client but it was actually the opposite. It turned out his eleventh strategic objective was to use the sport to engage with their inner cities. The results I was showing him demonstrated they weren't achieving this objective. While this may seem a bad message to receive, it is better than continuing down the wrong path while thinking it's the right one. Knowledge is power, and what the data shows can help you readjust your strategies.

Data standardisation

To support the third consideration of your data management strategy, the accuracy of your data, I'd like to talk about data standardisation. As I discussed above, sports rights owners will have different data sources, some internal and some external, so your data is being collected in different ways and in different formats. The principle of data standardisation is that a layer of processing can be added that ensures all your data ends up in a common format. Once processed, the data can then be aggregated and transformed into a Single

Customer View (SCV) that, in turn, can be used across your organisation for analysis and communication.

Data standardisation is an incredibly important part of your data strategy. It involves keeping your data clean, in the correct format and verified before you do anything with it. Imagine how important it is to have the correct email address for a fan before sending out any campaigns, or the right data points before you try and find your actionable insights. If you ever want to merge your databases together in an SCV (or any other type of data warehouse) the relevant data fields must match up. They must use the same pattern.

Here are some easy examples that clearly demonstrate the principle, with some tactics to help minimise the occurrence of incorrect formatting:

1   **Date of birth**: Here in Europe and in many other regions of the world we use the format DD/MM/YYYY but, as you'll be aware, in the US the date and month fields are reversed to MM/DD/YYYY. If you're not paying attention to the input format of the date of birth field in the different data collection forms around your business, you may be collecting records in both formats. Consider if the same person is asked to complete two different forms. I was born on November 2nd 1966 so imagine if I register to be a volunteer that uses the DD/MM/YYYY format, but then I enter one of your competitions via an independently hosted landing page and they use MM/DD/YYYY. If you're using an SCV, or even if you just use an email campaign platform that houses all your email marketing data, depending on how you import your records and the business rules you set, you could end up sending me a birthday card on February 11th. Here's another point to consider: if you ask for a customer's date of birth and allow users to free type instead of using a calendar format, you could end up with 2nd November 1966, 2 Nov 66, 2 Nov 1966, or any one of a number of spellings and formats.

The value in a correct date of birth can't be understated. First, there are digital birthday cards – a great tool for fan engagement that only need to be set up once a year and will then provide you with 12 months of activity. If you include a discount coupon for your online store or a sponsor offering, they'll help with your commercial objectives. Second, if you want to pitch to, say, Heineken for a sponsorship, they'll inevitably want to know how many adults aged 18 to 25 you have in your database, as it aligns with their target demographic.

2   **Gender**: Another data area that is incredibly important to your business but prone to errors is your gender field. Options for a customer to choose often include M or F, male or female, boy or girl, but the way in which a database may interpret this could also include a 0 and 1, or 1 and 2. If this isn't standardised when the individual data sources merge, you'll end up with a 'dirty' gender field when you really want 100% usable information. It's interesting to note that many organisations now use a broader gender definition than male or female.

3   **Country of residence**: I always recommend when using a country of residence field in your data collection forms that you use a drop-down menu that enables the customer to select their specific country. If you don't, can you imagine how many different spellings of any individual country you might get? Consider someone who lives in London. Their self-type options could be UK or United Kingdom, GB or Great Britain, or indeed they could write England. If they mistype or have a problem with spelling you could end up with Untied Kingdom, Grate Britian or Englend.

You can see from just these three easy examples that, if you don't pay attention to your data standards, you could end up with a database that contains a lot of unusable information. This will skew your statistics and result in incorrect messaging sent to your fans. Creating a data dictionary that lists each data cell in each of your data sources, its format and purpose, will help you stay on top of this.

Ensuring an organisation operates with the same data standards can be a challenge. One rights owner has managed this for over 16 years, resulting in a wealth of uniform information about the reach and impact of its movement: Special Olympics International.

Case study: Special Olympics International

With over 200 million people around the world with Intellectual Disabilities (ID), Special Olympics International (SOI) has a huge task. It uses the influence of sports to empower its athletes, working to change social perceptions and helping to improve the lives of those with ID by creating healthy environments. Special Olympics International also works to increase involvement for people with ID in communities, using its valuable data not only to improve the services it provides but also to help inform health initiatives to work with those with ID.

Special Olympics International spans the globe with 220 programmes worldwide and runs over 100,000 events yearly, providing athletes with the opportunity to compete in a variety of sports from alpine skiing to figure skating, football to basketball and everything in between. Special Olympics International has been collecting data on its community for over 16 years, keeping track of the number of athletes, volunteers and family members participating in its programmes around the world. The wealth of information SOI can provide through what it calls its 'census data' is second to none for both the people who work and participate in the organisation, but also in the form of valuable health data on its participants that can be used to monitor and maintain the health of athletes with ID.

While SOI has been collecting this anonymised athlete participation data for a long time, the use of that data at an individual level as opposed to an aggregated one has been overlooked. To progress this, SOI is implementing a new process for collecting participation data. This new bespoke system will enhance the depth of the database, enabling SOI to better track its progress in various business areas, engage directly with the SOI global community and provide all its stakeholders with valuable information that will support data-driven decision-making.

SOI and the changing use of data

As with any new initiative, there were hurdles when SOI first started to seriously collect census data. With a global network, it was challenging to communicate to everyone the how, why and what was involved in data collection. It takes time to implement training programmes and really get to grips with facilitating change within the business when people are so used to doing things a certain way. I interviewed Mary Davis, SOI's Chief Executive Officer, via email on 19 December 2017 and she shared some valuable insights.

> At the time, back in 2002, there was an understanding that capturing this information would be essential for the movement but how important and to what extent it could and couldn't be used has evolved, along with the evolution of technology and our use of data generally.

The initial data collected was relatively basic. The 2002 Census included information on participants such as sport played, gender, age group and whether they took part in the Athlete Leadership Program, which enables young athletes to become mentors to encourage their peers, training them to become leaders both within the organisation and within their community.

Over time, the requests for data grew to encompass more of SOI's individual programmes. On the Athletes Participation Summary (APS), it included data for programmes such as Young Athletes (a sports initiative for children both with and without ID), Athletes in Training, coaching programmes for six- and seven-year-olds and the Certified Coaches programme. The census also included information for SOI's Unified Sports initiative that works to join people with or without ID to build inclusive sporting communities. For this it needed data on both the athletes and the partners (the SOI term for athletes without ID who participate in Unified Sports), data on the three Unified Sports models (Recreational, Player Development and Competitive), as well as the number of coaches participating in the initiative.

By laying this foundation over the course of the past 15 years, SOI now finds itself able to align its resources with its observed and forecasted participation levels. It can look at the efficacy of new sports and programmes that have been added on a local level and compare that with how they perform both regionally and globally. With a centralised census implemented, the resulting data is more reliable, giving a better understanding of SOI's footprint in individual sports by gender and age group as well as by region. This information is vital in safeguarding the future growth of SOI as it helps with receiving grants for individual programmes as well as creating sponsorship and campaign opportunities.

The importance of CONNECT

Building on the success of its Census data, SOI is looking to implement something entirely new, replacing the current system that produces its data with bespoke CRM software that has been built and designed to suit SOI's needs. It's called CONNECT and will be used to register athletes, volunteers, family members, staff and other stakeholders engaged with the management of its sports, programmes and events.

> We call it a game and volunteer management system. It's basically a database that holds information about participants: who they are, where they live, what sport they participate in, what events they've attended, their results, personal details such as height, weight, disability, etc. It's web-enabled, and all our stakeholders can access it, from an athlete and parent to an event director. They can use it to input and update information and find data relating to performances and events.

The CONNECT system will give SOI the opportunity to gather more data than ever before, not only of the sports that athletes participate in but the events they attend in each sport. This would be of enormous benefit for the World Games quotas. On a single level, CONNECT will give SOI the ability to track an athlete's growth within the organisation's programmes. It can show what sports and events an athlete started with and how they've progressed over their lifetime within the organisation. It can show how sports relate to the overall health of participating athletes, give data on coaches, athlete's families and volunteers, and ultimately help SOI to better understand its impact and opportunities worldwide.

> When CONNECT is fully developed, we will have a tool that can provide us with accurate numbers for all the information we gather. We could drill down to the tiniest detail, like our athlete's different medical conditions and how that relates to their sport and event participation. We'd also be able to see a

full demographic profile of each individual program. We could see how many family members are coaches, serve on the board, or as volunteers. This would be true for volunteers as well. What is the volunteering doing for the program and community? We will have a much better way of tracking of the reach of Healthy Athletes screenings and see the impact that this has locally and worldwide.

Healthy Athletes is a programme that is of huge importance in SOI. It offers healthcare and services to athletes in need all over the world including free health screenings. To date, 1.7 million free health examinations have been conducted in more than 130 countries, making SOI the most significant global public health organisation dedicated to serving people with intellectual disabilities (Special Olympics International, 2017). These screenings encompass everything from free dentist check-ups to podiatry and opticians, just to name a few.

The CONNECT system will allow SOI not only to capture the results of these screenings but also follow up with the athletes personally, as well as their family members, to monitor improvement and pinpoint areas that may need additional follow-up. Healthy Athletes already has the world's most extensive database of health data for people with ID and, by partnering this data with the power of CONNECT, SOI will be able to impact the way that its services can improve and benefit the community.

But how will CONNECT achieve this?

Collecting data in this manner serves multiple purposes. Firstly, it enables us to understand our numbers. We will know how many athletes are participating in what programs. This allows for better planning and management. But when you have this much data collected over such a long time, it also enables you to predict growth. This also supports better planning and management. For example, if we know how many athletes there are in Australia, we'll know how many volunteers we'll need to provide support at events. If you see how the number of athletes has grown over the last ten years in Poland, you can analyse and predict how that growth might continue over the next ten years.

What Davis is referencing is time-series analysis. This type of analysis can be used to extract meaningful statistics from current data, as well as forecasting future trends. But regression analysis can also be used to improve the accuracy of this projection. Essentially, regression analysis boils down to adding observed factors to modelled scenarios such as the impact of economic crises, civil unrest in countries in which SOI has chapters, change in management or structure of SOI in different countries and so forth. However, I will discuss regression analysis in more detail in Chapter 4.

The CONNECT system doesn't just offer big-picture opportunities. It allows SOI to connect with its athletes on an individual level. The current system that hosts the census data doesn't include personal details on individual athletes, volunteers or family members. The CONNECT system will allow for the collection and storage of distinct contact data, enabling SOI to engage with its participants, their families and volunteers directly; something that will prove valuable in reaching a broader audience, engaging the community and liaising with potential sponsors and donors.

But if we've learned anything so far, it's that simply collecting the data is not enough. It's only as good as the way it's going to be used and, as such, the management of it can be a major challenge and dictates attention and focus. While there may be a department responsible for gathering the data, it's important to make sure that information is shared and implemented across the entire organisation. The people who collect the data are likely not the ones who will feel the most impact of what that data may be telling them, so it's important to have everyone on board. Reports need to be developed and shared with other departments, not only within SOI's headquarters but also at a regional level.

To overcome natural cultural barriers that appear within an organisation, SOI has started to present their data visually to more easily identify opportunities and challenges. By displaying the data in this way, it ensures that all departments are not only able to access it but to understand and act on it.

> Over the last few years, I think we've gotten better at collecting our data. However, there's still a lot that needs to be done. Areas for improvement are that we can look at resources better to see where we need to allocate our limited resources. We can really consider our program quality by looking at athlete-to-coach ratios as well as seeing how many coaches involved are certified head coaches. However this type of information is only as good as the way we use it, so by presenting the data – not in Excel charts but in colourful graphs – we're able to quickly identify both the challenge and the opportunity.
>
> Collecting and storing our data has been an ongoing process of development – knowing how to use software to present that data in a way that generates discussion across our business has been immediate. We know we've only scratched the surface of our use of data so it's exciting to think about our future and how it will be positively impacted as we make progress in this area.

Far-reaching benefits

Special Olympics International isn't the only organisation responsible for growing and developing their sport. So many organisations are just now starting to tackle the daunting task of counting their participants and learning more about them on an individual level. Davis has the following advice:

Make sure you're providing the right tool to ensure accuracy in all that you do. The numbers have to be precise and easy to collect. These tools aren't just software or databases, but making sure that you've got the right staff to support these programs and that everyone is on board with clear guidelines on how each data point needs to be collected.

By ensuring the accuracy of data and its accessibility, SOI has managed to develop and extend a number of its health screening programmes. They are in a unique position to collect data that will impact the health of their participants, which makes the accuracy of even greater importance to them. Their primary health programmes are:

- **Fit Feet** – a programme that offers podiatric screenings to evaluate ankles, feet, lower extremity biomechanics, and proper shoe and sock gear to participating athletes.
- **FUNFitness** – offering physical therapy to Special Olympics athletes to address their ongoing health needs.
- **Health Promotion** – focusing on healthy living, lifestyle choices, health screenings and education programmes.
- **Healthy Hearing** – offering comprehensive hearing analysis and recommendations.
- **Opening Eyes** – providing free eye assessments, prescription glasses and sports eyewear to people with ID.
- **Special Smiles** – offering comprehensive oral health care information and free dental screenings to increase dental health and awareness (Special Olympics International, 2017).

The data collected so far has been invaluable to these initiatives, helping build partnerships with corporations who have CSR (Corporate Social Responsibility) programmes. For instance, Essilor donate lenses and Safilo give frames to provide SOI athletes with free eyewear through the Opening Eyes initiative. Other sponsors and donors include Bank of America, IKEA, who support the Young Athletes Program, ESPN, who are the global presenting partner for Unified Sports and Microsoft, the official Technology Partner which has helped make CONNECT possible.

Moving forward, the use of CONNECT will help them build on their already rich database of information and enable SOI to engage directly with the athletes, family members, and volunteers, telling them about these partnerships, so they understand the benefits they bring.

Special Olympics International's broader CRM plan aims to have CONNECT integrate with their health screening data allowing follow-ups once their athletes have participated in programmes. This will let them see if, and how, their recommendations are being followed by athletes and ultimately see how health has improved as a result. With this integration it won't just be a general overview, SOI will be able to pinpoint individual athletes and engage with them directly. By working in conjunction with partners without having to share this data directly, SOI will be able to carry any partner's messages on their behalf.

(Source: Davis, 2017, 19 December.)

Key chapter ideas

1   Your data could be viewed as a business asset with its own value and it should be protected, nurtured and utilised in the same way you monetise your logos, trademarks, images and media rights.

2   You need a data management strategy to guide you through key considerations as you become a data-driven organisation. These include understanding what data you need, where you'll find it, securing and maintaining its accuracy, applying specific rules and processes to the way you manage it and, finally, identifying your KPIs so you know when you're on track to achieving your data-related business objectives.

3   Your data will only deliver its true potential to your organisation if it's in a format that ensures it can be readily used across the business. Implementing a process of standardisation that's applied to every individual data source will enable you to merge all your data and produce an SCV.

4   Collecting participation data in sports has a tremendous value for the development of the sport, but adding personal data at an individual contact level will add greater value – enabling you to track participants' performance to ensure progress and communicate directly with the individual.

References

Connelly, T. (2017). Manchester City get smart with data to create personalised fan experience platform [online]. *The Drum*. Available at: www.thedrum.com/news/2017/08/07/manchester-city-get-smart-with-data-create-personalised-fan-experience-platform.

Davis, M. (2017, 19 December). Email interview.

Econsultancy (2015). *The Promise of First-Party Data*. London: Econsultancy.

Heinze, J. (2016). *Business Intelligence vs. Business Analytics: What's the Difference?* [online]. Better Buys. Available at: www.betterbuys.com/bi/business-intelligence-vs-business-analytics.

Hellweg, E. (2012). 2012: the first big data election [online]. *Harvard Business Review*. Available at: https://hbr.org/2012/11/2012-the-first-big-data-electi.

Humby, C. (2006). *Data Is the New Oil*. *ANA Senior Marketer's Summit*, Kellogg School of Management, Northwestern University.

Kolowich, L. (2016). *Email Analytics: The 6 Email Marketing Metrics & KPIs You Should Be Tracking* [online blog]. HubSpot. Available at: https://blog.hubspot.com/marketing/metrics-email-marketers-should-be-tracking.

Lewis, M. (2003). *Moneyball*. New York: W.W. Norton.

McCandless, D. (2010). *The Beauty of Data Visualization* [video]. Available at: www.ted.com/talks/david_mccandless_the_beauty_of_data_visualization.

Nagle, T., Redman, T. and Sammon, D. (2017). Only 3% of companies' data meets basic quality standards [online]. *Harvard Business Review*. Available at: https://hbr.org/2017/09/only-3-of-companies-data-meets-basic-quality-standards.

Petraetis, G. (2017). How Netflix built a House of Cards with big data [online]. *CIO*. Available at: www.cio.com/article/3207670/big-data/how-netflix-built-a-house-of-cards-with-big-data.html.

Pudwell, S. (2017). Machine learning is the future of sports data [online]. *Silicon*. Available at: www.silicon.co.uk/data-storage/bigdata/machine-learning-data-206762.

Ray, Amie B. (2018, 11 January). Telephone interview.

Reichheld, F. (n.d.). *Prescription for Cutting Costs* [ebook]. Boston: Bain & Company. Available at: www.bain.com/Images/BB_Prescription_cutting_costs.pdf.

Ritson, M. (2017). Spreadsheet jockeys are misunderstanding the marketing funnel [online]. *Marketing Week*. Available at: www.marketingweek.com/2017/09/20/mark-ritson-collapse-marketing-funnel.

Roberts, D. (2017). Amazon's NFL streaming is all about collecting ad data [online]. *Yahoo*. Available at: www.yahoo.com/amphtml/finance/news/amazon-streaming-nfl-games-collecting-ad-data-110006168.html.

Special Olympics International (2017). *Providing Health Services Worldwide for the Most Underserved* [online]. Special Olympics. Available at: www.specialolympics.org/healthy_athletes.aspx [accessed 28 November 2017].

Chapter 4

Business intelligence and data analytics

In this book I've referred to Amazon being aspirational, but it's important to remember that most rights owners – in fact, probably all rights owners – won't have the same data-related requirements as the leading pure-plays. Tech companies such as Google, Netflix and Spotify aren't just generating rows and columns, they're in the business of big data. They're already leading the way in Analytics 2.0 (often called 'big data') while we're still trying to make Analytics 1.0 work for us (as in structured data). But, even so, there is so much that can be written about the use of business intelligence (BI) and data analytics in sport, its challenges and the opportunities, that the intention of this chapter is to provide a helicopter view of the subject area and highlight directions for further exploration.

These data-driven strategies, all focused on helping you make decisions and engage with fans on a more personalised basis, have become more important over the last decade as we've realised that the principle of 'if you build it, they will come' no longer applies. When your season's going well and you're winning, or you've secured the services of superstar athletes, it can be like Christmas: your tickets sell themselves, merchandise flies off your shelves and sponsors come to you looking for an association. But we, the business folk, can't control what happens on the field of play and have no impact on the decisions made in that area. We need to focus on what we can do and affect. That's the way we use data to fend off the competition for our fans' time, attention and money. Restaurants, theatres and the cinema are just a few of our competitors, and we need to learn how to keep our fans engaged and keep their attention.

BI and analytics: what's the difference?

In the same way the growth in the use of data has been exponential, so too has the proliferation of new and often confusing terminology related to the use of data. Googling 'what is business intelligence' gives you 15 million results in 0.63 seconds. Do the same for data analytics and you will find a further 13 million results in 0.61 of a second.

If the analysis of data generally means the way you look at the information you hold to help understand more about your business and to make decisions based on that data, how do we define the difference between analytics and BI? This is my favourite definition, reported in *BetterBuys* and provided by Mark van Rijmenam, CEO of Datafloq:

> Business Intelligence is looking in the rearview mirror and using historical data from one minute ago to many years ago. Business Analytics is looking in front of you to see what is going to happen. This will help you anticipate what's coming, while BI will tell you what happened. This is a very important distinction as both will provide you with different, not less, insights. BI is important to improve your decision-making based on past results, while business analytics will help you move forward and understand what might be going to happen.
>
> (Heinze, 2016)

The key thing for me, and for my team at Winners, is that any form of analysis, whether backward- or forward-looking, should provide actionable insights. We refer to the importance of ensuring that when we present our analysis we're not asked 'so what?' This is the area that seems to be confounding most organisations. A study undertaken by Gartner in 2016 suggested that while 74% of firms say they want to be 'data-driven', only 29% say they are good at connecting analytics to action (Hopkins, 2016). But that's where the value is: being able to convert your findings to your next steps. Without this, it's just data for data's sake.

In the following pages I will take you through some of my favourite types of analysis and how you could apply them as a rights owner. There are many being used by sports and non-sports organisations around the world, but if you're one that hasn't yet started to use data, or are seeking ideas for further analyses, you might like to start with these.

Email campaign analysis

> It can be argued that it doesn't really matter how optimized your emails are if you are unable to see the results of your efforts and cannot measure that performance against set targets.
>
> (Kolowich, 2016)

Your email campaign performance data (the 'so what?') tells you two important things: first, how you can plan your next campaign better because you know what worked and what didn't and, second, you can better understand your recipients' interests by tracking their engagement with the different content areas in your campaign.

As with everything we've discussed thus far, setting Key Performance Indicators (KPIs) is important within your email campaign planning, as they provide you with success and failure barometers. However, these KPIs need to be aligned with the most valuable metrics for this channel. Depending on whether your objective is reach, awareness, engagement or even direct sales, they could be:

- **Delivery rates**: displayed as a percentage of the number of emails that were received after sending. This demonstrates how clean your list is. A low delivery rate suggests too many old addresses that have resulted in a bounced email.
- **Open rates (OR)**: displayed as a percentage of the number of emails opened after receiving. Your subject line and even your preview text have the biggest impact on whether your email will be opened. In Chapter 6 we look at the use of multivariate testing to improve this metric.
- **Click-through rates (CTR)**: displayed as a percentage of links clicked in the campaigns after receiving. This metric demonstrates how relevant and interesting your content is to the recipient. At Winners we also like to report on the click-to-open rate; something that is presented in some email campaign platforms but not in others. We find it more relevant than the CTR as it's not possible for a recipient to click on a link if it's not opened. A more apt analysis is to look at those that opened the campaign to discover what percentage found the content of interest and relevant.
- **Unsubscribe rates**: displayed as a percentage of recipients who opened the campaign and then went on to unsubscribe. This informs you that they no longer wish to receive your emails. This is an important metric as it demonstrates how good or poor a job you're doing and, most importantly, if you need to improve.
- **Your campaign conversion rate**: that is the percentage of people who completed your desired action or campaign goal after opening it. This is another statistic you can report on, but it is not limited just to email marketing. The advent of technology has ensured this measurement is the *de facto* metric of our digital marketing efforts.

As with all of these metrics, or any others you choose to focus on within your email marketing campaigns, the key is to watch them over time, looking for a positive trend line to demonstrate that you're continuously improving and, if you see a downward trajectory, take remedial action; looking at what you've been doing and testing an alternative approach.

Population mapping

Putting the location of your fans and customers on to a map using their postal code enables you to see in a clear visual manner where they live in relation to your activity or need. A visual map is easier to understand and therefore more effective than searching rows and columns in a spreadsheet for postcodes and street addresses. If you haven't taken this step for any of your datasets, I would highly recommend it. The impact of geographic relevance can be quite immediate when you see how far your fans travel to get to your stadium or their distance to other locations such as your grassroots clubs or sponsors' retail outlets (an example of this is included in Chapter 7: The role of CRM and data in sponsorship).

Case study: the Polish Football Federation

At a workshop with the PZPN (Polski Związek Piłki Nożnej) on 7 September 2013 we produced two separate maps. One showed the location of its former membership data, Klub Kibica; the other focused on its participation data, the players, coaches, referees and other volunteers. The results are shown in Figures 4.1 and 4.2.

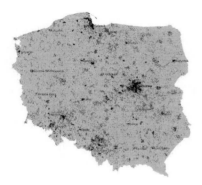

Figure 4.1 Population mapping of Klub Kibica members. (Source: Winners FDD Ltd using data from the Polish Football Federation, with permission.)

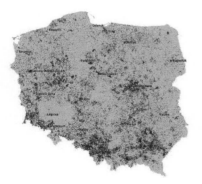

Figure 4.2 Population mapping of PZPN registered participants. (Source: Winners FDD Ltd using data from the Polish Football Federation, with permission.)

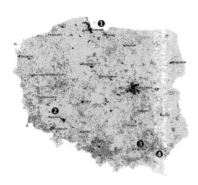

Figure 4.3 Population mapping of Klub Kibica members and PZPN registered participants. (Source: Winners FDD Ltd using data from the Polish Football Federation, with permission.)

Membership of Klub Kibica provided guaranteed access to tickets for the men's national team matches, so the map in Figure 4.1 clearly shows regions of the country where individuals with a strong interest in professional football live in greater or lesser quantities.

The map in Figure 4.2 shows where the areas that have the greatest interest in participating in football at the grassroots level are around the country.

The two maps already provided value as they were. The PZPN management could see at a glance where they should focus their marketing efforts, increase the number of grassroots coaches or clubs and where to stage events for maximum attendance. However, by overlaying the two sets of data, it showed something of even greater value, as you can see in Figure 4.3.

Interpreting the black dots (Klub Kibica) and the grey dots (participation) suggest that:

1   The Gdansk (1) and Legnica (2) regions may provide opportunities for increased participation through the development of more coaches and the establishment of football clubs.
2   The Tarnow (3) and Rzeszow (4) regions may be prime target areas for sales of Klub Kibica membership (and other PZPN products), as there are high levels of participation in these areas.

The patches with no dots also point to areas where the PZPN might choose to focus its future development activities, as there are small numbers of both members and participants.

Bartosz Bury from the PZPN's marketing department had the following to say:

This map helped us to understand the huge potential our database has and how easy and helpful segmentation is. Mapping our data allows us to identify and select the information we need for a particular purpose. It also shows us what region has the most growth potential, so we can focus our sales and marketing efforts, and it will help us plan the location of future events.

(Bury, 2013)

Ticketing timelines

One of my favourite forms of analysis that we apply in the sports industry is the use of a ticket-buying timeline, as it supports several opportunities.

If you have enough historic ticketing data, knowing the purchase pattern of your fans will enable you to predict when they're likely to buy for the next match. This can help in a multitude of ways:

- **Cash flow**: if you're a rights owner that has to work within a tight cash flow, the insight you can get from analysing the pattern of your historic tickets sales will be invaluable to your planning.
- **ROI tracking**: when you plan your ticket sales marketing campaign, knowing which tactics work and which don't can save you money and increase your efficiency. Tracking peaks and troughs in your sales figures against your activity such as social posts, website advertising, flyer distribution, email campaigns, etc., enables you to hold these activities to account.
- **Performance tracking**: knowing your target number of sales at any given time before an event, and comparing this to the progress you're making, will enable you to understand whether you're likely to hit your target. If you're not, then you can go back to your ROI tracking (above) and invest more in those tactics that have been identified as working for you.
- **Understanding ticket-buying behaviour**: when, why and how much is also useful for the implementation of dynamic ticket pricing (the practice of setting ticket prices based on real-time market demand and other

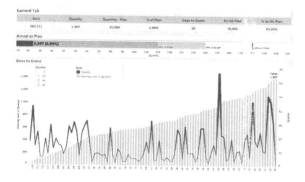

Figure 4.4 Ticket buying timeline. (Source: Winners FDD Ltd, data used with permission.)

datasets). While in Europe we're used to seeing this with airline and train tickets, we haven't yet adopted it in sport. In the US, 25% of NFL teams now use this approach to provide prices that 'reflect the fair market value' (Young, 2017). This type of real-time pricing strategy relies on demand information that can be forecast. Understanding historic ticket purchase behaviour can assist in developing the logic that's applied to the process. Ticketing behaviour at an individual customer level is also needed for RFV analysis.

Customer churn

Working with data in the sports industry, I find that I'm constantly checking myself: do I use the term customers or fans? Sometimes I even consider using stakeholders, although that can sound a little too corporate to represent someone with so much passion, and data subjects is just far too sterile. Many of our fans don't like to be considered 'customers' but, at the same time, a rights owner's customers include more than just the fans. This is particularly true for a National Governing Body that includes players, referees, coaches and volunteers among its most valuable group of customers. I find myself using the words interchangeably, depending on the context and the audience. But when it comes to the discussion of churn, we can't refer to fans because they don't churn. Or do they?

Churn is the calculation of how many people are left in your environment that are still customers and haven't dropped away from you during a given period. This could be your email newsletter subscribers, ticket buyers, grass-roots players, coaches or volunteers during a particular season. The two metrics we care about are the number of customers lost and the percentage that they represent of your initial total. This is referred to as your churn rate.

To be able to calculate churn you need to know two dates: when the customer first became a customer and when they stopped being one. But do fans ever really abandon their team if they really are a fan? Can consecutive relegation ever really cause a football fan to abandon their team? Does a Mariners fan ever get despondent enough to walk away in search of a team that will one day appear in the World Series?

In this case, churn can be applied to a fan but only when it refers to a specific action, such as the purchase of tickets or merchandise, but not the state of fandom itself.

But why is churn analysis such an important topic for rights owners? We've all heard that acquiring a new customer is more difficult than retaining an existing one and can be anywhere from five to 25 times more expensive depending on which report you read. Bain & Co, one of the biggest management consultancies in the world, also suggests that a 5% increase in customer retention produces more than a 25% increase in profit (Reichheld, n.d.).

We have a number of tactics at our disposal to reduce customer churn, but the key principle I subscribe to is that rights owners should proactively and consistently communicate with their fans and customers:

- When you've lost a match or a game, the temptation might be to ignore the result and look to the next event, but a better idea is to address the fact in a well-worded email to your ticket buyers, thanking them for their support, apologising for your lack of performance, and asking them to return to help you push through your losing streak.
- When a coach has secured their Level 1 badge, you could consider informing them how they can progress to Level 2, perhaps setting up a series of digital interactions that, over a period of time, perhaps six months, lead them to the relevant registration page on your website.
- When one of your grassroots players reaches 18, the change in their lifestyle as they move to university or enter the workplace could cause them to forget about registering to play again for the following season. A timely email reminding them of their performance record last season, where their club finished in the league thanks to their goals, assists or saves, could remind them why they love playing your sport, resulting in a repeat registration.

The customer life cycle

The customer life cycle (CLC) is a term used to describe a series of steps that a customer goes through when considering, purchasing, using and maintaining loyalty to a product or service. It includes the journey that customers take as they lose interest in you, move away and then come back to you at a later date.

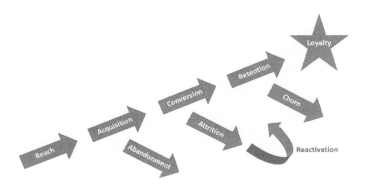

Figure 4.5 Sterne and Cutler Loyalty Model. (Source: Cutler and Sterne, 2000.)

When discussing this with colleagues or clients, I like to refer to the Sterne and Cutler Loyalty Model (see Figure 4.5) as it throws up all sorts of contradictions when it comes to sports fandom (Cutler and Sterne, 2000).

How can we position loyalty as the end game, especially as most fans of a sports team are inherently loyal, having been 'born into' a particular allegiance? As discussed earlier, do sports fans really ever walk away? Do they ever actually abandon their team?

Generally not, but this isn't to say that a fan's purchasing habits won't be affected, because they will. As the economy hits a rough patch, their personal circumstances change, or their choice of leisure activity is dictated by factors other than their fandom; their habits might change. Should these circumstances occur, while their inclination to stay with you may be very high, you will still need to use your targeted engagement activities, aligned with their position in the customer life cycle, to retain them as loyal customers not just as loyal fans. In this instance, the Sterne and Cutler Loyalty Model dictates that by providing excellent customer service, communicating with them in a way that is relevant to their needs and understanding their stage in the customer life cycle, your chances of retaining them and their interest will increase. This is specifically relevant for Europe where many of our sports clubs are over a century old, so the parallel with the US industry where teams can be moved from one state to another, requiring fans to switch their allegiance without breaking a stride, deserves to be explored as a separate dynamic that may affect the way the customer life cycle is defined.

Customer lifetime value

Building on your CLC, Customer lifetime value (CLTV) is the total financial value of a customer to your organisation over the lifetime of their relationship with you. When you identify the lifetime value of a customer who sits within one of your customer groups, you can calculate the value of that group as a whole.

Understanding the CLTV of different customer groups helps to decide where and how to focus your marketing. By combining CLC with CLTV you can identify the customers that are of most value to your organisation – your most profitable customers – and communicate with them in an appropriate way.

As a next step, identifying the most common characteristics of your most profitable customers will help you to identify which of the other customers within your database share some but not all of those characteristics. These can be considered your next most valuable customers and, after identifying them, you can communicate with them in a way that will encourage them to respond in the way you would like them to respond. For example, if you've been able to identify that your season ticket holders are predominantly male, aged 28 to 35 and attending 12 matches per season immediately before buying a season ticket, you can look for other 28-to-35-year-old males in your database that have attended 10, 11 or 12 matches. A well-designed email sent at the right time in your season could induce them to consider becoming a season ticket holder for the following season.

In participation, it's important to know the age at which your athletes stop playing. If you determine that males stop playing when they reach 18 (as they discover other interests) and girls stop at 16 (as they decide it's no longer 'cool') you can set up a process to ensure that 17-year-old boys and 15-year-old girls receive encouraging messages and reasons to continue in the weeks or months leading up to their birthdays.

Recency, frequency, value analysis

Recency, frequency, value analysis (RFV; also known as RFM, recency, frequency, monetary) is used to determine, in quantitative terms, which customers are your most valuable. It looks at how recently a customer has purchased (recency), how often they purchase (frequency) and how much money the customer spends (value). The outcome of RFV analysis usually confirms Pareto's principle that 80% of your business comes from 20% of your customers (Ultsch, 2002).

The RFV allows you to identify your best customers, not just on the basis of the quantity or value of sales, but on the basis of a combination of 'how often', 'how many' and 'how much'. Sometimes your highest-value customers only come once a year and spend a lot, or come often and buy in small amounts. The RFV analysis enables an understanding of this and could result in the creation of ticketing customer segments for single-visit customers, occasional attendance, regular attendance and avid attendees.

Other applications of RFV for a rights owner could include:

- Identifying the customers who would be most likely to upgrade their match ticket to a VIP hospitality product.
- Predicting the quantity of a limited edition high-value piece of souvenir merchandise that you could reasonably expect to sell.
- Predicting how many of your customers might be interested in hearing about your sponsor's goods and services.

The RFV analysis and the segments you create as a result can also form the basis of your loyalty programmes as you consider what behaviour you will reward and what you can give in return for those behaviours, as well as the use of all sorts of predictive analysis models.

Predictive analysis

When we use predictive analysis we're looking at current and historical data to make predictions about the future. For this reason, predictive analysis is considered the closest thing we have to a crystal ball. We look at what happened in the past and understand why it happened. We then look at what is happening now, applying it to the model, and from this we can predict what's going to happen in the future.

For rights owners, this could include understanding how to price match tickets to ensure maximum take-up, how many special events to stage and what quantity of merchandise to make available for sale. Rights owners that run a membership or fan club can also use predictive models to identify when a customer is likely to terminate their membership and take proactive steps to prevent this from happening. It can also be used to determine the quantity of memberships that you are reasonably likely to sell at a certain price point within a specific time frame. This leads to a greater conversion rate and lower marketing costs.

The level of accuracy in predictive analytics is dictated by the quantity and accuracy of the data available, but, as we take things even further and apply machine learning and artificial intelligence, the process will become more time-efficient and even more accurate.

Correlation and regression analysis

Correlation analysis is used when you need to understand the strength of a relationship between two variables. For rights owners this could be the projected calculation of a match attendance based on a combination of the ticket price and the weather. Regression analysis is used to understand which variables have the most impact on a given result.

At Winners we were asked to use correlation and regression analysis to quantify the link between participation and consumption in European football, that is, how much more money does a grassroots player spend following and supporting football versus a fan who has never played or used to play, and what factors affect the value of that relationship. In the study we looked at the frequency of match attendance, the amount spent on match tickets, how long ago players attended a match or played football, how much they spent on televised football or channel subscriptions and also how much they spent on football merchandise.

The purpose of this analysis was to demonstrate that a deeper understanding of a participant's spending behaviour could help sports organisations better target marketing communications, predict future revenues, provide an ROI model for participation development programmes and help rights owners make commercially focused decisions relating to marketing investment.

Methodology

Over 5,800 survey participants across six different countries answered a set of multiple-choice, rating-scale and open-ended questions. These questions ranged from basic identifications such as age, gender, occupation and annual household income to such questions as: 'how much do you spend when you attend a live professional match?', 'which sports do you play?' and 'which of these sports have you played in the past?'

The question 'how much of a football fan are you?' was also asked, and participants ranked their interest on a 1-to-7 scale, with 7 being a 'huge football fan' and 1 being entirely uninterested.

The data was translated into a common format and, after conducting a preliminary inspection of each variable to pinpoint correlations and relationships, all compiled data was analysed using simple and multivariate regression testing.

Overall, the general statistics, based on the six representative sample countries, were as follows: people who currently play football spend 6.3 times more than people who never played and 2.2 times more on match tickets than people who used to play. Regarding the purchase of merchandise and licensed products, people who currently play spend five times more than people who never played and double that of former players. When it comes to the amount spent on TV football channels, people who play spend three times more than people who never played and 1.2 times more than people who used to play (See Figure 4.6).

In addition, by using single and multi-variate regression analysis to identify the relationship between the variables, it was found that:

1   Participants who played football recreationally attended five more games per season on average than those who didn't play recreationally.
2   There is a relationship between frequency of match attendance, spend on football and 'fandom' rating assigned by the participant. For every unit increase in fandom (on a scale of 1–7), it is expected the participant will attend one additional match per season, spend an additional €2.50 on tickets, €4 on merchandise and €2.60 on TV content.

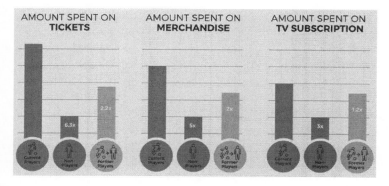

Figure 4.6 Quantifying the ratio of spend between players and non-players. (Source: Winners FDD Ltd using UEFA data, with permission.)

3   Among football participants, an increase of €13 on tickets, €22 on merchandise and €10 on TV content is evident.
4   Football participants spend an additional €13 on a match ticket, €22 on merchandise and €10 on TV content than a non-player.

Additional findings to note involved the gender and locale of football's biggest spenders. Specifically, men attended one to two more games than women, while urban residents attended one extra game per season than those in rural regions. Somewhat surprisingly, we found no correlation between age and income on a fan's interest or match attendance frequency. This suggests that attendance and spend have little to do with someone's income bracket or age.

How can the sports industry use this insight?

As I've previously discussed, with tighter wallets and more choice, consumers are now more selective about how they spend their money and their time. The rise of eSports demonstrates that younger fans frequently favour video games over spectator or team sports; a marked contrast to their parents' and grandparents' generations, who grew up on the field and in the stands.

Where and how sports development and marketing budgets are allocated has become more important than ever. This type of analysis offers valuable insight that rights owners can exploit to grow revenue regardless of the changing economic and consumer landscape. Sports development teams that need justification to secure a bigger budget can point to this data, which clearly demonstrates that having more people playing results in more revenue directly into the sport.

Combining predictive and regression analytics

One of our rights-owner clients at Winners wanted to understand how far it would be from its 2020 participation growth targets if nothing changed in the way it managed the development of its sport, i.e., if it continued to attract new registrations and lose current ones at the same pace as it had experienced since 2007. Using simple time series analysis it was easy enough to plot the trend to demonstrate this. However, in order to provide additional context, we added the natural movement of population within that country over the same period using data provided by the World Bank. This can be seen in Figure 4.7.

We had already identified a strong positive or negative correlation with the annual revenue of the rights owner, so we overlaid this data on the time series line to see what impact this had (Figure 4.8).

Unfortunately for this client, in both instances its natural growth pattern would leave it short by nearly 15% or 25%, depending on the worst-case or best-case scenario. But, as the client had control over its revenue, unlike the impact caused by population movement, they could put strategies in place to

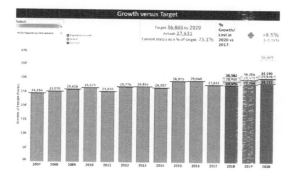

Figure 4.7 Growth based on time series analysis. (Source: Winners FDD Ltd using UEFA data, with permission.)

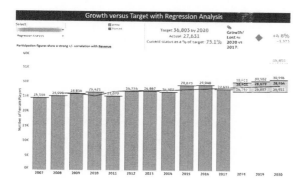

Figure 4.8 Growth based on time series analysis with correlation impact. (Source: Winners FDD Ltd using UEFA data, with permission.)

manage this. Considerations could include either amending its targets to be in line with its projected revenue movement or plan to increase its revenues by the relevant value necessary to hit its predetermined target.

Propensity modelling

Propensity modelling is the form of predictive analytics that tells us which customers are most likely to buy and, in the case of National Governing Bodies (NGBs) and International Federations (IFs), which are most likely to play or become a referee or coach. My favourite example of how powerful this can be is the case of Netflix and *House of Cards*, an online-only, multiple-Emmy-award-winning television series. The decision-makers at the online streaming service committed a reported $100 million investment without seeing a single episode of the show thanks to their use of propensity modelling. They combined the data available for viewers of the original *House of Cards* series from 1990, viewers of movies with Kevin Spacey (the show's then-golden star) and, finally, viewers of other movies directed by David Fincher (the show's executive producer). The intersection of the Venn diagram they produced was sufficient for them to believe the show would be a hit (Petraetis, 2017).

Consider how this can be used for a rights owner when addressing season ticket sales. You could start by creating the different segments of your customers based on combined demographic data, including their distance from your stadium, with RFV analysis formed from your ticketing data. You would then classify these customer groups based on how likely you think they are to become season ticket purchasers. For example, a fan who's purchased tickets for 70% of your home matches and lives less than 20 km away is more likely to purchase a season ticket than someone who's been to 20% of your matches and lives 70 km away.

When you segment your customers in this way you can then create marketing plans for each of the different groups, measuring the applicable ROI. As the first segment examples above are your 'hot leads', you can expect to use less effort to convert them into becoming a season ticket holder. The second example, your 'cool leads', will need more effort. Perhaps a series of automated email campaigns set up to nurture the recipient to a purchase will be sufficient for the hot group, but the cool group will also need a follow-up phone call.

In Chapter 6 on data-driven marketing I look at the different communication channels we use and how we combine them with the different analyses we use and the insights they generate.

Customer loyalty

Building on the question of churn in sports – and if we accept that when it comes to fandom, we don't really lose them, we lose their interest in acting on it – we need to look at the subject of loyalty and what it means to you. That's the starting point for this discussion: that loyalty means something different for every team, club, governing body or international federation and it's defined across a host of different variables.

In many cases, loyalty may not be financially driven nor based on how many matches or events a fan may have attended. This is even more the case if you're a global sports brand with a fan base size that exceeds the capacity of your stadium. In today's digital world loyalty can include metrics such as the length of time a fan stays on our websites, the frequency with which they visit, their interactions in our social channels, their frequency opening our email campaigns and clicking on the links, the number of times they visit our sponsors' websites or watch our broadcast partners' digital streams. This can be added to more traditional metrics such as number of matches attended, quantity of merchandise purchased and, from a participation standpoint, number of training sessions attended.

In addition to choosing attributes you consider to represent loyalty, the calculation of that loyalty can also be done in a number of ways. I've already referred to RFV analysis: scoring the three individual factors or the total scoring across all three could be used as a straightforward loyalty calculation. Another method is looking at the multiple relationships you have with an individual, i.e., how many different source databases do they sit in, which other departments also have a relationship with that individual? Are they a home *and* away fan? Do they buy merchandise as well as play your sport? Do they follow you on Facebook and open your emails? The more relationships an individual has with your organisation, the more you could consider them 'loyal' to you and your sport.

At Winners we introduced the concept of a Super Fan to a group of clients that shared a common business model within the same sport. The Super Fan was a simple loyalty analysis identified on a monthly basis throughout a season, using whatever metrics the client could access. Generally, it included:

- number of matches they attended
- number of tickets they purchased
- total value of ticketing spend
- any other purchases made: merchandise, stadium tours, summer schools, etc.
- number of emails they opened
- number of times they clicked on email content
- social media following status (did they or didn't they?).

The intention behind the monthly Super Fan was that in addition to introducing the client to a simple form of loyalty analysis, the output could then be used in a variety of ways from directly rewarding the fans to producing content for their digital channels. The concept could even encourage other fans to change their behaviour with the aim of becoming that month's Super Fan themselves.

We performed this exercise at least 20 times in one year with 20 different rights owners and my most memorable moment was when we presented one client with their Super Fan of August 2016. He was the best friend of one of the client's team members who was in the room. He immediately sent a message to that friend to tell him his face was displayed on a large screen in their stadium boardroom. His pleasure was palpable!

Fan/customer loyalty programmes

The key point I want to make about loyalty at this point is that understanding the loyalty you have among your customer or fan base is not the same as building a loyalty programme. Conversely, a loyalty programme is not something that you launch to generate loyalty.

Earlier in the chapter I discussed the cost of acquiring a new customer as a comparison to the cost of retaining an existing one. This results in a clear understanding that, notwithstanding the natural fan loyalty we've also looked at, we should do what we can to keep our customers coming back to us. In this regard, a loyalty programme should be a vehicle you use to reward that behaviour and extend it.

It's important to consider that any loyalty programme you launch should be grounded in analysis. Your starting point has to be to understand current behaviour so you know what will work. It's the reason this section has come at the end of this chapter to emphasise my point above: that the launch of a loyalty programme should come after you've performed the previous analysis, not before.

One reason this is important is because according to *The Loyalty Report 2017*, North America's largest loyalty study, the average consumer has registered for 14 loyalty programmes, but is only actively engaged with seven of them (Bond Brand Loyalty, 2017). If you don't understand what your fans or customers want from a loyalty programme your chances of becoming one of those 50% that aren't used beyond registration are very high. This will mean wasted resources (budget and time), loss of reputation (who wants to spearhead a programme that's failed to deliver?) and possibly fatigue and future lack of interest from your fans (they'll ask themselves how much you actually care or know about them).

An effective loyalty programme uses various tactics to drive the customer behaviour that you desire and the collection and analysis of relevant data as outlined in this chapter will provide you with the knowledge needed to identify the right tactics to use. To reiterate, while a loyalty programme should not, in itself, be considered your answer to revenue growth, it is a useful tool to reward existing customers and generate new ones, and should be considered at an appropriate stage of your data-driven development.

Case study: UEFA GROW

With 55 national associations belonging to the Union of European Football Associations (UEFA), there has never been a greater need for a clear centralised growth plan. With 16 million players in Europe and armies of fans all over the world, the use of data-driven processes is essential to supporting both targeted communications and increasing engagement for local associations and UEFA as a whole.

Noel Mooney is the Head of Business Development for the National Associations Division at UEFA and is responsible for the rollout of UEFA GROW, a support programme designed for all of UEFA's member nations. The programme relies on four key business objectives, or pillars:

1   **Image**: nurturing the public image and perception of the game.
2   **Engagement**: reinforcing engagement with the football family at a local and international level.
3   **Participation**: increasing and retaining participants of the game at all levels.
4   **Revenue**: increasing the commercial revenue of all member associations.

In an interview on 13 September 2017, Mooney described the UEFA GROW programme to me and talked about the way data is used to support both UEFA's delivery of the programme and the way the member associations use it.

UEFA GROW is our vision for how we can support our 55 national associations to increase the love for football across Europe, based on consultation and working closely with our members. We will support the national associations to create a clear marketing growth plan.

By utilising these four pillars, UEFA GROW hopes to achieve the development of robust marketing plans to back the member nations in their business objectives, supporting their goal with work streams that cover brand communication, strategic planning and public affairs.

Within UEFA's National Associations Division, the term CRM is replaced with FRM, with the 'F' representing not fans, but football (and, understandably, removing the reference to customers — have you ever met a football fan who wants to be called a customer?). The 'F' represents the whole of the football family, from grassroots players and volunteers, coaches and referees to national team ticket-buyers, sponsors, media partners, even local governments who play an important role in donations and funding for many local football initiatives.

Football relationship management and data are crucial in achieving UEFA's aims for the growth of football across Europe. They allow for informed and supported decision making, highlight clear markets to inform targeted communication and allow for increased engagement with the national associations' fans both at home and abroad.

For the time being, UEFA is utilising FRM in its **participation** and **engagement** pillars, encouraging its members to analyse and generate actionable insights. This data reveals challenges but also highlights areas of great opportunity that can be maximised across different business areas.

Some national associations are already quite advanced in this area, but UEFA GROW aims to support all associations, even those who are still in the early stages of this approach.

Focus on participation

Traditionally, football clubs and leagues have focused on sales rather than engagement. Sales might include match tickets or shop merchandise; however, for the national associations, this is not always the best way to foster fan relationships to a sustainable level. For governing bodies of the sport, Mooney believes that the focus should naturally be on participation rather than sales.

The associations are, after all, responsible for the growth and reputation of the sport in their respective countries.

That isn't to say that revenue isn't important, but it can be seen as an end rather than the means. The more people who play football, the more individuals who are engaged and interested, the more revenue will come as a by-product.

As we've already demonstrated in this chapter, there is a relationship between playing football and spending money supporting football. Collecting data and analysing it helps to support this. Other businesses have embraced data as a way of creating actionable insights, and Mooney believes the sports industry should move in the same direction to create a sustainable business that can continue to develop and expand.

Achieving growth

The FAF (Football Association of Finland) gives a perfect example of growth achieved through data and insight. Mooney and UEFA GROW helped FAF implement a strategy that would allow it to send targeted messages to the fans that engaged with the national association.

Email marketing was a digital channel not previously used by the FAF, which Mooney encouraged it to use, while simultaneously looking at its participation data to understand how its players were registered and what activity was recorded.

Despite not previously having needed them, the FAF had been collecting email addresses from all registered participants. These records were then integrated into its email-marketing database, along with match ticketing and online store sales data. What this showed was a fantastic overview of how their registered players were engaging with them, and what kinds of relationships were being fostered. This data could help the FAF understand if its players both played and watched matches, whether they spent money while following football, and how much they were spending. In turn, this enabled them to begin sending out targeted and personalised emails.

The first three email campaigns were issued in November and December. Rolling out the new campaigns so close to the Christmas period had an enormous impact on the size of their databases, and Mooney stated that the fact they had never before directly addressed their fans was instrumental to their success. These email campaigns achieved 400% of their annual sales targets for the online store, while also getting more players to register.

> At a time when structured sport is facing a decline, [the FAF] managed to not only achieve their annual growth target of 6.5% but exceed it and deliver an 8% growth in registered footballers.

The FAF has continued its email campaigns, sending out an email once every two weeks and supplementing it with targeted campaigns for specific projects and events. Player registrations are personalised with reminders to re-register two weeks in advance and, for those who still haven't registered, sending out a reminder the day after and again two weeks after the registration date.

Consistency in approach is key to email marketing and personalised targeted messages helped produce this outstanding result. Implementing this new data stream was relatively straightforward and, according to Mooney:

> The key was to get the FAF using email and their data in the first place and, once we did this, the results they achieved led them onto further developments.

Changing culture

Getting associations to change the way they operate is one of the biggest challenges for Mooney and UEFA GROW. It is a common problem across many industries that work with participation, not just sports. The departments that deal with participation often work separately from marketing and sales teams, so it has become imperative for UEFA GROW to address FRM as a cross-organisation strategy, rather than an initiative belonging to a single department.

> I guess our situation is no different to an international company with country offices, all of whom are using different systems and processes to do the same job. Within UEFA GROW we're aiming to understand these differences so we can help them progress.

The ultimate goal is to have a full audit of people, processes and systems in place among all 55 of UEFA's national associations. Mooney aims to have UEFA operating under a system similar to Gartner's CRM Maturity Model tackling activity, pursuing tactical objectives, implementing strategy and ultimately linking their business strategy to the realisation of their goals and objectives.

> [UEFA GROW] will help us be more strategic about the support we give our members, ensuring our investment is spent in areas of greatest need across all their different business units.

Not only will this help develop grassroots participation like playing, coaching and refereeing, but will also branch out to see gains in ticketing, online merchandise sales, sponsorship and marketing.

(Source: Mooney, 2017, 13 September.)

Key chapter ideas

1   Business intelligence and data analytics refers to two different forms of analysis – the former looks at historic data to understand why things happened, the latter uses historic data to understand what will happen next.
2   The purpose of analysis is to produce actionable insights and not leave you asking 'so what?'
3   Analysing your campaign performance metrics is important to ensure you consistently improve your processes.
4   There are many forms of analysis that can be performed on data. Most popular for rights owners are population mapping, ticket purchase timelines, RFV analysis, customer lifetime value and customer lifecycle.

References

Bond Brand Loyalty (2017). *The Loyalty Report*. Ontario: Bond Brand Loyalty. Available at: www.bondbrandloyalty.com.

Bury, B. (2013, 7 September). Personal interview.

Cutler, M. and Sterne, J. (2000). *E-Metrics: Business Metrics for the New Economy* [ebook]. NetGenesis. Available at: www.targeting.com/wp-content/uploads/2010/12/emetrics-business-metrics-new-economy.pdf.

Heinze, J. (2016). Business intelligence vs. business analytics: what's the difference? [online]. *Better Buys*. Available at: www.betterbuys.com/bi/business-intelligence-vs-business-analytics.

Hopkins, B. (2016). *Think You Want to be "Data-driven"? Insight is the New Data* [online]. Forrester. Available at: https://go.forrester.com/blogs/16-03-09-think_you_want_to_be_data_driven_insight_is_the_new_data.

Kolowich, L. (2016). *Email analytics: the 6 Email Marketing Metrics & KPIs You should be Tracking* [online]. HubSpot. Available at: https://blog.hubspot.com/marketing/metrics-email-marketers-should-be-tracking.

Mooney, N. (2017, 13 September). Personal interview.

Petraetis, G. (2017). How Netflix built a *House of Cards with big data* [online]. CIO. Available at: www.cio.com/article/3207670/big-data/how-netflix-built-a-house-of-cards-with-big-data.html.

Reichheld, F. (n.d.). *Prescription for Cutting Costs* [ebook]. Boston: Bain & Company. Available at: www.bain.com/Images/BB_Prescription_cutting_costs.pdf.

Ultsch, A. (2002). *Proof of Pareto's 80/20 Law and Precise Limits for ABC-Analysis*. Available at: www.uni-marburg.de/fb12/arbeitsgruppen/datenbionik/pdf/pubs/2002/ultsch02proof.

Young, J. (2017). Dynamic ticket pricing use takes off, and teams hope it'll lure fans back into sports stadiums [online]. CNBC. Available at: www.cnbc.com/2017/12/01/dynamic-ticket-pricing-use-takes-off-and-teams-hope-itll-lure-fans-back-into-sports-stadiums.html.

Chapter 5

CRM technology stack

The theme of this book has been to address the more evolved definition of CRM that, unlike its origins in contact management software to track sales activity, is not just about technology. Many consider Customer Relationship Management a philosophy; it can incorporate and impact strategy, process and organisational culture. This means that implementing CRM, or addressing digital transformation, should not be led by your IT departments but by your business requirements. We shouldn't think about technology first. While it is undeniable that the right software can make things work more efficiently, without the other elements of the perfect circle, the right culture and stream-lined processes, clean data and a clear strategy, the best technology in the world will be unable to deliver what you set out to achieve. Consequently, it will become a costly mistake and an expensive lesson. However, it is also a truism that the more you advance in the development and delivery of your strategy, the more your need for technology will grow. Therefore, there is, without a doubt, a role for technology as an enabler.

This chapter will look at the different supporting technologies that are rel-evant to the business model of a sports rights owner, an SCV, digital marketing, analytics and data visualisation. Sales force automation, customer service, and business process management have not been included in this section.

At the end of this chapter the NBA's San Antonio Spurs provide us with an insight into their technology stack.

A CRM eco-system

In Chapter 2 I referred to the approach we take at Winners where we talk about CRM *eco-systems*; the technical environment you need to enable data-driven marketing and address digital transformation, composed of multiple pieces of software, platforms or channels that work together. While they will all have distinct roles (and sometimes the same product will have several roles), your objective should be that, between them, they enable targeted marketing, customer journeys, and interactions across the multiple channels that our fans and customers now use.

Specifically, your technology stack should enable:

1   **A customer-centric approach to marketing and service**. You want to put your fans and stakeholders first and to do this you need to know more about them.
2   **A customer experience that encourages your fans to come back**. You want them to stay longer and to engage deeper.

Moreover, the right eco-system will also provide non-customer facing benefits such as:

3   **Better cross-organisational collaboration**. While technology alone can't achieve this (I discuss this more in Chapter 8 on Business Change), it helps if the software, systems and processes your organisation uses are aligned from one department to another.
4   **ROI tracking**. A quote often attributed to the nineteenth-century Philadelphia retailer John Wanamaker is, 'Half the money I spend on advertising is wasted; the trouble is I don't know which half'. You want to know that you're spending your money in the right direction and ROI tracking can help you with that.
5   **Time efficiencies**. Without wanting to open a discussion on Artificial Intelligence and Machine Learning at this point, the more automation you can deploy in your marketing processes, the more time you have to think strategy.

To achieve all of this you need more than just traditional CRM software for tracking the sales process. You also need to consider data management, profiling and analytics, and digital marketing.

Data warehouse vs Single Customer View

I don't mind admitting that when I first entered the world of data at the end of 2011, I didn't quite understand the difference between a data warehouse and an SCV, often using the references interchangeably.

I referred to SCV in Chapter 2 as a centralised database that houses your structured and personally identifiable data: individual and unique customer records that provide the information your marketing, sales and customer service teams need. Conversely, a data warehouse collects high volumes of both structured and unstructured data. It's usually an enterprise-wide tool, doesn't need to match to a unique customer, and therefore does not include any additional processing to make the data usable to marketers.

In Chapter 2 I also introduced the concept of a DMP and a CDP, but as there are still many rights owners who have not yet managed to achieve an SCV, I'll focus on that for now. According to a 2016 report by Experian, a global consumer marketing services provider, 81% of marketers report having challenges in trying to achieve an SCV (Experian Marketing Services, 2016).

The importance of your SCV really can't be overstated. It's one of the most crucial elements of your technology stack. Without it, any other contributory components cannot function with full efficiency or efficacy. Imagine your marketing campaign platforms attempting to send the right message to the right person, when the data in your SCV is incorrect, or your analytics count your fans twice, or three times because of the presence of duplicates. Your SCV provides the hub of your CRM and data-driven activities. When you combine your unique records with marketing technologies you can generate insights that support your marketing decisions. You can easily visualise and analyse your data at speed to identify the perfect audience for your targeted marketing, but only if it's been processed in the right format to make it usable.

Master Data Management: data in, data out

Master Data Management is the term given to the processes and technology that get you to your single point of customer reference. Within the process you will need to identify the data that you need, collect it in a way that conforms to data-related legislation (more on this in Chapter 9) and, finally, you'll probably need to transform and repair it to meet the format and standards of your database schema (the way your database is structured and designed).

The process of collecting data from your individual source databases (such as your ticketing systems, online store, website, landing pages, social channels, etc.) for input into your SCV, whether through an automated integration or a manual process, is commonly referred to as ETL – Extract, Transform and Load.

Extract

Within the extraction phase the aim is to convert the outgoing data into the appropriate format for the transform stage. This is relevant whether the process is automated or manual. For example, your source database may provide you with the option to extract or export with a comma or pipe separator. Dates may be entered in a dd/mm/yyyy format but the default on the extraction may be set with an mm/dd/yy rule.

Creating a data dictionary for each of your data sources (and the destination SCV) is a useful process that will help you identify the validation rules that need to be in place for efficient data extraction. When you write a data dictionary the purpose is to identify each data field within a database, describing the content and purpose, defining the format and field size, and identifying if they're needed within the extract process.

They can be produced in a spreadsheet, and are used to map out different stages of the ETL process, starting with the requirements of the business (e.g., what data does your marketing department want to collect?), aligning with the design of your database, through to mapping into the appropriate field of your SCV.

Transform

In this stage of the process, the validation rules we identified in the extract phase are enhanced with further rules that enable the outgoing data to be integrated with, or imported into, the target database. In this case, your SCV. Some of your data won't require any transformation and is referred to as 'pass through' data, but the remainder will be cleansed or 'normalised'.

Cleansing can include various steps depending on the data in question, the processes used in the source systems, and its intended use. For example, for your email marketing campaigns you will want to ensure all email addresses are valid. If double opt-ins or captcha (a process used to tell whether or not the user is human or a machine) were not used in the data collection process, then I'd highly recommend running your imports against an email validation list. I talk about the importance of this in Chapter 6 on Data Driven Marketing.

An example of normalisation is that certain character sets that are available in the source database won't be available in the SCV. A common example is Cyrillic characters used in Eastern Europe and Asia. Another example is date fields as previously mentioned, or perhaps the use of US dollars in a source system and euros in the SCV.

Another common issue for rights owners, particularly IFs and NGBs, is the country field for those sports where teams from the UK compete as individual nations. This is the case for UEFA who store data using England, Scotland, Wales and Northern Ireland but whose third-party suppliers may use Great Britain, United Kingdom or even the British Isles, all of which are different to each other.

An important point to note at this stage is that, if your data fails the validation rules, it will mean there are errors in the format. An easy temptation is to amend the offending records and continue with the process, but a better approach is to make corrections in the source database to avoid the need to constantly repeat the amendments. While this could be easily rectified in your own digital estate, when using third parties to provide services it can be a little bit more time consuming to achieve the correct format. But, time spent at this point will save a lot more in the future. I refer to the need for following processes in Chapter 2, and this is a classic example.

Load

The load, or import, phase requires further rules that deal with the manner in which your data is added into your SCV. These rules will differ widely, not only within each organisation, but also within each rights owner's source system. For example, when it comes to setting the frequency of the process, if you are a club that stages 20 or 40 events per year, your ticketing system data may need to be loaded on an hourly basis, 365 days per year. But, if you're an IF or NGB with just four to six events per year, the process may occur daily during the month of the event, but increase to hourly in the few days immediately prior to the event. If you register your participating athletes on an annual basis, but provide just a small window of opportunity for those registrations, for example one month, the ETL from your registration platform to your SCV may only need to be daily for that specific month.

When deciding what rules to put in place you need to look to your business needs and the intended purpose of the incoming data. Using the examples above, ticketing data may be needed to ensure your management can track sales performance, marketing may need it for promotional campaigns, and your online store may want to cross-sell some merchandise.

Deduplicating your records

Having cleansed and normalised the data in the *Transform* phase, deduplication rules now need to be put in place. This is an SCV, the one place where you'll be able to see the 360-degree relationship your fans or customers have with you, so you need to be as sure as you can that each individual fan, participant, customer, or stakeholder is represented just once in the database.

Once the rules have been identified, algorithms can be designed to produce the required result by first identifying those records that could be considered duplicate. The identification of duplicates could be based on a number of different fields in the database, with the most common being email address. If there are multiple incidences of the same email address in a source database, it's reasonable to assume the same person has been represented multiple times. However, this might not necessarily be the case. The same email address may have been used by different members of a family, different friends in a group, or different participants in a grassroots club.

Another consideration is that not every customer in your source database has an email address. While half of the population of the world uses email there's another 3.7 billion who don't. In addition, the average user has 1.7 accounts, so you need to ensure you identify records that are duplicates even though email addresses are the same (The Radicati Group, 2017). You do this by considering additional data attributes, the most common being first name, last name, postal address and date of birth. It's unlikely further validation is needed after this point, after all, how likely is it that more than one record will have the same name, live at the same address, be of the same age *and* use the same email address? But, there may be an instance when all the identified fields are not populated, or populated in a different manner, for instance, John Smith in one system may be Jonathan Smith or J Smith in others. If your matching rules are too strict, these three instances will produce three different records even though they most likely belong to the same person.

One final point to highlight is that when the data is imported and deduplicated based on your matching rules, you then have to consider your merging rules. Using the example above, when you import a record with J Smith you don't really want the "J" to overwrite the existing field that may say 'Jonathan' or 'John'.

I've used the date of birth field as an example as it occurs often. In your SCV you may want to store the date of birth field in the dd/mm/yyyy format if that's what's needed for your analytics programme to identify age, and your email campaign platform to issue those all-important birthday cards. The *Extract* process has ensured the right format has been exported, but if the data collection form at the source didn't use front-end validation to ensure correct dates are used, you could be attempting to import 12/09/0000 or 12/09/2030, neither of which are possible ages for your fans and customers.

I've highlighted here some data management issues to be concerned with when creating your SCV, but not the solution to addressing them. As with the rest of this book, the intent is to bring to the forefront areas for further consideration, putting them into context with your CRM or digital transformation strategy. As your ETL processes are pivotal to this, I hope they receive the attention they deserve as you move forward. Your objective should be to constantly acquire more; *more* customers, and *more* information about those customers. Your data management processes should ensure the quality of your data is not compromised as you seek greater quantity.

Off-the-shelf vs bespoke build

While The Gartner CRM Vendor Guide 2017 states that only 25% of new projects involve bespoke solutions, I'm comfortable admitting that for some of my rights owner clients I do advocate the use of a bespoke build, specifically when it comes to an SCV or data warehouse. If you've read Chapter 2 you will know that MLS took this approach, building on a SQL database with additional off-the-shelf software and apps. Some of you might question this when there are long-established, market-proven, even industry-leading, products that are out there and readily available, so I'd like to qualify my rationale:

1 While there are multiple products that are off-the-shelf, specifically when it comes to data warehousing, they're very rarely (in fact, I'd go so far as to say never) available as a plug-and-play. They need to be formatted to suit your current data sources and your business needs. They also need to be integrated with your incoming and outgoing data feeds. Some of you may be reading this thinking I'm stating the obvious, but there are many unsuspecting individuals who will be sold on a dream, who believe there's a silver bullet and will be genuinely shocked when they learn a software license can be only a small percentage of the budget required to establish an SCV.

2   If you scope your build to meet your specific business requirements you can ensure you're only paying for what you need; you won't be paying for a Ferrari if all you need is a Volkswagen. While I don't want to get too technical, if you use an open schema approach to your database it will be easier to build on it as your requirements, data flows or data quantities grow.

3   The key is that while you're all in the sports industry you're all rights owners with largely the same business models and the scale of your data requirements will vary significantly. Consequently, as with every element of your approach to CRM, you need to think about your business requirements first. List and detail out your use cases and then apply them to your resource and budget situation.

A requirement that all rights owners have is the need for deeper engagement with your fans, customers and participants, so now I'll look at the layer of your tech stack that delivers targeted marketing.

Digital marketing platforms

When I think about the digital marketing channels that are informed by data and can provide a personalised experience (subject to the right data being available), I consider email, mobile app push messages and banner ads (web and social). I also include SMS marketing and personalised web content. I review each of these in the next chapter on Data-Driven Marketing but, in the context of this chapter, I'd like to tell you where they sit and how they interact within your technology stack.

All these digital channels mentioned above operate independently of each other to get the right message to the right person at the right time. They can all be personalised with the data you have in your SCV so *ideally* they will all be integrated into your centralised database so you can use your SCV to create segments of the fans or customers with whom you wish to communicate, then 'push' that list into the distribution platform. Note that I use the word 'ideally' as opposed to 'definitely'. This is because, as with many tasks in the world of technology, there are manual workarounds that can be used temporarily to achieve the same aim. I say temporarily because the objective with your technology stack is to use automation that saves you time on certain tasks, freeing you up to spend your time in areas that can't be automated. Setting up automated integrations adds another layer of cost to your development and, while the time you save will more than pay that back, if you need to throttle the way you spend your budget, or need to demonstrate some quick wins before you ask for more, using manual processes as a temporary measure could assist with that.

So, if you now have all your digital marketing channels sitting on top of your SCV you're in a perfect position to use them in a multi-, cross- or omni-channel manner. Confused?

In the previous chapter I referred to the proliferation of different terms that can be sometimes confusing. Here's another case in point.

Since the term 'digital marketing' was initially used in the early 1990s with the launch of Archie, the first search engine (Shedden, 2014), or when the first clickable banner made its debut in 1994 (Edwards, 2013), reference to multi/cross/omni-channel has grown at an incredible pace with *The Huffington Post* claiming it to be one of the 'Top retail buzzwords for 2013' along with 'personalisation' and 'mobile' (Cherwenka, 2013). But what do they actually mean? Are they the same thing or are they different?

Multi-channel marketing means engaging with your customers using a combination of channels. For some rights owners this includes both online and offline (remember those days of stuffing catalogues into envelopes, processing paper order forms with cheques stapled to them?) but, for many, the focus will be like this book; purely on the digital experience. Going back to the definition I use of CRM – right message, right person, right time, right platform – multi-channel is knowing which channel to use at any given time, using multiple touch points to reach audiences and customers.

Cross-channel has a slightly different meaning. While it also refers to engaging across any channel or any device to suit the customer, cross-channel takes it one step further and takes the perspective of your customer. They see no distinction in the way they engage with you. For them, they just see the digital world as one big technology-enabled channel. Your fans might read a squad announcement on your optimised website, receive goal alerts through your mobile app, vote for their MVP (Most Valuable Player) in your Facebook account and then click on an email link to buy their next match ticket. They really don't know, or care, that they're in your cross-channel workflow, or that it's automated based on their last action.

Having highlighted the difference between multi-channel and cross-channel, where does omni-channel fit? The key difference with omni-channel is that actions can be happening simultaneously; because that's the way your fans behave. The second screen has been a talking point for the sports industry for some time, for example, using a laptop or a mobile to check for stats while watching a live broadcast. Another example could be your in-stadium point-of-sale tracking a fan's purchase while their loyalty account in your mobile app is updated with the points earned, triggering a 'thank you' email to their inbox. With omni-channel, one platform serves another. They complement each other with the information they have about your fans and customers, providing the continuous and seamless experience they want and now expect.

Behavioural data from your marketing channels can funnel back into your SCV. This can then enhance the records you have about your fans and customers, produce insights into the efficiencies of your campaigns, and provide you with knowledge that enables improvements to your systems and processes.

Analytics

I've already talked at length about the importance of acquiring and analysing data in previous chapters, reviewing the key areas of insight that are of use to sports rights owners, from marketing campaign metrics, to transactional behavioural analysis, including predictive analytics and RFV analysis. Here, I'll summarise where your analytics platforms sit within your eco-system and the relative role in the data-in, data-out process.

Many of your digital channels will provide a level of data demonstrating the effectiveness of your content and campaigns and the way your fans respond to them:

- Your email platform will show you how many of and which of your fans opened your campaigns.
- Google Analytics provides a comprehensive level of analysis you can use to understand and improve the user experience, acquisition rates, and other actions taken across your website and mobile app (although the ability to do this at a user level and match that back to your CRM system isn't 'out-of-the-box' functionality).
- Your ticketing system and online store provider will be able to provide you with the information you need to understand more about your fans' buying habits.

However, when it comes to creating a full picture of your fans, customers, participants or other stakeholders across your multiple business units and digital touchpoints, the automated quantitative processes you can do with SQL will not be sufficient: you'll need to use an analytics platform across your SCV.

As I discussed earlier, each of your source systems and databases will push data into your SCV, and the matching rules will ensure all incoming data aligns to one unique record. Depending on the type of individual unique user insight you're looking for, these comprehensive records can then feed into your analytics software, appending each record with the relevant tagging that can be used in your digital marketing campaigns.

Not all analysis relevant to a rights owner involves individuals. Understanding the movement of your fans around a stadium concourse (see Figure 5.1), how they might respond en masse to your next home match if it's raining, or how many fans might travel to your next away match are informed by different sets of data from individual source systems. Your SCV can pull all this together so your analytics application can do its work. The benefit of having this centralised analytics environment is that you can look for insights at a cross-organisational level. With one central repository of the key data points needed for your analysis, the task of producing comprehensive dashboards becomes instantly more achievable.

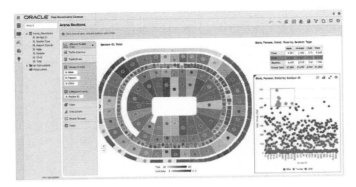

Figure 5.1 Tracking fan movement around a stadium. (Source: Oracle.
com – www.oracle.com/technetwork/middleware/bi-foundation/
dvdarena-2997628.jpg.)

Data visualisation

The role of data visualisation is exactly as it sounds. It's the visual presentation
of your data, using graphs, charts or other formats that enable the following:

- Communication of information clearly and efficiently.
- Easier and quicker analysis and assessment of situations.
- The identification of patterns or trends.
- Complex and copious datasets become more accessible.

Data visualisation is considered both an art and a science. It's an art because it
involves the ability to draw focus and attention through the use of carefully
considered graphics, and knowing which graphics to use for which datasets. It's
a science because it draws on the data you have in your SCV or other source
database, so you need to know which data will provide you with the visual you
want to create. Or, more importantly, the insight you want to present.

Thanks to technology, not only do we have more data to inform these visualisations, we also have the ability to produce these graphs and charts for review
in seconds and, more importantly, view them dynamically, constantly in real-
time and with the ability to drill down, going deeper into different areas.

Many applications or software products will include a level of reporting, or
dashboarding functionalities, to support their core functionality. They know
that users need to understand what's happening within their systems. But, this
is very different from having a dedicated and centralised reporting function that
looks cross-organisationally and cross-platform.

For example, knowing your conversion rate once a fan is in the ticketing
section of your website is great, but if you can link it to the responses your

email campaigns or social posts generate, then your insights will have so much more value. Imagine the value of your insights if they are also linked to behaviour within your sports registration platform. When considering multi-, cross- and omni-channel marketing, the right data visualisation set up can provide you with information about the customer journey across each of these.

Why is data visualisation so important?

According to the Visual Systems Division of 3M, the global conglomerate whose business areas range from health care and highway safety through to office products and adhesives, visual aids can improve learning by up to 400%. We can also process visuals up to 60,000 times faster than we can process text, so when it comes to ensuring we get value from our data work, and that our management and marketing teams can make the appropriate decisions, we need to ensure it's as easy as possible for them to see the insights we're producing for them (3M, 1997). I illustrated this in Chapter 4 using images to demonstrate the point, but in this chapter I'll highlight some of the key considerations when using data visualisation.

Your audience: who are they and what are they looking for?

In the same way that you have hierarchical levels in your organisation, and staffing levels with access to varying levels of company information, you can set up your dashboards to provide different information to specific users and user groups. You can imagine that your senior management have a need to stay abreast of key statistics like KPIs that provide a helicopter view of how each of the business units is performing, all available in one view. But, at a department level, you need to look at much more granular information. Knowing 'how much' won't be enough, you'll want to know how, why, what type, how often, and by whom.

Your visuals: what's the best format for the specific message?

Choosing the right chart for your particular message is important. Different views do a better job than others at presenting information. Graphs and charts should be used to show the information about data relationships, patterns, or how things are changing over time. Tables should be used when you have to show precise value, and numeric data is best presented using dots, lines or bars if you're looking to present a quantitative message. Maps are used when a physical location is key to the information you're presenting, and heat maps are used when different values within a map are shown through the use of colours.

Correct and clear labelling is important when creating visual reports. Your objective is to ensure that the words you use are clear enough to explain what the visualisations represent, but at the same time minimise the quantity of words to let the graphic speak for itself.

Choice of colours

Research shows that different colours generate different responses. The University of Melbourne demonstrated that the use of green boosts concentration (Calligeros, 2015), while Feng Shui dictates that the colour orange is best for productivity (Ecker, 2013). However, in the sports world, it's more likely that team colours will dictate those choices. It's unlikely the German Football Federation would use orange in their reports, or that Rangers Football Club would make green their prevalent colour, but there are still some principles that could be easily followed:

- **Red versus green**: If you use these colours, make sure your red is for negative values and green for positive because of their natural association with traffic lights (stop and go).
- **Light versus dark**: It's easier to read text when light colours are used in backgrounds and if you use dark colours to represent a specific finding the reader might give unnecessary weight to it. I also recommend never using more than eight colours in your dashboard as they can become distracting at that point.
- **Colour differentiation**: While you want to use different colours to differentiate data points, it's important to use the same colour when referring to the same type of data. For example, the colour used for month-on-month comparisons should be consistent; year-on-year should use a different colour.
- **Use of axes**: You can use the same chart in your dashboards to present comparisons, correlation or causality between two entities (periods, products, personas, etc.) instead of producing a different chart for each entity. However, it's important to remember to label your left and right axes clearly.
- **Order of data**: There should be a logical hierarchy in the way you present your data. If it's not appropriate to do it by value, you can do it alphabetically or chronologically. As with choice of colour, it's important that whichever order you choose, you remain consistent.

At the end of this chapter you'll read about the platform San Antonio Spurs use for data visualisation in their technology stack, and how it quickly started generating insights, even within the first few months of their CRM implementation.

Where to go next

As a technology-neutral consultant I'm not here to advocate one vendor over the other in any of these areas. For those readers who want to know more about the vendors that could meet your requirements, I recommend two sources of information:

1   *The Gartner CRM Vendor Guide*, which is published annually by Gartner, Inc., the world's leading information technology research and advisory company.

In the report, Gartner reviews and evaluates multiple vendors that provide the different components of a CRM eco-system. In the 2017 edition they also provide the worldwide market forecast through 2021 predicting that in the digital marketing category alone there will be an 18.5% growth and, in sales automation, 10.8% (Gartner, 2017).

You have to be a client (or a student) to access the *Guide*, but some of the vendors featured in the different categories will publish a licensable copy, you just have to provide some details to access it (a classic example of the value exchange I referred to in Chapter 3).

2   The CRM Watchlist is produced by Paul Greenberg, Managing Principal, The 56 Group, LLC, a customer strategy consulting firm, and the author of the best-selling book *CRM at the Speed of Light: Social CRM Strategies, Tools, and Techniques for Engaging Your Customers*.

Greenberg presents the CRM Watchlist as an 'impact award', identifying the strength, mindshare and market share a company had in their market the previous year, along with the expected impact in the following three years.

The 2017 Watchlist was the award's tenth year and it's now published for all to view on ZDNet.com, a business technology news website. The 2017 categories included Lifetime Achievement, won by the aforementioned Gartner, along with Elite, Winners with Distinction, and Watchlist Winners. Most usefully, the Watchlist provides a link to each company enabling you to read more about them (Greenberg, 2017).

Both of these sources will provide you with the direction to look in to understand which vendors support different functional requirements.

Case study: San Antonio Spurs

The San Antonio Spurs are a professional basketball team based in Texas, and five-time winners of the NBA Championship. Within the NBA, team performance is a critical factor in determining success, both on and off the court. Just as the players must perform well to keep winning their games, the CRM team behind the scenes must hold their edge as digital innovation sweeps the industry.

When it came to creating their tech stack, the Spurs opted to work with KORE Software, a global software solutions provider specialising in the needs of the sports industry. The centralised data warehouse was provided by KORE, along with various ready-made integrations and applications that would work in tandem to provide the Spurs with the insights they needed to deepen fan engagement and increase revenue.

Jordan Kolosey joined the Spurs as Director of Business Analytics and Insights in 2016 with the immediate responsibility of building a data warehouse. In a KORE Software webinar held on 12 December 2017 Kolosey shared his approach to such a major project.

> This data warehouse project was important to the early success of our department, particularly with me only recently joining [the Spurs]. So, it was really important to move quickly and to stay in budget. With that in mind we just got to work so that something could be presented to the executive staff in the first week.

The Spurs' philosophy on data analytics revolves around an easy-to-understand three-step process. When presented to senior executives, it helped them understand more about the project and the process. The use of simple language to get stakeholder buy-in is reiterated by Mic Conetta, Head of CRM at Arsenal Football Club, in our case study from Chapter 8. Kolosey, however, describes his process below.

> The first step is the data collection process which is very time consuming, not very much fun, but important to getting the end result. Then you get to analyse the information – the fun part – when you scour out what the insights are and what they are telling you. And then you have to implement whatever it is you learn to demonstrate why you are doing this in the first place. Just spelling out this three-step process really helped demystify what analytics is and showed that it's a science and not a magic trick.

In Chapter 2 we discussed the importance of ensuring you have the right staffing capabilities. Kolosey had similar concerns, and describes the infrastructure he has within his own team to help keep on top of their CRM needs.

The data management analyst is really a data engineer type role. We've all had data feeds fail on us, we've all had those connections and implementations take a lot longer than they needed to. So, it's very important for us to have somebody on the ground who can hold our partners accountable, and be able to decipher our business needs to the data engineers.

Our Manager of Business Analytics is responsible for structuring our data, the tip of the spear so to speak, and comes from a pricing scientist background, very well groomed in a lot of the very raw, more traditional areas of statistical and predictive analytics. Then we have a research coordinator to help provide more of the qualitative consumer-type research to layer in with the heavy statistical skills of our Manager of Business Analytics.

Finally, we have our marketing automation team who jump in after we've gained the insights and seen the different avenues that we could take to improve our business. They use AB testing in campaigns, generate the leads, and get them to the appropriate sales reps, and so on and so forth. Once we get the results back of those campaigns, we make sure there's a lot more interaction between our team and our data management analyst who's able to help us digest that information.

So, with the right people in place, the Spurs assessed various vendors to identify how they could scale quickly and, from that process, identified KORE Software, a company who also service several other NBA teams. This approach enabled the Spurs to benefit from the knowledge and integrations that KORE already developed for Orlando Magic, Oklahoma City Thunder and the Denver Nuggets, providing them with what Kolosey refers to as a 'solid foundation' and a strong level of confidence in the way they moved forward so that, from day one, they were more or less able to go live.

Kolosey highlighted another benefit of working with a provider so closely aligned with other NBA teams. He was able to support his second objective; staying in budget.

We were able to share the cost burden with the other teams, and so it was much more cost effective for us. So, not only were we getting started fast, with actionable data that we could actually utilise, we were able to do it for a lower cost.

Moving on to their tech stack, with their centralised data warehouse in place, Kolosey was able to gain more information about the individual feeds (see Figure 5.2 below).

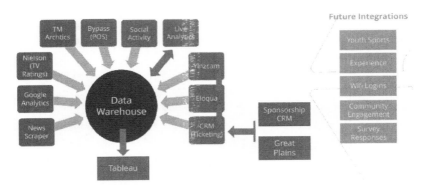

Figure 5.2 San Antonio Spurs – technology stack. (Source: San Antonio Spurs using KORE software.)

This is a snapshot of the current data feeds we have active within our system. A number of these were native from day one and you can't take for granted how important it is to have a reliable ticketing feed, and having a reliable feed from your CRM. It just makes all the difference. Bypass (point of sale) was provided by KORE as an application with an existing integration, with Tableau for live analytics as well. Now we've been able to move to an on-demand scenario and our data engineer has a checklist of different feeds we want to get into the warehouse. He's just been ticking them off one at a time from Nielsen data, Google Analytics and a proprietary news scraper he's built out.

Other data integrations include Eloqua, which provides the campaign management platform. This allows the Spurs to create very dynamic campaigns and use the response data from those campaigns along with other data points relating to demographics or behaviour to trigger follow up campaigns.

Kolosey highlights the benefits of this when it comes to targeted campaigning.

Previously when we would do a week of campaigns to call single game buyers in order to warm them up for eventual pitches on either group nights or anything else, we wouldn't really have any idea if we were producing quality leads for our sales reps or not. So any business processes that we built out based on lead distribution for lead quality would break, and we had to come up with different scenarios, which doubles the work. So being able to take for granted that every sales lead now has the same level of information allows us greater

> visibility and ubiquity with the processes that we put in place. This ultimately allows us to operate a little bit more efficiently when we don't have to create different scenarios for each [customer record] if they have data or not, if they're appended or not.

The Spurs have also integrated a YinzCam mobile app that provides valuable in-stadium behavioural data (something European teams continue to struggle to secure) and enables highly personalised push messages.

When asked about how he determined the order of their integrations (that is, which feeds to focus on first), Kolosey says it was a combination of the demands and vision of their various stakeholder departments.

> We wanted to get a) quick wins and then b) find our external evangelists in other departments; those that seemed much more engaged and forthcoming with needs and had kind of got the process. We were able to spin up quick wins for those individuals, even if it was supplementing the work that they were doing manually, so that we could point to clear victories for the executive staff. Obviously it was the revenue-generating departments; anything you can do to make more money and make the business better overall.

When considering how long it took the Spurs to create their data warehouse, Kolosey suggests that a project like this is never really complete, but is proud that the time it took from first appointing KORE as their supplier to getting their first data visualisations up and running was just three months.

Data visualisation

For Kolosey, the main focus of the tech stack was Tableau for real-time reporting that was up and running so soon after their project start. This is a sentiment shared by Momin Ghaffar, who fills the role of Business Analytics Manager.

The Spurs have created different rules for specific user privileges that match to the three different types of reports they produce and the different purposes behind them. Ghaffar describes them as follows.

> First, you've got your standard bread and butter reporting for executives, the highest level of reporting, that shows how we look at the business in three major revenue buckets: tickets, suites, and sponsorships. A lot of teams will look at tickets and their subtypes – plan, group and gate sales – as well. And

(continued)

(continued)

what becomes pretty informative, something that the end user can really pick up on, is what proportion of the overall budget is comprised by plan and group and gate sales, and, specifically, how do we perform as an organisation by those plan, group and gate subtypes.

Then we have our game-by-game reports that show what [ticket] scans we saw for a particular game, what the Nielsen rating was, how these trend over the entirety of the season and also from a food and beverage perspective. We can see on a game by game basis who are the marquee opponents or the non-marquee opponents, where we reach our budget goals, or miss our budget goals, and, specifically, what tends to be the huge revenue gainers from a food and beverage perspective, and what seasonality component figures into the equation here.

And so we have a very bird's eye view at a very high level. We're able to measure very specifically, game by game, and then we're also able to see things like the heterogeneity of ticket types in the arena bowl. How does this mix look from game to game? Is it something that's influenced by strategy, where you may want to be selling a certain type of ticket for a higher yield for certain opponents? Moreover, I think this report also starts to engage folks that may be on your service and retention team where our season ticket members, our plan holders, are not scanning [as they go into games], that should raise an alarm. What exactly may be driving that apathy or how do we maybe try and deliver even more value so that they're showing up to games and scanning in?

And so what I really like to look at here is that sort of tandem effect that this type of visualisation illustrates. Breaking it out by plan, group and gate, ticket types and seeing what types, or how many folks, scan into those types of games. And then where I think it gets really fun to look at this is comparing certain marquis opponents vs certain non-marquis opponents.

In Chapter 2 I referenced the need for cross-organisational collaboration. For the Spurs, the use of dashboards that combine data from multiple departments brings the focus of the different business units into one area, for example, using Google Analytics to identify where and how a sale was generated, whether it be through Spurs.com, Ticketmaster, through a search engine, or via social channels. Individual business units can use daily sales reports to see day-to-day changes and isolate where the organisation can see quick wins and track against budget on a year-to-date and month-to-date basis.

When it comes to the value of sales management, Ghaffar was able to offer further insights.

> We're able to specifically point out different products that reps are selling and where they're tracking against their goals. And something like this really elucidates what exactly it is that we're doing from a sales force effectiveness standpoint. I think where this becomes incredibly powerful is being able to slice and dice different reps' names and come up with some sort of general conclusion about the effectiveness of the sales force and how they may be achieving sales force excellence, how they may be really leveraging their different skill sets to be able to sell different types of products and do it in a relatively effective manner.

Tech stack developments

Ghaffar is quite clear about what he thinks is next; the ability to look at different business efficiencies, specifically the area of what he refers to as the 'industrial engineering' that goes into staging an event and parking efficiencies around it.

> There's undoubtedly a tremendous amount of ingress and egress, and I know vendors have popped up here and there with artificial intelligence products to help teams and organisations better manoeuvre or better navigate how to configure an arena so that it's conducive to revenue maximisation. And so where we really want to go is, by using something as simple as looking at concessionaires and kiosks and realising where there may be certain transaction depressions and densities in the arena, and really be able to understand perhaps an underlying consumer behaviour or consumer psychology that could unearth an entire new revenue stream. How might we configure our arena so that more and more folks are able to get their burger on time, get to their seat on time and ultimately improve their fan experience? I think that's something that we'll always be marching towards and that's quite honestly where we're trying to go next.

He also believes sentiment data will be the next set of information that rights owners will try to integrate into their tech stack, proposing that game-by-game analysis could open up a new avenue of opportunities.

> Perhaps a cold hot dog led to some kind of engagement attrition in subsequent games. Or perhaps a parking concern was raised. Those are the types of sentiments that we would hope to be able to capture. It's something that we have an eye for, something that we would like to build toward, and something that we've put on our data roadmap.

Kolosey sees the value in the integration of concession data as the start of a drive to provide one universal truth for the organisation.

> With this kind of integration everyone's on the same page, there's no level of scepticism by our executive based on rosy reports they're receiving. The reports show the way it is, and then the conversations can begin based on that one universal truth that everyone understands. And from there it allows us to have a little bit more of an organisation of strategists and implementers really focusing on how we are working, as opposed to having so many man hours in so many different areas of the business spent collecting reports and then publishing them. That turnaround time makes things that much more sticky, and so it allows us to be a lot more flexible and dynamic in both of those realms.

(Source: KORE, 2017, 12 December.)

Key chapter ideas

1   There is no single piece of software or a stand-alone CRM system that will provide you with all your needs. Instead you need to think about a CRM eco-system that incorporates different products and platforms.

2   The holy grail of CRM is the Single Customer View. This is a centralised database that enables you to have a 360-degree view of all your fans, customers, participants and other stakeholders.

3   When you are a data-driven business there is a constant movement of data around your environment so you need a data management strategy to inform the way you approach this. The strategy document will inform the processes you need to maintain a uniform approach to the way you acquire, transfer, store and use your data.

4   Your eco-system should be future-proofed to deal with the vast pace of digital technologies. As you move forward with your development you'll want to integrate your technology stack with other applications.

5   Planning, designing and implementing your technology stack is not an IT project and should be led by your business. Technology is an enabler not a driver.

References

3M (1997). *Polishing Your Presentation*. Austin, TX: 3M.

Calligeros, M. (2015). Seeing green boosts your concentration, research shows [online]. *The Sydney Morning Herald*. Available at: www.smh.com.au/technology/sci-tech/seeing-green-boosts-your-concentration-research-shows-20150525-gh8udh.html.

Cherwenka, A. (2013). Top retail buzzwords for 2013: omnichannel, personalization, mobile [online]. *HuffPost*. Available at: www.huffingtonpost.com/andrew-cherwenka/top-retail-buzzwords-for-_b_2506997.html.

Ecker, S. (2013). *Best color for concentration and productivity is orange* [online]. *HuffPost*. Available at: www.huffingtonpost.co.uk/entry/best-color-concentration_n_3949427.

Edwards, J. (2013). *BEHOLD: the first banner ad ever — from 1994* [online]. *Business Insider*. Available at: www.businessinsider.com/behold-the-first-banner-ad-ever--from-1994-2013-2.

Experian Marketing Services (2016). *The 2016 Digital Marketer* [online]. Nottingham: Experian Marketing Services. Available at: www.experian.co.uk/assets/marketing-services/reports/report-digital-marketer-report-2016.pdf.

Gartner (2017). *The Gartner CRM Vendor Guide, 2017* [online]. Gartner. Available at: www.gartner.com/doc/reprints?id=1-43163S2&ct=170613.

Greenberg, P. (2017). And the winners of the 2017 CRM Watchlist are. . . [online]. *ZDNet*. Available at: www.zdnet.com/article/and-the-winners-of-the-2017-crm-watchlist-are.

KORE Software (2017, 12 December). Data warehousing in action: spurring efficiency & collaboration with the San Antonio Spurs [webinar]. *KORE Software Customer Insights*. Available at: https://info.koresoftware.com/data-warehousing-in-action.

Shedden, D. (2014). Today in media history: the first Internet search engine is released in 1990 [online]. *Poynter*. Available at: www.poynter.org/news/today-media-history-first-internet-search-engine-released-1990.

The Radicati Group (2017). *Email Statistics Report, 2017–2021* [online]. Palo Alto, CA: The Radicati Group. Available at: www.radicati.com/wp/wp-content/uploads/2017/01/Email-Statistics-Report-2017-2021-Executive-Summary.pdf.

Chapter 6

Data-driven marketing

In Chapter 1 we introduced the definition of CRM as getting the right message to the right person at the right time. We also included Don Peppers' definition of treating different customers differently, as well as Gartner's longer, more detailed definition ('A business strategy optimises revenue and profitability while promoting customer satisfaction and loyalty'). When you get to Chapter 8 you'll also read the following definition from Mic Conetta, Arsenal's Head of CRM: 'the automation and technology to better deliver fan experiences, customer interactions and the provision of services'.

Each of these definitions represents the core essence of data-driven marketing: ensuring your marketing is customer-centric. This means securing, maintaining, analysing and using your customer data, then actively segmenting it to enable better targeting and engagement with your customers. As we discussed in a previous chapter, your analysis could be used to predict future behaviours, but the intention at all times is to enhance and personalise the experience for your customers.

But why has this suddenly become such a big deal? I don't think there are many people out there who would disagree that marketing has experienced a fundamental shift, that many of the techniques and approaches that worked for the past 50, 40 or even 30 years are no longer relevant in today's digital world. The shift has been driven by the customer's demands that we now listen to them and, more importantly, give them what they want, not what we think they want. It's been enabled by technology and the data that it generates. In turn, marketers are expected to quantify and measure their actions like never before, demonstrating data-driven decision-making and customer-centric campaigns. In the same way a CFO looks at the decimal points in his analysis of profit and loss, so too are CMOs expected to assess the ROI of their actions. They now have the tools to track this information and so they're expected to do so.

The collapsing marketing funnel

The digital marketing funnel is usually described as **awareness**, **consideration**, **conversion** and **retention**. At the 2017 dmexco, the international exposition and conference for the digital industry that takes place every September in Germany, Sheryl Sandberg, Facebook's Chief Operating Officer, made the following announcement:

> The marketing funnel itself is collapsing. It used to take time to go from research, to discovery, to awareness, all the way through a purchase. But now with digital and mobile, that's happening faster than ever. And that means that from the largest brands, to the corner coffee shop, to the smallest companies in the world, to non-profits, the way you work on your brand, the way you communicate who you are has never been more important.
>
> (Sandberg, 2017)

Sandberg's key point was not that the funnel is collapsing altogether, but that it's contracting, not at different stages, but at the pace in which a customer might go through it. I had first-hand experience of this at the start of 2018. I'd visited a friend who served me a coffee from one of those machines that used little pods or discs. While still there I had a look at similar models on my phone, musing whether we might use it if we had one in our own kitchen. Later that night my husband and I started looking for holidays using my laptop and I saw a few adverts for the same coffee machines I'd looked at earlier. To cap it off, my Facebook notification the next morning led me to check out my sister's latest photo and there was the exact coffee machine I wanted. I bought it. In less than 24 hours and just a few clicks.

Liverpool Football Club is no stranger to digital remarketing to collapse the marketing funnel. With its merchandise operation generating an eight-figure turnover, it's easy to understand why the club would apply this practice to its online store. Its remarketing campaigns incorporate website engagement driven by user data, supplemented by email and display retargeting, using customised dynamic messaging. In a case study published by Ve (Ve, 2017) automated abandoned shopping cart messaging was used to encourage fans to complete their online store purchases and achieved a click-to-conversion rate of 55.8%. That is, 55.8% of all email recipients who clicked on the message to continue their transaction went on to do so.

What customers really want

I'm often asked by clients, particularly when delivering workshops that provide an introduction to CRM, if fans and customers really want us to know who they are. Do they like us to have this level of awareness or do they find it 'creepy'? If you recall, in Chapter 1, I referred to the Orwellian 'Big Brother is watching you' notion that is no longer the theme of a book but an everyday reality.

My response to this question is always the same and is two-fold:

1   If your fans, customers, participants or any of your stakeholders don't want to be part of your engagement strategy, they don't have to be (at least that's the case if you're following the appropriate legislation and implementing a best practice approach). They can opt-out of your email campaigns, cookie retargeting, profiling, web and social remarketing, and indeed any of the data-driven activities you use.

2   According to Salesforce's 2016 report *State of the Connected Customer*, 63% of millennial consumers and 58% of GenX consumers are willing to share data with companies in exchange for personalised offers and discounts, with 72% of the belief that companies should understand their needs and expectations (McGinnis, 2016).

There's a big difference between watching your customers because you can, versus watching them to enable you to provide them with great customer service, and it seems our fans and customers might agree with that. So, let's look at a few examples that could resonate with rights owners:

- **Timing is key**: if a fan has just purchased a season ticket, he might not appreciate being asked if he'd like to buy an individual match ticket. But you could expect an email with a 10% discount for your online store the morning of his birthday to be greeted with delight. Sending a congratulatory message to a coach who's completed your Level 1 might also be followed up by a message to let them know they can progress to Level 2 at the click of a button. If you have a goal to increase participation, one of your registered players might stay in the game after they've moved house if you advise them that their nearest club is located just two miles away from their new location and is looking for members.

- **TripAdvisor-style recommendations**: while a fan would never pay attention to someone else's recommendations when it comes to which team they should support, they might appreciate being advised that the matching shorts are a perfect complement to their recent purchase of the replica shirt, or that upgrading their ticket purchase to a one-off corporate hospitality pass would provide them with the opportunity to meet their favourite player.

- **Make their lives just that little bit easier**: advising your event attendees of the location of the concession stands in relation to their seats and which one has the shortest queue at half-time might be appreciated by your fans keen to get back to their seats as quickly as possible. If local highways management is aware of the distance they're likely to have travelled, they can ensure the traffic flows minimise the risk of jams or other disruptions to their journey. Liverpool FC's example above could also be considered under this category. Have you ever been halfway through making a purchase when your phone has rung, causing you to forget to complete your purchase even though you wanted to?

- **Joint benefit and value**: this is the exchange value: when a customer feels they'll receive something of value as a result of you having their data, they'll be more receptive to the notion of sharing it. This of course includes content and is more relevant in the sports industry than many others. Behind-the-scenes footage, interviews with star athletes, exclusive competition entries and previously unseen footage and photos are just a few things that can entice a fan to tell you what you need to know. Privileged access to tickets for that all-important event or a meet-and-greet with the team is sure to entice people to the hit the 'submit' button if they've previously resisted.

This chapter is going to look at how we take the data we're now collecting and analysing to apply it to the way we market to or, more importantly, engage with our fans and customers. I'm going to take a look at the different formats of marketing that are enhanced with this data-driven approach and the different channels that can be driven by data. I'll focus on those that enable the use of segmentation and personalisation, specifically those that are considered online as opposed to offline.

I had been selling and optimising the benefits of sponsorship, merchandise and TV rights in the sports industry for over 25 years before I moved into my current field. When I did so, I recall surprise at the constant chatter about the death of email marketing. I also met several social media marketers who were so obsessed with their own field they couldn't see the danger in placing all their marketing focus in this area.

The reality is that email isn't dead, nor is it dying. Email continues to be a requirement for registration of social networks, app stores and online purchases. But, as with all communication methods, the challenge is to do it well; to use email for the right message, the right person and at the right time. This is a view shared by leading CRM practitioner Russell Scibetti, President of KORE Planning & Insights and founding editor of *The Business of Sports*, a blog dedicated to discussing new ideas and current events in the sports industry. Scibetti shared the following with me in a discussion in January 2018:

> People like to make the comment that 'email marketing is dead', which I vehemently disagree with. One of the main premises of that belief is that email has been overtaken by social media as a primary communication channel to fans and customers, and while we shouldn't underestimate the impact of social media, different channels are better at different things.
>
> One area where email marketing still has a clear advantage is in direct consumer monetisation, so whenever this topic comes up in a group setting, there's a simple exercise I love to run. First I ask everyone in the room to raise their hands if, in the last 12 months, they've purchased an item directly from clicking a link on Twitter or Facebook, and very few hands are raised. Then I ask the group to raise their hands if, in the last

12 months, they've purchased an item directly from clicking a link in an email, and nearly every hand pops up. This creates a clear demonstration of email marketing and direct marketing in general maintains its effectiveness in generating sales.

When I start working with a rights owner client who hasn't yet used any form of data-driven marketing and has no CRM capability within their organisation (there are still many out there), I introduce them to email marketing as a starting point. My reasons are:

1   **Email marketing is cheap**. I know that term is relative but when you compare it with the other digital channels like SMS, mobile app push messages, web and social retargeting or remarketing, the cost of entry to develop and to deploy are all lower with email (assuming you've selected the appropriate platform for your needs).

2   **The skill needed to begin email marketing is not great**. Most commercial platforms provide a drag-and-drop option, meaning that anyone in marketing who knows how to use PowerPoint can quickly adapt their skills.

3   **The database format (usually) allows you to replicate some CRM functionality**. As an example, building list segments based on data attributes, merging lists on a unique ID to create an SCV will introduce you to some key principles at a low cost-to-enter.

4   **The email campaign introduces workflow automation**. Functionality will (usually) include triggered campaigns and other formats that will introduce you to the efficiencies of this kind of automation.

5   **The reporting functions introduce you to the benefit of using actionable insights**. In turn this will help you to inform your decisions, for example, what to do differently, or the same, in your next campaign.

6   **The landing page functions introduce the importance of data standardisation and correct data mapping**. This is usually available on commercial platforms.

The point I'd like to make here is that if you're at the beginning of your journey into the use of data-driven marketing, starting with email campaigns is a great place to be and everything you learn will be applicable as you continue to progress. It's important you select a system that is future-proofed, providing you with enough bandwidth to grow in capability for at least 12 to 18 months. If your website developer offers you an email tool within their website build, unless they're referring to integration with an external provider I'd recommend you turn them down. You'll never get the appropriate level of email function from a company whose core role for you is to build your website.

Key considerations for email campaign planning

I'm going to talk you through some key steps when using email marketing because, as I mention above, this process, once adopted, can then be readily applied to the evolution of your use of data.

Aligning with business objectives

In Chapter 2 we talked about the importance of a strategy to ensure your individual business units are all heading in the same direction and your operational delivery is aligned to your business objectives.

We practise the same approach when planning email campaigns. Each broadcast represents one minor cog within a significant wheel and should be treated as such. The individual purpose of the campaign, the action, or the 'why', should align directly or indirectly with your business objectives.

List segmentation

After determining the purpose of your campaign, the next step is to consider the target audience. To whom do you want to send it? This is where the use of list segmentation comes into the planning. While you can send emails to your full database, and there may be occasions when this is both necessary and desired, sending your emails in a more targeted manner is a key way to increase engagement and therefore ROI. Even if you're not yet at the stage where you have customer personas, you'll probably know who buys your tickets and who doesn't, who attends your events or volunteers at them, who has previously opened a campaign and who hasn't.

Building on this, the different types of segmentation considered could include gender, age, geography or purchase history. For example, if you're promoting last-minute ticket sales to an event in London, your fans in the US are less likely to respond to a request to 'buy now' than those that live in the UK. If your objective is to seek out female coaches or referees, your message should exclude the males in your database (unless, of course, you include a message to that segment that starts with 'do you know a woman who'd be interested in this?').

Testing content and design

In Chapter 1 I highlighted how our attention span is now less than that of a goldfish so, when it comes to the content and layout of your email, you need to be thinking about how you can grab your customer's attention before they get a chance to move on to their next email. Most importantly, you need to make the content interesting. If your objective is to sell tickets, use content to support this instead of just using a blatant sales message. For example, if the match you're focusing on is against a team you've played before, remind your fans of the result the last time you met, or your total history if you've met them more than once.

'Less is more' is often the case when it comes to email content. The recommended approach is to include a small section of the story and provide a web link to the remainder on your website or an alternative destination page as this is the objective of your email campaign. This should be through a clear call to action (CTA) button that inspires a clear action such as 'Buy Now', 'Read More' or 'Watch Here'. Never expect your recipients to be curious enough to click anyway. You have to pique their interest.

In the image-rich world of sports, the use of high-quality images consistently throughout your email campaigns will draw your recipients' attention and help keep them engaged. If you include ones that aren't published on your website or social channels you can expect higher open rates as your customers start to expect this unique content.

Finally, the type of content you include should be varied to reflect the multiple opportunities the digital world presents. People love to interact, even more so when it comes to their sport, event or club, so you can expect links to videos, polls, quizzes and competitions to be a big hit with your fans.

Personalisation

There are three main types of personalisation to consider when planning your email campaigns:

- **From name or subject line**: These two elements are the most prominent in an inbox so it makes sense that they'd have a significant impact on your open rates.

  I haven't yet met any team that uses a reference to its manager in the 'from name' field, but maybe the club nickname or its mascot might have an impact. Dale Carnegie, the author of *How to Win Friends and Influence People*, believed that a person's name is the sweetest sound in any language for that person, and that it was important to use it whenever possible. He stated that as a name is the core part of our identity, when we hear it being used it validates our existence, which makes us feel more positively about the person using it (Carnegie, 2006 [1936]).

  Try using the recipient's name in a subject line and see if Carnegie was on to something. Experian Marketing Services suggests that personalised subject lines generate 27% higher click-through rates and 11% higher click-to-open rates (Experian, 2016). The personalisation doesn't have to be limited to the recipient's name. You can refer to their favourite athlete or team (if you know it), their response to your last campaign (if your system provides it) and even their transactional status (if they have or haven't bought a ticket to your next game).

- **Content**: expanding on the themes above, you can personalise the text and images within the email content to reflect what you know about the recipient. While beginners can use a simple manual process to do this, advanced marketers can use dynamic content to reduce the amount of time needed to achieve this.
- **Date and time of send**: if the campaign you're sending is not time-critical, unlike a squad announcement, then you can segment your list so that different recipients receive the email at a different time. Imagine providing a window of opportunity for your most loyal fans to be able to purchase tickets to the must-attend match or the launch of a new piece of merchandise in your online store.

When it comes to personalisation, you're only limited by what you know about your customers, the data you have in your database and the functionality of your email broadcast platform. Your objective is to ensure that every person in your database feels like they are an individual; that you are marketing to a segment of one.

Case study: Bristol Rovers FC – personalisation based on data

Tom Gorringe, Commercial Director for Bristol Rovers FC, a club currently in England's Football League One, is an experienced email marketer and knows he needs data to turn his email campaigns from ad-hoc messaging to personalised engagement. In a meeting on 8 December 2017, Gorringe said:

> Data is vital. From a football perspective we need to know as much about our supporters as possible because ultimately we're here to serve them. So, the better understanding we can get of them, their behaviours, the way that they interact with us, the better we can service those behaviours, and ultimately then commercialise them. Every email campaign that we send would be targeted to a specific group. We wouldn't go to somebody who's never been to a game before and say 'here's a season ticket'. It's about getting them to their first game. We couldn't do this without data.

Gorringe used personalisation to great effect at his previous club, Brighton and Hove Albion. An end-of-season email campaign to the club's ticket buyers included the distance the recipient travelled across a whole season, calculated from the address data they held. To this the email added information about the matches they attended, the goals scored or the goal scorers in those matches, resulting in multiple versions of the same campaign; one for every user with a different postcode and attendance record.

> The most important element of the email was that it was specifically non-commercial. It contained no mention of any sort of sales messages. This was to ensure that it was authentic and received in the manner in which it was sent. However, what we found was that following the receipt there was an increase in season ticket sales, which in the first instance amounted to £30,000 within 48 hours from those that received the email. This we believe is due to the reminder of why supporters do what they do and the development of the feeling of loyalty and thanks given for their efforts.

At the Memorial Stadium, Bristol Rovers' home ground, Gorringe has a 'green field' and intends to take the time necessary to get the foundations in place to use email effectively.

> Because we haven't done anything for so long, we effectively need to start getting a lot of these supporters and making sure we're communicating with them from day one and getting a real understanding of what their preferences are, and that we're only communicating with them in the way that they want us to. But it is a bit of a blank canvas so again, it's a nice place to be in.
>
> I think the main thing in the next 12 months is to get a better understanding of who's coming into the stadium. Even if we only get their email address at busy times, we can build forms to use and go back to them for further information after the game. It'll be a slow process but we'll get there if the engagement level is right.

The club is still in the early stages of pulling its data streams together. By early 2018 Gorringe expects to have the email system set up in order to send tailored messages to the Rovers' fans.

> I think the most important thing is, we start with a nice welcome email that explains the changes and what we're looking to do. We need to make sure that everyone's details are up to date and then, from the start of next season,

once we've done a bit of a survey and got some more insight on the supporter base, made sure all of our data's clean and that we're compliant, we can really start to push this strategy. We'll particularly aim to utilise our email channels to bring it to life.

(Source: Gorringe, 2017, 8 December.)

Digital ad retargeting

Unlike normal website banner ads, retargeting ads are presented specifically to people who have already visited your website or are in your contact database (perhaps your email marketing database, athlete registration database or your centralised database/SCV if you have one).

There are two main forms of retargeting: pixel-based and list-based. Both work on the principle that a customer visits your website, leaves it without completing the action you wanted them to take (for example, buying a ticket, visiting your sponsor, or registering to play) and they continue visiting other websites. Your digital ad is then displayed on one (or many) of the websites they visit, which draws them back to your site so they can complete the target action.

Pixel-based retargeting allows you to show your advert or message to any of your website visitors, whether they're anonymous or known. When someone visits your website, assuming you have your cookie policy in place and your user accepts it, a pixel will be dropped into their browser. This will follow them as they browse your site, and other sites, allowing ad platforms to serve your adverts to them. These ads can be personalised based on the pages they visited on your website. For example, if they visited your ticket sales page but didn't purchase, the ad you can serve them will promote your next match. If they visited the section of your website that discusses how someone gets into your sport but they don't register or complete any forms, the ad you serve can invite them back to your site to sign up.

Pixel-based retargeting can generate fast results as web visitors can be retargeted almost as soon as they leave your site. However, subject to the way you manage your site, it may take some time to implement the coding on the different pages that you want to include in your retargeting campaign. Bear in mind that if your website doesn't generate a lot of traffic, then you won't be retargeting many users through this method.

With **list-based retargeting**, your list of customer email addresses is used to identify those users who are to be served your ad. While this form of retargeting is less common than pixel-based, your campaigns can be more targeted because you choose, at an individual level, who sees your advert. This allows you to use more than just behavioural data as targeting criteria. For example, you can create a list of email addresses for fans who read your email campaigns but haven't yet purchased a ticket for the next match, pre-ordered the new home shirt or registered to play for your club next season. You could also use this tactic to re-engage your customers that aren't responding to your emails, such as if you use a list from your email platform of anyone who hasn't opened a campaign in 90 days. Use a digital ad to remind them of the great news and exclusive content they can get from you.

Your list is imported to an ad platform where the data is anonymised (usually through a process called hashing). The ad platform then uses that list to find these fans on other websites so your advert can be served. This is important as it means your targeted segment will naturally be smaller than the original list. Not only is it expected that not all users accept cookies or may delete them, but the retargeting platform has to match your email addresses with users of other digital platforms, and the email address they gave you may be different to ones they've used elsewhere.

Unlike pixel-based retargeting, it takes time for the ad platform you use to match email addresses, so advance planning and preparation is very important here. Another difference with list retargeting is that you are in charge of uploading and maintaining the lists you use, so this form of retargeting, for all its benefits, is less automated and takes up more of your time.

It's also important that your email list has opted in for digital retargeting, although you could consider whether using 'legitimate interest' would enable you to use your lists without the need for a further opt-in. There will be more about this in Chapter 9 on data and the law.

Retargeting can also be used in social channels such as Facebook, Twitter, Instagram and LinkedIn, as well as in mobile apps and based on keywords used when using a search engine. As with email marketing, dynamic content can be used to ensure the message can be personalised to a very granular level.

You can use a dedicated retargeting platform for either of these retargeting techniques, or you can go directly to the ad networks or exchanges themselves (i.e., advertise directly with Google, Facebook, etc).

Unlike email marketing, while you can get general overall campaign tracking data, you can't get individual response data. This is because your targeted customers are either anonymous or you've used email addresses that have to be anonymised before they can be used by the retargeting platforms.

A big advocate of Facebook's list retargeting services is the NFL's Miami Dolphins, having transferred 80% of its marketing budget from 2015 to 2017 to using Facebook's Custom Audiences, Lookalike Audiences and Lead Ads. According to Jeremy Walls, the team's senior vice president and chief marketing officer, 'Overnight, Facebook has become our largest lead-generation source for season tickets' (Ourand, 2017).

The Dolphins' strategy is based on creating unique content and using Facebook as the distribution platform. During the 2016 season the Dolphins created 11 online shows that ranged from two-minute videos to a three-day-per-week podcast, supplemented by montages of the season's most popular videos accompanied by music from artists such as Ella Fitzgerald and Johnny Cash.

> Instead of buying a TV commercial or radio ad last season, we bought music rights for social media for a week or two weeks at a time . . . Millions of people would watch that, then we would retarget them with an ad to generate a lead for us . . . That was a big shift for us on the marketing side. We were reaching a lot more people doing that versus making a 30-second TV commercial that was outdated a week after we started airing it.
>
> (Ibid.)

Not only does Walls credit the Facebook campaign with generating 30% of all season ticket sales, the Dolphins generated about $10 million in sponsorship revenues around the content. And because the programming has been so well received, the strategy provided sponsor opportunities as well. Walls always intended to seek sponsorship for the shows, but he was keen to ensure they approached this in the right order.

> We wanted to build really good content franchises first — build them up, build up the audience and then assign a brand to it, not the other way around.
>
> (Ibid.)

SMS marketing

While costing more than email marketing, the use of text messages is nevertheless a valuable channel that supports the use of segmentation and personalised messages. While there is a natural limitation on how much content can be used, SMS is great for last-minute notifications, when your fans or customers are on site, or when they're not responding to your emails and you need to get them engaged.

As with email marketing, response tracking is possible at an individual level but, unlike email, text messages don't run any risk of getting caught in spam filters. As with any form of targeted marketing, your SMS recipients must have opted in and must have the ability to opt out at any time.

Mobile app push messages

A mobile app push message is content that is 'pushed' through a mobile app to alert a recipient to news, events, special offers or any other content you wish to share with your fans or customers. While the app user has to set their push messages to 'on' (the equivalent of opting in for an email), messages will be sent even when the app is closed. As with SMS, if your users have opted in, they will get to see your messages and they won't get caught in a spam filter.

As with email and SMS, if you've used a login process so you can identify individuals, behavioural responses to push messages can be tracked including interaction times and device used, as well as the content that produced the most engagement. However, while the actual cost of mobile app push messages is negligible, unlike with the use of email or SMS you have to start with a mobile app, so the costs to get going are more significant.

Moving from silos to multi- or cross-channel

Each of these channels on its own can provide incredibly powerful results when used in conjunction with data to deliver a personalised experience. But when they work together to provide a multi-channel experience, then the experience for the user is greater and your results are improved.

As I discussed in the previous chapter, multi-channel marketing means engaging with your customers using a combination of channels and knowing which channel to use at any given time. Taking this principle one step further, is cross-channel, that is, continuing the conversation with your customers as they move from one channel to the next, and picking up that conversation at the last point you've left it: if they were looking at buying a ticket or joining a club on your website, then their next mobile app push message or social post they see will progress that discussion.

Moving from a silo approach in digital marketing to multi- or cross-channel can be challenging, but it's not just factors such as an absence of collaboration, commitment or integration that prevent progress. It's a reality that getting the right team with the right skills can also be difficult. By its nature, the use of data in marketing is still a niche role so securing the type of staff that specialise in areas such as data analytics, particularly with the types of budgets and head counts that rights owners have, can be difficult. However, there is a process in your approach to digital marketing, the use of data and multi- or cross-channel marketing that can help increase your chances of success: the use of testing.

Test and learn

Elon Musk, the billionaire founder of PayPal, SpaceX and Telsa, said:

> I think it's very important to have a feedback loop, where you're constantly thinking about what you've done and how you could be doing it better. I think that's the single best piece of advice: constantly think about how you could be doing things better.
>
> (Ulanoff, 2012)

Musk wasn't talking about data-driven marketing when he made this statement, but it's still highly relevant. One of the many benefits of marketing in the digital world is our ability to test our theories or ideas before we commit to them.

Consider the process of printing a poster to promote ticket sales for your event. You produce the design based on all the information you have at the time. You show it around to colleagues in your office and maybe to a few other people whose opinion you respect. Then you order 100, 1,000 or 10,000 of them and have them printed. At this point, you're committed. The poster includes an offer code, so when your fans book their tickets you can track your ROI. But what you don't know is your conversion rate; how many people saw the poster and then went on to use the code. Further to that, you don't know how much your conversion rate would have increased had the wording or imagery been different, if you'd placed the posters in different positions, or placed them on a different day.

Compare that with the process of producing an email campaign, a banner ad, a landing page, or indeed any piece of digital content. In any of these instances, while you will again produce the digital asset based on the information you have at the time, by using a testing process you'll be able to amend it based on the information you gather as your customers engage with it. In many instances you can automate that process for added efficiency.

When you use testing you make an informed decision based on an objective, not subjective, data-driven process. You'll increase your chances of making an incredible breakthrough and reduce your chances of implementing a bad idea.

A/B test versus MV test

In an A/B test you set up two different experiences, with A representing the current state or the champion, and B having been amended to reflect the elements you want to test and therefore considered the challenger.

The A and B versions of the digital asset are served up randomly, and the key metrics are compared to see which performed the best. The winning version is then used. Multivariate (MV) tests are based on exactly the same principle but more than two versions are used, meaning you have one champion and multiple challengers.

In email marketing you first select the quantity of recipients you want to use in the test samples, for example 10%, then consider the amount of time you want to run the test for. A key consideration here is that if an email campaign is time sensitive, for example a squad announcement or exclusive window of availability for ticket sales, the period of time you select for the test will mean a delay in the time your recipients receive their campaign. I know that sounds obvious, but I've seen clients get so excited at the thought of using testing protocol they forget that certain tests only work in certain conditions.

The KPI tests that can be impacted in email marketing are:

1 **Open rates**: using different subject lines, preview text, date of send, time of send and personalisation can all have an impact on a recipient's propensity to open. Interestingly, among our sports clients at Winners we have

been surprised to find that when it comes to the subject line, 'Official news from. . .' often outperforms text that actually describes the content within the email. We wonder if this is representative of the importance placed on the value of official status when 'fake news', the *Collins Dictionary* Word of the Year for 2017, is now so commonplace.

2   **Click-through-rates**: placing content in different positions within the email, using different text or colours on your CTA, using different images or text, and even using a recipient's first name in the content, can produce different results.

One final point to note when using testing in email marketing is that most platforms provide this as an automated process. That is, the test segments are picked randomly by the system and, at the end of the test period, the winner is automatically sent to the remainder of the database who were not included in the test segments. This is referred to as the roll out.

Testing data collection forms

My clients regularly ask me how much information they should ask for in their sign up forms. My answer is pretty much always the same: test different versions and see what your fans think.

As with the email testing process above, you can apply the same logic to your data collection forms. Produce any number of versions, using different tactics, see which one performs the best over a period of time and then 'switch off' the other versions. Different tactics include the number of questions you ask, the use of mandatory fields, personalisation if you're using dynamic content, different CTAs, and opt-in consent wording, among others. If you add Google Analytics to your landing page, not only can you look at which format of the form produces the most opt-ins, you can also track conversion from visitors to the page itself.

While I've specified two particular use cases, the principle can be applied to pretty much anything within your digital estate like text content, images and videos, but a key consideration is that, in any test, you should only focus on testing one particular element. You can't test both a subject line and a CTA in the same email campaign, or the number of data collection fields used as well as the imagery in a landing page. You won't know which of the different elements impacted the result. While setting up tests increases the amount of time needed to deliver a campaign, the results more than outweigh the additional resources requirement.

Most importantly, you can see the results of digital marketing test really quickly so, not only are you able to fail and then improve, to use the different mantras of Silicon Valley you can 'fail fast, fail often', 'fail better' or 'fail forward', all of which put you in a stronger position to deliver your target KPIs.

A/A testing

Advanced digital marketers may also consider the use of A/A testing. This is a process used before A/B or MV testing to check the validity of the test you're about to implement. In this instance, you use two versions of exactly the same asset to ensure that the tools or processes you're using are running correctly. When using an A/A test you should see no difference between the two variations, and can be confident there will be no external factors impacting your A/B or MV tests.

I discussed the principle of digital marketing testing with Dave Callan, Head of Partnerships & Business Development at Team Sky, five times winners of the Tour de France, in a phone call on 8 January 2018:

> On the bike we've always been obsessed with making the best informed decisions. The application and use of data has always played a crucial role within this and now we take the same approach to the way we engage with our fans. The use of testing what we do to see how our fans respond is a major part of that. For example, when we're running a digital competition that has a data collection element in it we typically run a minimum of three different versions to make sure we get it right. We take a look at the conversion rates and choose what to drop, amend or change accordingly. It's interesting that what we've learned from doing this isn't just really valuable, it often tells us the opposite of what we thought we knew. Fans will answer questions if you give them the reason to. These answers then help me plan content, engage partners and continue to build the trust between the Team Sky brand and our fans around the world.
>
> (Callan, 2018, 8 January)

From last action to next best action

In Chapter 4 we talked about the role of predictive analytics to help you understand what's likely to happen in the future. When you apply this process to digital marketing you're able to move from just tracking a customer's last action to predicting their next one. Most importantly, you can prepare for it, anticipating their needs and presenting them with the right message at the right time and on the right channel.

This process works by assessing all the potential next best actions for your fan or customer (for example, buy a ticket, upgrade to VIP hospitality, extend to a season ticket, buy the matching shorts, train to be a coach) and selecting the one that they're most likely to take given the results of your analysis. Irrespective of your customer's response (i.e., did it work or didn't it), you'll learn more about that customer. This in turn will improve the efficiency of this process as you continue to use it. The key to successful use of this process is ensuring you strike a balance between what your customers expect from you and what you're trying to achieve.

Data-driven marketing: the utopian state

The extent to which you use data-driven marketing will depend on a number of factors relevant to your specific organisation, the most important of which is your business need. As with any form of marketing, the costs have to be taken into account and considered against the potential gains. For example, if your objective is to sell 5,000 tickets and you have 100,000 previous ticket buyers in your database, you can be relatively confident of a 5% conversion rate using some basic processes. However, if the numbers are reversed and you have 100,000 tickets to sell and a starting point of just 5,000 customers, your plan will change. In addition to converting existing customers you'll be looking for new ones.

Thinking more strategically, if your mid-term organisational objectives include increasing your engagement within a specific segment of fans, extending your global reach into new territories, or doubling your participation base, then it's reasonable to assume you'll need the appropriate resources to deliver this.

Some rights owners have gone beyond data-driven marketing and are talking about complete digital transformation. This is the change associated with the application of digital technologies across the whole of a business. This digital usage inherently enables new types of innovation or creativity, as opposed to simply enhancing and supporting an existing method. I've already discussed how the sports industry is moving at a slower pace than other industries, not just the pure plays, but let's assume that this is your objective: to achieve digital transformation that delivers significant increases in KPI over a five-year term. In this case your utopian state would be fast and accurate cross-channel and cross-device engagement with attribute tracking at every touch point. This would enable you to know the exact contributing factor at every step of the customer journey, so you could continue to improve on the efficiency of your processes.

In reality there's no one actually achieving this yet, not even Amazon, Netflix or Spotify, and the reason is the pace of technological change, which is providing our customers with more choice, more frequently. According to Scott Brinker's annual review of the marketing technology landscape, 2017 saw an increase in 40% of solutions resulting in a total of 5,381, provided by 4,891 companies (Brinker, 2017). The key for every rights owner is that you're finding the appropriate ways to optimise the channels you use to achieve your KPIs and that, along the way, you're improving the level of engagement you have with your fans, customers or participants. Equally as important is that they feel valued along the journey, and that you know and care about them and are talking to them individually.

Case study: Derbyshire County Cricket Club

Derbyshire CCC (County Cricket Club) is one of 18 first-class county clubs that play within the structure of the domestic game in England and Wales. In March 2017 Derbyshire CCC appointed Sportego, a Dublin-based consultancy, specialising in fan engagement in the sports industry, to design a personalised communication strategy with the creation of key supporter personas at the heart of it.

In a telephone interview on 18 January 2018 Chris Airey, Media and Marketing Manager of Derbyshire CCC, talked to me about the process they used with Sportego's support.

> We started with six years of ticketing, merchandise and membership sales data that was audited and normalised to enable the creation of a Single Customer View. Once that was in place, the data was then analysed with specific focus on the timing and types of the ticket purchases.
>
> We then looked at any possible factors that could have affected ticket sales such as the competition format, the weather, and the day and time of the match. We even looked at how, if at all, the team performance at the time affected our fans' loyalty — we looked at any relationship between our sales and our results.

Specific attention was paid to new fans; how they were captured, the type of tickets they purchased, the games they attended, and the timing of their purchases. The RFV analysis, described in Chapter 4, was applied with specific focus on the results for lapsed fans. The records were cleansed against the UK PAF (Postal Address File), a database owned by the Royal Mail that provides all known postal delivery points in the UK (30 million addresses and 1.8 million postcodes). Running a database against PAF returns a file of addresses in the correct format as the process detects and corrects corrupt or inaccurate records.

Once cleansed, Derbyshire's database was then matched against Acorn, a UK consumer classification segmentation tool developed by CACI, a global IT consultancy firm. Acorn stands for A Classification Of Residential Neighbourhoods, and is based on the premise that people living in similar areas generally present similar lifestyle and spending habits. Acorn classifications are created by analysing demographic data, social factors, population and consumer behaviour to provide six categories, 18 groups and 62 demographic types. In the end, Airey achieved an Acorn match rate of 94% with useable classifications for 83% of their database.

Thanks to our fast start it meant that just two months later we were in a position to create six key customer personas, using our supporter behaviour as one of three to six key attributes. For personas with three or four attributes, there had to be a 75% match rate for fans to be allocated that persona – for personas with five or six attributes they had to match the two key attributes and two of the remaining three or four. One of these was 'Friday Night Out', fans who met at least three of the following: they previously bought tickets to a Twenty20 Friday match, a limited overs/one day Friday match, matched the key age profile of 18 to 35, and fell into the Acorn group that identified younger sports fans. Given the different formats of cricket that we compete in, we used these as one of the key attributes and, unsurprisingly, T20 was the most prevalent.

Airey agreed that the use of customer personas increased the efficiency of Derbyshire's approach to personalised and targeted campaigns, both through email and direct mail, and will continue to build on them to create segments based on loyalty and longevity.

Now we have a greater understanding of who our supporters are and what they look like, and have created these personas that aid in the way we refer to them, we can start to expand on new areas of opportunity such as pulling supporters in from neighbouring counties. One of our next stages will be to get a clearer view of the influence team form and weather has on them. We're also looking at stadium entry mechanisms to build even further on these personas.

Airey and his team learned a lot going through this process and, while he concedes not everything they did was executed to perfection, he's pleased with the approach they took, using both Excel and Alteryx for data processing, and Tableau for analysis and visualisation.

The results speak for themselves. We achieved the most advanced sales ever in the club's history and we had the earliest ever advance sell out for a T20 match. We also saw the highest ever average attendance across T20, an 11% increase, as well as the highest ever aggregate attendance – 33% increase on last season.

This was the first time Derbyshire had used data-driven insights to formulate their marketing plan, and to use personas in their first project was a great achievement. With a record year behind them and a renewed contract with Sportego, Airey will build on what they've achieved so far, continuing to deliver personalised campaigns that add impact and increase their conversion rate.

Key chapter ideas

1   There is no single individual digital channel that will provide you with the platform to engage with all your fans, participants, customers and stakeholders. As you evolve, you will aim for a multi- or cross-channel approach that will deliver your messages through the appropriate platform for the fan, participant, customer or stakeholder with whom you want to engage.
2   If you are not yet using data for personalised communication then start with email marketing as it enables you to think about all the key elements of a data-driven approach. You'll be able to use segmentation, a Single Customer View, analytics to inform your future approach and tracking to understand your ROI.
3   While your data-driven campaigns will be focussed on delivering your business objectives, they must also provide value to your fans. Thinking of your customers' needs first will ensure you achieve this.
4   Digital technologies allow us to test and learn, fail fast, then test again. Don't be afraid to make mistakes and then learn from them.
5   More advanced digital marketers will be able to implement next-best-action planning. When you know your fans well enough, you can predict their next action and make it easy for them to say yes to your ticket sales message, merchandise offer, hospitality upgrade, next coaching badge or sponsor offer.

References

Airey, C. (2018, 18 January). Telephone interview.
Brinker, S. (2017). Marketing technology landscape supergraphic (2017) [online]. *Chief Marketing Technologist*. Available at: https://chiefmartec.com/2017/05/marketing-technology-landscape-supergraphic-2017.
Callan, D. (2018, 8 January). Telephone interview.
Carnegie, D. (2006). *How to Win Friends and Influence People*. London: Vermilion.
Conetta, M. (2017, 16 December). Telephone interview.
Experian (2016). *New insight from Experian Marketing Services helps brands prepare for the holiday season* [online]. Experian. Available at: www.experianplc.com/media/news/2016/q2-2016-email-benchmark-report.
Gorringe, T. (2017, 8 December). Personal interview.
McGinnis, D. (2016). Please take my data: why consumers want more personalized marketing [online]. *Salesforce Blog*. Available at: www.salesforce.com/blog/2016/12/consumers-want-more-personalized-marketing.html.

Ourand, J. (2017). Dolphins plow marketing budget into content and get results [online]. *Street & Smith's SportsBusiness Journal*. Available at: www.sportsbusinessdaily. com/Journal/Issues/2017/03/27/Media/Sports-Media.aspx.

Sandberg, S. (2017). *Building Community and Discovering Growth in a Mobile World.* dmexco, 13 September, Köln.

Scibetti, R. (2018, 22 January). Personal interview.

Ulanoff, L. (2012). Elon Musk: secrets of a highly effective entrepreneur [online]. *Mashable*. Available at: https://mashable.com/2012/04/13/elon-musk-secrets-of-effectiveness/#DDVq740.3aqt.

Ve (2017). *Liverpool FC* [online]. Ve. Available at: www.ve.com/resources/case-studies/liverpool-fc.

Chapter 7

The role of CRM and data in sponsorship

I started selling sponsorships in sport 30 years ago. From shirt, match and ball packages for Notts County FC, the oldest Football League club in the world (remember that – it's now a *Trivial Pursuit* question), through to European Championships and World Cups on behalf of UEFA and FIFA. Two of my last major deals in this area were the 2003 signing of Thomas Cook as the shirt sponsorship for Manchester City, the catalyst for the launch of their sports travel business, and the 2008 naming rights to Sophia Gardens, home of Glamorgan Cricket Club, to the utility brand SWALEC. But these were many years ago and a lot has changed in the sponsorship industry since then. One of them is the role of data.

Looking back to the negotiations between City and Thomas Cook, the Blues' fan base played a vital role. The driver of Thomas Cook's sponsorship wasn't the ad boards, match tickets or meet-the-players opportunities, it was the ability to sell holidays to City fans. And boy did it work. When Thomas Cook went on to renew the deal two seasons later, they reported that 'the club's supporters are four times more likely to choose Thomas Cook over their rivals' (Gibson, 2005). But, while we talked about City's fan base, we didn't talk about their database. We referred to more traditional above-the-line advertising methods to engage en masse and, as we looked for one-to-one opportunities, it took the form of a leaflet in the club shop's carrier bags or placed on the seats in the stadium.

Skip forward five years, and Paul Russell, the former Chairman of Glamorgan, was going through his sponsorship wish-list. He wanted a Welsh company (he was, and probably still is, very patriotic), a brand that would work as a naming rights sponsor (short and not a word that could be considered 'descriptive') and, finally, a company that could help extend the reach of his favourite sport, which was overshadowed by Welsh Rugby. It couldn't have gone better. The company SWALEC, a regional brand of SSE (Scottish and Southern Energy), met all the criteria and, on the last point, had a customer base of 1 million residents in Wales. Most importantly, as part of the sponsorship deal, they agreed to help promote the Glamorgan Cricket brand to their customers via their monthly bills and statements.

Looking back, I didn't realise then that what I had successfully negotiated with Thomas Cook for Manchester City and for SWALEC on behalf of Glamorgan Cricket would resonate so closely with where I am now – knee deep in the use of customer data to support a rights owner's business objectives. In this chapter I'll be looking specifically at sponsorship, one of my favourite areas of the sports industry, and one to which every rights owner in sports will be able to relate.

To reiterate my words in Chapter 1, when I deliver client workshops I start the section on sponsorship by saying, with tongue-in-cheek, that had I known at the time the impact the use of data could have on sponsorship sales, I'd have made a lot more commission. I'd have sold sponsorship far quicker and a lot easier. In reality, 10 to 15 years ago, the industry didn't have quite as much access to data as we do now but I use the statement to make a point and to grab the attention of the salespeople in the room.

Here's when I usually have to revisit the meaning of CRM. If you recall from previous chapters, the term has evolved from the use of software to manage the sales funnel to the definition that we use at Winners: getting the right message to the right person at the right time and incorporating five key elements, of which software is just one. So, while the right software can ensure the process is more efficient (it helps you track your actions, highlights next step tasks, manages your inventory), the bit that makes the real difference is when you can match your fanbase to a prospective sponsor's target market, demonstrate how you can engage with them on a one-to-one basis, and show how your sponsorship proposal enables the direct delivery of their message to your fans, individually and with relevance.

Sports Outlook from PwC summarised this approach as the following:

> Data continues to reveal increasingly valuable consumer insights, dissected and used to expand and customize marketing strategies to deliver relevant customer interactions and enhance lifetime value.
>
> (PwC, 2016)

Let's take Heineken as an example. They have a target customer audience of males aged 18 to 24 (*InfoScout*, 2017) so imagine how much more powerful your sales pitch is when you can tell them how many of that audience you have in your database and that you can ensure they see your co-branded message. You are then able to give Heineken a reason to look closer at your proposal and, as many sponsorship salespeople know, sometimes just getting in the door is a challenge.

Let's look at some examples. The checkpoints in Figure 7.1 represent the location of Hertz Car Rental offices in Portugal. The heat map in Figure 7.2 shows the distribution of this rights owner's database, at a postcode level, relative to the Hertz offices. This rights owner can go to Hertz and show them the relationship between rental outlets and their fan database and, in this case, it shows that 70% live within 20 km. That's quite a powerful message to incorporate into a sales pitch. It shows that the rights holder understands the potential sponsor's

Figure 7.1 Hertz Car Rental offices in Portugal. (Source: Winners FDD Ltd using data from Hertz, with permission.)

Figure 7.2 Rights owner's geographic mapping of fans database. (Source: Winners FDD Ltd using data from Hertz and client, with permission.)

objective to get more consumers renting their vehicles. Later I'll look at the next stage; supporting the leverage of sponsorship through this type of fan data.

Let's look at a few more examples to further demonstrate the point. In 2012, just before they signed a £150 million extension to their sponsorship of Arsenal, Boutros Boutros, the divisional senior vice president for corporate communications at Emirates Airlines, made the following public declaration:

> Data on customers is important to us like it should be for any business. The price of media is increasing every year and having detailed data on customers allows us to work out where we spend our ad budgets and who we target as well as what markets we focus on through the club's channels.
> (Joseph, 2012)

It's probably an exaggeration to say that Emirates invested this amount just because Arsenal were starting to understand who their fans were, but it went a long way in helping secure the deal. Emirates is interested in people with a relatively high disposable income such as long-haul travellers who like business class, or business travellers whose employers are footing the bill. With their approach to CRM, Arsenal would be in a position to give Emirates what they wanted; sight of their target customers and the ability to communicate with them directly.

Manchester United, Arsenal's competitors on the field, but their peers off it when it comes to commercial prowess and aspirations, are just as gushing about the role of data when it comes to making decisions in their sponsorship strategy. As Tom Hill, former Head of Partnerships and Operations at Manchester United, advocated at the 2016 SportsPro The Brand Conference:

> When 20th Century Fox (a global partner since February 2016) wanted to create awareness for their films on a global scale we adopted a non-traditional route, working with them to create content that would appeal to our fans. With 10 seasons' worth of TV viewing data we had valuable insights into our global fan base of over 659 million followers.
>
> (Hill, 2016)

This informed the decision to create a video where United player Wayne Rooney met the superhero Deadpool. That video was viewed over 12 million times on social media. Showing it during a match resulted in a 39% increase on searches for the film compared with on non-match days, with a further 15% increase in the 60 seconds after the promotion of the film on Old Trafford's digital advertising boards. Hill went on to say:

> The key thing for Fox was the ability to analyse how good the relationship with Man United was film by film and how successful the promotional activity was compared to traditional advertising. This enabled them to convince their CEO in LA that this was a good use of money.
>
> (Hill, 2016)

Case study: the Warriors and NBA jersey sponsorship

The Golden State Warriors and Rakuten were able to use their data to secure a sponsorship deal worth $60 million. In 2017 the NBA (National Basketball Association) created a ruling that would allow the placement of a 2.5 square inch advertising logo on jerseys above the left breast (NBA, 2017). They started looking at the option back in 2012 because, while kit advertising may be commonplace in other parts of the world (most notably in European Football), it was still rather unprecedented in major American sports with just teams in MLS presenting a full complement of shirt sponsors.

The WNBA (Women's National Basketball Association) adopted jersey ads back in 2011 and these did generate an increase in revenue, but the NBA still hesitated to give the advertising proposition a green light. The WNBA has less than half the fans of the men's game so, for the NBA, it was much harder to anticipate how fans would react, with the key consideration being their backlash to this commercial move. With the NBA already making significant use of branding opportunities for sponsors, from stadium names and mid-game entertainment to arena panelling and branding in special seating sections, there was concern that jerseys were the last bastion of non-commercialisation.

At the time of writing, the Warriors are just one of 16 out of the 30 NBA teams to have already brokered a deal for their jersey patch. They've reached an agreement with Japanese ISP and e-commerce giant Rakuten; a deal projected at being worth $20 million annually over a period of three years. This deal is the highest patch agreement to date, doubling that of the Cleveland Cavaliers and Goodyear, the next placed deal in terms of value.

The players

So, who are the players in one of the NBA's most lucrative new sponsorship deals?

The Golden State Warriors, founded in 1946, are currently in their 72nd season and are a charter member of the NBA. They moved to their current base in Oakland, California, in 1971, and have a history that includes five NBA Championships, an NBA record 73 wins during the 2015–2016 season, the greatest post-season run in NBA history (16–1 in 2017), six of the NBA's 50 greatest players and 27 members of Naismith Memorial Basketball Hall of Fame.

Founded in 1997, Rakuten is the biggest e-commerce site in Japan with 90% of Japan's Internet users registered as customers. That's more than 100 million users. It currently hosts 40,000 different businesses and services, all of which know they need to be on Rakuten to reach Japanese residents. In addition to its globally renowned Viber messaging app, Rakuten acquired leading Canadian e-reader Kobo and, despite the fact that they established their American headquarters in the Bay Area in 2015, Rakuten remain a largely unknown quantity to many American sports fans. They recently became the shirt sponsor of Barcelona FC, as well as a broadcast partner of the NBA providing live coverage of the sport in Japan, so these deals will help increase their European and American brand awareness.

But the Warriors deal will provide further exposure for Rakuten, and not just through the placement of their logo on the NBA team's jerseys. The Warriors' practice facility will be renamed the Rakuten Performance Center and they will be the Warriors' official e-commerce, video-on-demand and affiliate marketing partner.

Chip Bowers, the Warriors' chief marketing officer, revealed that Rakuten's offer was not the most lucrative that the team received, but in order to grow their global vision they had to align themselves with a global brand.

How data helped broker a deal

Despite their successes and star power, the Warriors had to make sure that they had real data to support key elements of their sales pitches to any potential sponsors. While their celebrated players are one element of their value, according to Bowers they also had to ensure the right processes were in place to show the added value of both their team and their fans.

> The Warriors organization wanted to look at this through a very responsible lens. This is not a typical sponsorship asset. You're placing a brand on the chest of your players – the most valuable asset of your organization.

To support their approach, the Warriors teamed up with the Wasserman Media group and, by using their proprietary Scorecard Analysis and Regression Analysis metrics, built an estimation of the team's value to potential sponsors. They looked at market dynamics, fan purchase behaviour, team performance, franchise reach as well as visibility to their fans and within the sport. They compared the values of other sports properties both in the US and worldwide in order to compare trends of similar deals and make comparisons based on these markets and similar brands within the NBA. The jersey patch itself was analysed for exposure. The brands would be most prominent during televised games and via digital streaming channels and most notably when a player is at the foul line.

> It was really important to understand the Warriors brand both nationally and globally. We could see the return we and our partners were getting through our own channels and our own media, but the jersey sponsorship deal was all new. We kind of expected the league would want us to be one of the first to reach our deal, but we took a cautious approach to it [calculating the financial return].

Using Wasserman's analysis the Warriors were able to refine their sponsorship proposals to suit the needs of their potential partners. With a more in-depth knowledge of where their appeal was centred, it made them realise that what they were looking for was a global partnership, furthering this by performing international fan insights research to gauge their appeal to international brands.

> For Rakuten, it was about people alignment and philosophical alignment as much as brand alignment. They are very focused on the future, innovation and positivity. And when you look at our team, our players, our brand, they felt there was some natural alignments between their company and the Warriors.

Conversely, Rakuten's CEO Hiroshi Mikitani understood that his company lacked brand awareness in the US, despite their North American headquarters being based in San Francisco. A partnership between the two would provide good exposure for the sponsor. With the Warriors location near Silicon Valley and their use of analytics demonstrating a like-minded approach to understanding their customers, it was clear to Bowers that the partnership had potential.

> When you think about it, one of the biggest reasons for brands to wish to align with someone like the Warriors is the power of sports. We represent a region, and in many ways California. We need to make sure that our fans are going to be fine with a brand we align ourselves with, and Rakuten meet that criteria.

Over the course of their partnership the Warriors' deal will help Rakuten increase their brand awareness through television, digital and social media channels. With the Warriors' expansion of e-commerce platforms for ticketing, merchandise and digital content delivery, Rakuten deliver benefits back to the team and, more importantly, their fans. In addition to this, as the sports industry is pursuing more and more technological innovations, not only to improve the experience of their fans but also to collect valuable fan data through digital channels, the Warriors can expect to benefit from Rakuten's extensive knowledge, experience and technical infrastructure.

The future of NBA jersey sponsorships

The Warriors–Rakuten $60 million partnership is set to provide the blueprint for all future NBA deals of this type, with data informing the approach while also enhancing the rights owner's ability to generate and use data as an output of the relationship. But, rather than commit to jersey sponsorship in perpetuity, the NBA has instead decided to run the patch partnerships on a three-year trial basis. If fan backlash is detected they can change their minds with very little damage to their reputation. So, with the possibility of an extension after the trial period, it will be interesting to see how this data-driven partnership can help two global brands achieve their respective business goals.

With huge potential revenue and lucrative sponsorships on the horizon, it not only seems that patches will be here to stay, but that the NBA's decision may open the doors for other American major sports leagues, perhaps even the NFL, to take the plunge.

(Source: Brown, 2017a.)

Using data to capitalise on sponsorship

Moving on from data to *inform* sponsorship decision-making to data to *leverage* sponsorships, let's look to ESP's 32nd annual year-end industry review to understand which direction this is heading:

> As a growing number of properties pursue data-driven audience engagement plans – and the potential they bring for personalised marketing – sponsors rated access to audience data as one of the most important benefits their rights owner partners can bring . . . about one-third of sponsors rated the benefit a 9 or 10 on a 10-point scale of value, ranking it the seventh most valuable benefit.
>
> (ESP Properties, 2017)

So, how do you ensure you provide your sponsors with the opportunities they want, without compromising the rights owner's relationship with the fan? The industry of brokering data has been around for a very long time, whether it be collecting and selling information about your newspaper subscriptions, the type of car you drive, your choice of pet, holiday or breakfast cereal, whether you use credit cards and have a mortgage, even your contact details, but that's not where the value of data as part of a sponsorship programme lies.

Referring back to the ESP report, the right to use property marks and logos is identified as the third most valuable opportunity, confirming that building brand positioning through associative imagery continues to be a major driver (ibid.). With this in mind, we know that selling a fan database to our sponsors and partners won't achieve this drive. The message to the fan has to be carried by the rights owner, incorporating the sponsor's content for that association to remain intact.

Let's return to my Hertz Car Rental example seen in Figures 7.1 and 7.2. This particular rights owner has the contact details of fans, in this case an email address with an opt-in to receive direct communication. They can provide highly targeted messages on behalf of this brand, incorporating content that matters to the fan with a call-to-action that increases the chances of a sale. For example, consider the power of the fan receiving an email that tells him where his closest Hertz branch is, particularly if it's with a message that fans get a discount.

But, there are other forms of targeted marketing a rights owner can provide to a sponsor. In April 2017 it was announced that Coca-Cola had replaced

Pepsi as the sponsor of MLB, a move that, while not sending shockwaves through the industry, certainly did raise a few eyebrows. It wasn't just that two leading brands in their categories swapped position; it was the change in emphasis for Coca-Cola from their traditional '3 Ss' (seats, suites and signage) approach to sponsorship. Instead, they chose to enter into a deal based almost entirely on digital and empowered by data.

Bob Bowman, MLB President, Business and Media, had the following to say about it:

> This partnership is focused on . . . connecting Coca-Cola with our fans through digital, mobile and social.
>
> (Brown, 2017b)

Coca-Cola activating their sponsorships through digital channels is nothing new. London 2012 saw the emergence of this trend, where online and offline combined to provide the ultimate leverage programme. Indeed, Coca-Cola 'outdid themselves' according to *Forbes* (Peterson, 2012). The 2017 contract will still enable creative offline executions however, such as the Houston Astros 2017 World Series win commemorative edition can (Coca-Cola, 2017). But the focus of this deal will be the activation of tie-ins through MLB Advanced Media and their owned and operated digital platforms: mlb.com, their 30 club websites, their At Bat and Ballpark mobile apps, MLB's multiple social accounts and MLB.tv.

Similarly, in 2016 when Telefonica UK Ltd renewed their longstanding partnership with England's RFU (Rugby Football Union) for a further five years under their O2 brand, it was emphasised that the deal was a departure from the more traditional sponsorship objective of increased brand awareness, to the opportunity to engage more closely with rugby fans. According to Nina Bibby, the Chief Marketing Officer at O2:

> When we first partnered up years ago it was about raising awareness of the brand but we've moved beyond that so we're now looking to shape new experiences for our customers and engage with them through those experiences.
>
> (Connelly, 2016)

The telecommunications industry places a lot of focus on reducing churn, that is, minimising the number of service subscribers who discontinue their subscription within a given time period. Bibby credits O2's Priority programme as a driver of the reason their contract churn has halved from 1.8% to 0.9% over the last ten years. Not surprisingly, their Priority offering will play a key role in O2's partnership with the RFU moving forward, with a focus on creating integrated, connected and personalised experiences across mobile devices along with special offers such as tickets to England matches (ibid.).

The RFU's approach to CRM

To enable O2 to achieve the above, they needed the RFU to have a handle on their own fan data and, as described by Mark Killingley, formerly their Head of Digital and CRM at 2015's Festival of Marketing, this is an area they have been working on for some time (Davis, 2015).

The RFU's CRM technology stack includes an SCV from data integrations with their player registration platform, marketing data from their social channels and the RFU website and commercial data from England team matches and other related activity. With this in place, the RFU is able to know nearly all their stakeholders across multiple digital and non-digital touch points, identifying which customer falls into which profile, for example a coach, a fan, a pitch-side father, a club player, etc.

This optimised approach to customer data enables the RFU to send the right message to the right person at the right time, and it's this foundation and approach to engagement that will power their partnership with O2, providing them with the information they need to ensure their Priority offering for rugby fans is in line with their expectations; that it's what the fans want and what they need. Personalised opportunities will include pre-match content that's available 48-hours before anywhere else, behind-the-scenes and match-day digital content along with access to priority tickets for all England matches at Twickenham.

In addition to engaging with the RFU's fans, Bibby says that O2 witnessed an increase in interest in rugby among their customers, particularly after the 2015 Rugby World Cup that was hosted in England:

> We saw a big jump after the World Cup last year which tells us more of our customer base are becoming active fans. We know customers love live experiences we offer them with rugby and concerts so now we're focusing on how digital can enhance those experiences before, during and after [events]. That's really what we want to try and do more of, that whole end-to-end experience from live to digital and back.
>
> (Connelly, 2016)

For O2 this also means pushing their use of technology even further and exploring live streaming and VR (Virtual Reality) and it's in the implementation of the latter that the RFU's extensive archive of performance data will demonstrate its commercial potential.

Performance data for commercial use

I mentioned in my introduction to this book that, while data is an area I'll be looking at, it's not performance data that I work with. It's the statistics that enable a rights owner to make business decisions and send targeted communications. My caveat to this has always been that when the natural silos between sports performance teams and their marketing teams are broken, when we can use that rich player data to entertain and engage our fans, then we at Winners may start to enter that market.

A great example of this is in O2's VR offering, made possible by the RFU's Try Tracker, a web-based predictive analytics platform for rugby fans produced in collaboration with IBM through a partnership that started in 2013 (IBM, 2013). During live matches Try Tracker produces data to inform three dashboards that are displayed on the RFU's website; momentum, keys to the game and player influence. Each dashboard presents different datasets that provide real-time insight to fans. In describing their approach, Nick Shaw, Head of Digital at the RFU, says:

> We saw a major opportunity to bring the rich data we had on past rugby matches to life on RFU.com, and tell the story of a match in real time. By creating a platform for insight using the latest business analytics technologies, we realised that we could transform RFU.com into the destination site for anyone interested in rugby, and reach new fans around the world. The 'keys to the game' dashboard highlights specific areas where teams are over- and under-performing, and identifies three targets that a certain team needs to achieve to increase their probability of winning a match. On a match day, these three keys to the game are surfaced on the TryTracker hub page; if a team hits all three, then their probability of winning increases dramatically. This feature of TryTracker shows new fans exactly what to look out for as a match progresses – helping them to get more from the experience of watching live rugby.
>
> (Ibid.)

The 'momentum' dashboard provides a live interactive timeline of a match and shows statistics such as possession to show a fan which team is most likely to score next, with 'player influence' demonstrating the impact a player entering or leaving a match has on a team's chance of winning using historical data and the status of the current match.

So, having built this application over the last four or five years, the RFU is now able to enhance their partnership with O2 even further to power their VR offering with a deep archive of player and match performance data. Unveiled in March 2017, O2's VR rugby experience provides gamers with the opportunity to compete against England's best rugby talent in the form of interactive CGI characters, created using accurate player movement along with England players' weight, mass and average speeds (Ellison, 2017). Describing the initiative in marketing and advertising title *Campaign*, Gareth Griffiths, head of sponsorship at O2, said:

We believe in live, and using the latest VR technology we can showcase our live experiences to O2 customers in our stores across the country. Through a combination of world first CGI characters and unique interactive gameplay, each experience has been designed to give the user unprecedented access to our relationship with the England Rugby team. We're excited to roll our new virtual reality into O2 stores nationwide and at Twickenham Stadium on match days.

(Ibid.)

What can your sponsors do for you?

Securing the right value for your sponsorship has always been a priority and most of the time we want to steer away from VIK (Value-In-Kind) deals and instead focus on those deals that provide us with cash. But, as highlighted in the Warriors–Rakuten example, sometimes the right partner can support you in your own CRM and data-driven quests.

Sponsors who operate in the financial services, telecommunications, ISPs, travel and indeed any other B2C category where they focus on personalised offers and messaging, could provide you with different areas of support (of course always operating in compliance with the GDPR or any other relevant regulatory authority).

- **Data acquisition**: why not consider asking them to use a 'third party opt-in' when implementing co-branded promotions using your logos or trademarks through their channel? Or perhaps you can be a common data controller, giving you both the right to use the data they collect.
- **Data enhancements**: there's a very good chance your sponsor's technology stack will be more advanced than yours and the insight they carry on each of their customers will probably be deeper. In the same way you might use a third party such as Experian or Acxiom, perhaps your sponsors could help you in this area, enriching the customer profiles you have in common with the information they have in their database.
- **Knowledge sharing and training**: from assistance with ad-hoc data-related tactics to sessions on advanced use of digital retargeting, supporting with technology consulting to advising on an IT procurement process, your sponsors could provide a stop-gap of resource until you've managed to increase your own headcount.

Case study: UEFA sponsorship

The following case study demonstrates how all the considerations discussed in this chapter combined to help UEFA secure a major sponsorship deal with global pure-play Booking.com, and how the tactics discussed can be used by a sponsor to target the fans of the property with whom they associated.

In October 2017 UEFA and Booking.com announced a four-year global partnership to become the Official Accommodation and Attractions Booking Partner for all UEFA national team football competitions from 2018 to 2022 (UEFA, 2017).

Booking.com is one of the largest travel e-commerce companies in the world, with over 15,000 employees in 198 offices in 70 countries worldwide. A pure-play online retailer, their mission is to:

> Connect travellers with the world's largest selection of incredible places to stay, including everything from apartments, vacation homes, and family-run B&Bs to 5-star luxury resorts, tree houses and even igloos.
>
> (Booking.com, n.d.)

Their websites and mobile apps are available in over 43 languages, offer 1.4 million properties and cover 120,000 destinations in 228 countries.

One of the aims of the sponsorship for both parties is to help UEFA improve their fan experiences with tailored travel deals and recommendations. With ten competitions and more than 500 matches over the next four years, there are plenty of opportunities for advertising, promotion and digital engagement, but the focus will be on using data to ensure the experience is relevant for each football fan. Both parties will also collaborate to organise various campaigns and events to make the most out of their partnership over the next four years, with UEFA's database playing a central role in the planning.

In an interview that I conducted on 5 December 2017 with Peter Willems, the Head of Marketing Activities and Sponsorship at UEFA, at their headquarters in Nyon, he shared some interesting insights into the way that the discussion over this sponsorship differed to others. 'It was the first negotiation we've had where there was more talk about data and digital than anything else', he said.

Traditionally, negotiations for sponsorships have evolved around the more common rights that UEFA could provide, such as advertising, tickets, corporate hospitality packages and exclusive access. When partnering with Booking. com, it was the way that fans were digitally engaging with UEFA that played a significant role in brokering the deal.

We're in a very fortunate position. We could see the direction the sports industry was heading in the way it dealt with sponsorships, so three years ago we started to build our own data capabilities. As we progress through the group stages of our club competitions, as European Qualifying matches take place for our national teams, we continue to generate more traffic to our various platforms, adding more fans to our database in the process. And it's not just about the number of fans, but also the quantity and quality of information we have that allows us to improve their experience with us.

The collection of fan data is an on-going job, but UEFA can now pinpoint the gender of 70% of their fanbase, the age of 73%, the country of residence of 82% and the preferred language of 50%. Willems says that with such a strong foundation they are now able to focus their work in other areas, such as pin-pointing favourite clubs, national teams and the nationalities of their fans. Of course there are hurdles to overcome in any task of this scope, but he plans to use these to his advantage.

> It's quite possible that a person of a particular nationality could support a dif-
> ferent country while living in still another country. This provides us with three
> different references that can all be used to ensure we provide them with the
> content they want when they are most likely to want it.

Almost certainly UEFA has the most extensive database of known fans out of any sport that has provided direct contact details. Consequently, they truly do know who their fans are and can pinpoint their interests at a 'per record' level. This is invaluable information for a sponsorship deal and will be fully utilised by Booking.com as they seek to provide an individually tailored experience to UEFA's fans.

Two-way collaboration with sponsors

UEFA has a global fan network and tailoring their service to make sure that all fans feel involved and engaged is no easy task. As an example, stadiums can only accommodate a small percentage of the overall fan base, so UEFA has to tactically use their digital channels to ensure that, even if a fan can't be present, they still feel like they're part of the events that interest them. However, this service spans so much more than just match days and specific events. Whenever and wherever there are fans, all day, every day, the team at UEFA has to ensure that they can get their football fix and actively engage in their favourite sport.

To support this approach, UEFA has been exploring ways in which col-laborating with sponsors and partners can help them in their data acquisition and enhancement strategy. An early example of this came in June 2016, when Coca-Cola ran a co-branded promotion of their EURO 2016 Panini sticker collection. Using their own digital and offline channels, Coca-Cola and Panini targeted fans of the European Championship and, in doing so, were able to secure a significant number of opt-ins from football fans for UEFA's database.

Conversely, Booking.com have a very deep, very rich database, but a lot of their customers simply don't have the same relevance to UEFA as the fans collecting Panini stickers or that they organically acquire through their own channels. While there will be a crossover between the two companies, not every traveller is a football fan and not every football fan is a traveller. However, when a customer goes through a transaction on Booking.com, the action of the purchase will produce rich, up-to-date and relevant data that would be of use to UEFA, particularly when matched to their own database. Consequently, over the term of the sponsorship, both parties will benefit.

The more information that UEFA has on their followers, the better service and fan experience they can offer, tailoring news the fans want about the teams they support, their favourite players and their history in UEFA tournaments. And, when it comes to the fans that have bought tickets to attend UEFA matches, this collaboration with Booking.com will provide relevant travel information, further supporting the personalised approach.

Steps taken by UEFA

In the lead up to the Booking.com discussions, UEFA focused on learning more about their fans and implementing a centralised database, ensuring the on-going health and consistency of their data. Having started the build of an SCV, where each fan and their interests exists as an individual, to provide a 360-degree view they layered this with an interactive dashboard to present the data in a way that enabled immediate access to information. Most importantly, the data visualisation is presented in a way that's relevant for UEFA's team of marketers, providing the key insights that answer both their internal questions and the information relevant to their sponsors, as demonstrated during the Booking.com negotiations.

> We could tell you how many viewers in Brazil watched the EURO 2016 Final on their televisions, how many social followers we have in Indonesia, the age groups of our website visitors. But for Booking.com, and all our negotiations moving forward, we need to know more than that. We need to know our fans by their names, where each and every one of them lives, we have to understand their interests at an individual level, and we have to know how they like to engage with us. We're in an environment now where we're marketing to a segment of one. It's how Booking.com run their business, so to be a valuable partner to them, we had to do the same.

The partnership in action

Booking.com's ad management platform and algorithms ensure accuracy in their approach to remarketing and retargeting that, when combined with UEFA's active database, will be a powerful partnership. One of the challenges of being a great digital marketer is ensuring that the parameters or conditions that you set on your ad delivery platform work hard for you. When brands don't use experienced marketers, the results are often the opposite of those desired. Instead of effective targeted advertising, it's easy to fall into the trap of irrelevant messages or spamming the user with too many ads. This is a problem of which Willems is well aware.

> As any good digital marketer knows, we have to ensure a balance of providing the adverts that will genuinely benefit the fans and won't become intrusive or annoying. That's one of the many benefits of our digital world; we can track the number of times our fans see these adverts to ensure they're kept to a minimum, we can ensure they only see the ones that are relevant to them, and once they're no longer relevant we can turn them off.

By partnering with Booking.com, UEFA can use their vast experience to ensure their fans see only relevant messages.

> For the first time in history, the 2020 UEFA European Championships will be played across 13 different countries. Let's assume that Romania qualify. What if one of their games is played at the Millennium Stadium in Cardiff? There will no doubt be thousands of Romania fans, including their diaspora, needing accommodation in Wales. We will ensure Booking.com's information about their accommodation deals in Cardiff at the time of the Romania match gets to those fans seamlessly – making it easy for them to complete their travel plans.

Booking.com's message will be shared by UEFA in a way that's the most relevant to their fans through their chosen digital channels. For example, when fans have applied for tickets through UEFA.com, their email notifications to confirm success could include Booking.com's recommendations for accommodation. These messages can be tailored right down to the distance from the stadium that is hosting the match they're attending. This same approach can be taken through social channels, UEFA's website and even their web remarketing programme. They will be able to identify the customer segments that suit the message that Booking.com wants to share, and use their personal information on their fans such as location, supporting team and match preferences to make sure their fans get the right messages.

Fans first

But what is the cost of this tailored experience to the fan? With the growth of targeted digital marketing, consumers are now savvier about the security of their data and the way in which it's used. This negativity has the potential to cancel out any gains from a sponsorship deal like this.

To ensure the integrity of the relationship UEFA has with their fans, Willems states categorically that Booking.com will not have direct access to UEFA's database or their fans' information.

Our fans trust us with their data, and we're not going to do anything with it that could compromise our relationship with them. We won't sell their data, and we won't give their personal information to our sponsors. Everything we do is with our fans' express permission – not only do we comply with all the relevant regulations on the way we collect, store and use our fans' data, we use it to ensure the best possible experience for our fans. We put our fans first.

Instead, UEFA will maintain full control of their data, Booking.com will provide the message, and UEFA will ensure it gets to the right people at the right time.

So, what does Booking.com gain from this? The answer is simple: UEFA will provide the message, but Booking.com will provide a point of sale. Once a fan moves from UEFA's digital channels, they will become a Booking.com customer. This allows them to manage all transactions as they would with any other customer. They have, however, committed to ensuring UEFA's fans get the best service possible. Clearly defined terms in their sponsorship agreement outline the way they will engage with, and manage, their relationship with any customers brought to them via any of UEFA's digital channels such as website, email, mobile app and social accounts. UEFA don't just want to sell products and services to their fans; they want their fans to be provided with a valuable service. That makes these contractual terms a crucial part of the Booking.com agreement, and any other sponsorship deals they may secure in future.

Looking forward

Data-driven sponsorship for sole customer targeting is a long-term goal. Pure-play online retailers like Booking.com have a long history of collecting customer data and basing their business structure on these principles, but, in contrast, this is an area that's still quite new to the sports industry. Through this partnership, UEFA can expect to learn quite a bit about Booking.com's approach and methods, but, conversely, sponsorship is a very new area for Booking.com who can also expect to learn from the experience.

> We'll be looking to replicate the same type of opportunities for all our sponsors, based on their particular needs and, more importantly, what they can do for our fans. We'll be able to target their messages so they're relevant to the receiver and, in turn, provide greater return for the sponsorship dollars, ensuring their continued investment in football. However, we believe our approach to data is a two-way street. The more we have, the greater value our sponsors receive so a logical next step will be to work together to ensure we're getting more data, more insight and more knowledge with all our partners.

(Source: Willems, 2017, 5 December.)

Key chapter ideas

1   Using data in your sponsorship strategy can help you cut through the clutter of the many proposals your prospects receive by demonstrating you can deliver their target audience.
2   Once engaged, you can use your approach to targeted communications to increase your sponsor's ROI.
3   Sponsors can support your data and CRM strategy. Be sure to include some data-related obligations in your contract negotiations.
4   Performance data is valuable content for your fans and can be commercialised with your sponsors through innovative applications.

References

Booking.com (n.d.). *Booking.com: The Largest Selection of Hotels, Homes, and Holiday Rentals* [online]. Booking.com. Available at: www.booking.com/content/about.en-gb.html [accessed 27 November 2017].

Brown, M. (2017a). Inside the Golden State Warriors' $60 million jersey patch deal with Rakuten [online]. *Forbes*. Available at: www.forbes.com/sites/maurybrown/2017/11/27/inside-the-golden-state-warriors-record-60-million-jersey-patch-deal-with-rakuten/#72a34d307b59.

Brown, M. (2017b). Multi-year deal reached with Coca-Cola to be 'official soft drink of MLB' [online]. *Forbes*. Available at: www.forbes.com/sites/maurybrown/2017/04/03/multi-year-deal-reached-with-coca-cola-to-be-official-soft-drink-of-mlb/#4017fa075ae2.

Coca Cola (2017). Coca-Cola® releases commemorative championship can to celebrate the Houston Astros World Series victory [online]. *Style Magazine*. Available at: http://stylemagazine.com/news/2017/nov/03/coca-cola-releases-commemorative-championship-can-.

Connelly, T. (2016). O2's chief marketing officer on its digital plans for English Rugby sponsorship extension [online]. *The Drum*. Available at: www.thedrum. com/news/2016/10/29/o2s-chief-marketing-officer-its-digital-plans-english-rugby-sponsorship-extension.

Davis, B. (2015). How the RFU manages CRM & personalised messaging [online]. *Econsultancy*. Available at: www.econsultancy.com/blog/67180-how-the-rfu-manages-crm-personalised-messaging.

Ellison, H. (2017). O2 unveils new virtual reality experiences [online]. *Campaignlive.co.uk*. Available at: www.campaignlive.co.uk/o2-unveils-new-virtual-reality-experiences/ %7Bsubjects%7D/article/1427514.

ESP Properties (2017). *What Sponsors Want and Where Dollars Will Go in 2017* [ebook]. ESP Properties. Available at: www.sponsorship.com/IEG/files/7f/7fd3bb31-2c81-4fe9-8f5d-1c9d7cab1232.pdf.

Gibson, O. (2005). How the Thomas Cook/Manchester City shirt deal came about [online]. *The Guardian*. Available at: www.theguardian.com/football/2005/sep/22/ newsstory.sport.

Hill, T. (2016). *The Futures of Manchester United*. SportsPro the Brand Conference, Lord's Cricket Ground, London, 15 September.

IBM (2013). *Rugby Football Union Uses Predictive Analytics to Drive Fan Engagement* [ebook]. Portsmouth: IBM. Available at: www-935.ibm.com/services/uk/bcs/pdf/ RFU_YTC03611GBEN.PDF.

InfoScout (2017). Heineken consumer insights and demographics [online]. *InfoScout*. Available at: https://infoscout.co/brand/heineken.

Joseph, S. (2012). Emirates: 'CRM data key to £150m Arsenal deal' [online]. *Marketing Week*. Available at: www.marketingweek.com/2012/11/23/emirates-crm-data-key-to-150m-arsenal-deal.

NBA (2017). *Warriors and Rakuten Form Jersey Partnership* [online]. NBA. Available at: www.nba.com/warriors/news/rakuten-partnership-announcement-20170912.

Peterson, B. (2012). Beyond the logo: how to win at Olympic sponsorship [online]. *Forbes*. Available at: www.forbes.com/sites/onmarketing/2012/08/21/beyond-the-logo-how-to-win-.

PwC (2016). *PwC Sports Outlook: At the Gate and Beyond Outlook for the Sports Market in North America Through 2019* [ebook]. PwC. Available at: www.pwc.com/us/en/ industry/entertainment-media/publications/assets/pwc-sports-outlook-2016.pdf.

UEFA (2017). *UEFA Announces Global Deal with Booking.com* [online]. Available at: www.uefa.com/uefaeuro-2020/news/newsid=2511295.html.

Willems, P. (2017, 5 December). Personal interview.

Chapter 8

Culture and business change

At Winners we have a basket of fruit delivered every week from which the team can help themselves. One of my longest-standing colleagues, Callum MacGregor, recently bemoaned the absence of bananas. When the work day began there had been plenty, but, by the time he got to the basket, they'd all gone. I remember the resulting exchange his comments generated between the team members, so I made a mental note that Callum didn't like the other fruit. He only liked bananas. My intention was to ask HR to change the fruit choices to make sure everyone was catered for.

So why am I starting a chapter on Business Change with this seemingly unrelated incident? Because, in an article in the *Harvard Business Review* (*HBR*) titled 'To get people to change, make change easy', the authors start with a story about fruit choices. And guess what? Everyone wants the bananas! According to *HBR*, they're easy to peel and therefore easier to choose (Luna and Cohen, 2017).

This mirrors a research article published on *eLife* in February 2017 that suggests, in essence, that we're lazy, or at least that the path of least resistance really is the one most trodden. More accurately, it says, 'the effort required to act on a decision can influence the decision itself' (Hagura, Haggard and Diedrichsen, 2017).

In the second chapter of this book I highlighted process and culture as two key elements to implementing CRM as a business approach, and this is where Business Change and Change Management come in. Business Change is the process by which our employees (and other relevant stakeholders) adopt new ways of doing things, perhaps also adjusting their attitudes and behaviours and developing new skills as the business changes.

Change Management is about the way we support individuals affected by Business Change. The reason it's such an important part of implementing a CRM framework is because moving from an experience-driven business to one that is data-driven – one that uses evidence-based decision-making – involves a significant shift; a shift of attitudes, behaviour and skills. In line with the *HBR* article and as many change practitioners will attest, we have to make it easy for our stakeholders to change with our businesses.

The importance of change

I remember working with a client in early 2016 who said something that resonates with me to this day. My role was to assist with the production of a Request for Information (RFI) for a rights owner looking to develop its digital real estate in order to support a drive to become a more data-driven organisation. The new environment would be powered by a centralised database, enabling the creation and delivery of personalised experiences across multiple channels, from websites and social channels to mobile apps, SMS and email campaigns. The client was starting on a journey on which many of you have already commenced, and many more are yet to embark.

A few weeks into the project, a senior member of the client's team sat back and said, 'What if we don't actually have to do all this – what if all this talk about the need to provide a personalised experience and working with data is made up?' At first we laughed at that, but we also acknowledged that there could be something to it. In reality, we don't know what would happen to our individual businesses if we didn't 'get the right message to the right person at the right time'. We can all see the downward trajectories of our attendance figures and participation rates, but would the trend line really hit the x-axis if nothing changed?

That's the challenge that your senior management have when you go to them asking for investment in CRM. Whether you're asking for budget, people or time, ultimately it adds up to an expense that has to be accounted for, and an investment that has to generate a return. But as I've already discussed in Chapter 2, CRM is a journey not a destination. When it comes to Business Change, you're in it for the long term. It's a marathon, not a sprint. So, if you can't show your management an immediate return, it's reasonable to expect a tougher sell-in than if you're justifying the purchase of a new format ad display, more replica kit for your online store or the addition of a friendly event to your fixture schedule.

So how do you know that it is necessary? How do you convince your management of a need for change? I guess the answer to that is that if we didn't have to change, we probably wouldn't. But our fans and stakeholders are changing, and they're demanding that we change with them. Their expectations are being shaped by the digital leaders in other industries such as Amazon, Netflix and Spotify. These are the brands we aspire to emulate (but within our own frame of reference); the ones that are repeatedly held up as champions of the understanding of customer journeys in this omni-channel/cross-channel/channel-neutral environment. Users of these brands are used to the immediacy, entertainment and engagement that Facebook, Twitter and Instagram provide. They like being in control of what they watch, listen to and read. They also like being in control of when they do it and, when it comes to spending their time, their attention or their money, they have an abundance of choice.

In order to address this, to give your fans what they want when they want it, not what you want them to have in your timeframe, you have to change the way you work. You have to be agile. Being agile means being flexible and having the ability to rapidly adapt and respond. And this needs to be organisation-wide.

How many rights owners do you know that sound just like that? I'd guess not many. The transformation from a traditional hierarchy, formal meetings and committees along with the politics of voting in and voting out, the pressure of needing to win each match, each week or each season are just a few reasons why change in the sports industry can be so challenging.

Change in the sports industry

In the same way the use of data has been prevalent in sports performance for some time (see my reference to *Moneyball* in Chapter 3) so too has the consideration of Business Change and Change Management. In 2012, The University of Central Lancashire published 'Change management: the case of the elite sports performance team', which concluded that, with the intense pressure faced by incoming managers and coaches to create a high-performing culture at lightning speed, the role of Change Management is 'both an applicable and highly pertinent construct for the optimisation of elite sport team performance' (Cruickshank and Collins, 2012).

Earlier still, in 2005, authors at Nova Southeastern University published 'The examination of change management using qualitative methods: a case industry approach' where 29 sports managers from Australian national and state sporting organisations and clubs were interviewed to provide the industry case. The key findings in this paper suggested the following:

> Subject to the strategic whims of their leaders as well as the pressures forced upon them by their institutional environment . . . Australian sport managers were inclined to be flexible in both their view of the origins of change, and its effective management.
>
> (Evans, Smith and Westerbeek, 2005)

The paper went on to further define the different types of change prevalent within Australian sports organisations. Do you recognise any of them in your own environment?

1   **Fast change** – the paper cited that this typically occurs when sports organisations are under-performing to a significant extent. The changes made are in direct response to the perceived crises. This sounds to me like the classic change of team management when you're six games and no points into the English football season. To demonstrate that point, from the start of the 2017/18 English football season in August to the end of December, 19 of the league's 92 club managers were sacked.

2 **Slow change** – the paper defined this as the type of change that continues indefinitely on an almost daily basis in the form of minor amendments to policies and practices. An example could be the process used to issue a public ticket sale after an exclusive sales window has closed, or the warm-up routine associated with a training session.

3 **Accidental change** – the paper classified this form of change as something that didn't fit into either the fast or slow category where the change occurred without design or strategic intent, without specific thought to the outcome of the improvement or any other implications. A specific example provided involved a change in the way club merchandise was distributed (ibid.). Although the policy was to sell club merchandise from the club only, as a result of an accidental change where a mail order was accepted and discharged promptly by an unknowing work placement student, sales of merchandise almost doubled as additional mail orders arrived.

In my years in sport I've been witness to some significant change when it comes to revenue generation and event formation. Let's look at some examples.

1992: formation of the English Premier League

When Sebastian Coe, gold Olympic medal winner and a newly elected Conservative MP, said, 'I think it is wrong that only two million [satellite] dish owners get access to such major sporting events' (Nicholson, 2015), he set the tone for concerns about the changes to the traditional TV rights deals. With subscription TV operator BskyB securing a five-year contract for the best live matches, BBC awarded highlights and ITV leaving the table empty-handed, there was genuine concern for the future of English football.

One of Britain's leading newspapers, *The Guardian*, carried a piece that suggested fans would be the biggest losers. 'A lot of people who want to watch matches regularly in future are going to have to buy a bond or a dish' (Lacey, 1992).

Alex Ferguson, then Manchester United manager, also made his feelings known:

> A deal was stampeded without consultation with the most important people in the game, the managers and the players whose livelihoods are at stake . . . It's the most ludicrous and backward decision football has taken. We managers must seriously question its wisdom.
>
> (Potter, 1992)

But now, the Premier League is the most-watched sports league in the world. The UK-only TV rights to cover three seasons from 2019 to 2022 were sold in February 2018 for £4.46 billion and, with two rights packages unsold at the time of writing, there has been speculation that Amazon, Facebook, Netflix or Twitter might bid for the first time (BBC, 2018).

2000: creation of Major League Baseball Advanced Media

It's impossible to write about changes in the sports industry, particularly when we focus on digital technology and data, without referring to the behemoth that is MLB Advanced Media, or BAM for short.

Back in 2000, Bud Selig, the commissioner of Major League Baseball (MLB) at the time, created BAM as a vehicle for building the MLB clubs' websites and managing their digital rights. The approach was intended to ensure parity among the teams, regardless of their size or status within the sport, and BAM was set up as a stand-alone company with an initial budget of $120 million: $1 million per year from each of the 30 clubs for the first four years of operation.

From humble beginnings that included the broadcast of a game to 30,000 fans, BAM led the way in over-the-top (OTT) broadcasting in sports (i.e., using the internet to bypass traditional broadcasters). The next big step came with the evolution of MLB.tv, which launched in 2003 with a digital viewing package for $79.95. Over 100,000 customers signed up in the first year and now BAM streams to over 25 million digital viewers.

In my opinion, the real shift came when BAM stopped being just about baseball and started servicing other organisations including the National Hockey League (NHL), Home Box Office (HBO), World Wrestling Entertainment (WWE) Network, the Professional Golfers Association (PGA) and the New York Yankees' YES Network. It's this combination of services to third parties coupled with BAM's development of digital products for baseball that led *Forbes* in July 2014 to name it 'The biggest media company you've never heard of' (Brown, 2014).

As a demonstration of how much MLB's business really did support change, 2015 saw BAM create a spin-off, BAMTech, which focuses on providing streaming video technology, particularly for OTT content services. Then, in September 2017, Disney topped up its original $1 billion investment with a further $1.58 billion to take its share from 33% to 75%.

With a focus now purely on baseball, BAM retained a 15% share of BAMTech, but, according to Commissioner Robert D. Manfred Jr:

> Major League Baseball will continue to work with Disney and ESPN to further grow BAMTech as it breaks new ground in technologies for con-sumers to access entertainment and sports programming.
>
> (*Business Wire*, 2017)

2003: launch of Twenty20 cricket

With the global success that is Twenty20 cricket, it's hard to believe that the launch of cricket's short form almost didn't go ahead. In a 2003 interview for cricket website *cricinfo*, the chairman of the England and Wales Cricket Board (ECB), Lord MacLaurin, recalled the following:

> From the feeling there, we weren't going to win the votes. I had a list of chairmen and called them the night before. I said, 'All I ask is that you give it a chance. After three years we'll have a review. If it's not successful we'll pull the plug'.
>
> (Williamson, 2012)

The vote eventually went in favour of this change by just 11 clubs to 7.

The *cricinfo* article also covered the views of other press members, most of whom echoed the sentiment of *The Times* journalist, Simon Barnes, who commented:

> It's the trappings I can't stand. The garnish. The gimmicks. The wrapping, the ribbons, the packaging. The noise. Music should be banned from all sporting occasions, live and televised. Never mind keeping politics out of sport; if we can keep music out, I'll be happy.
>
> (Williamson, 2012)

While some believe the divide between Twenty20 and Test cricket (the longest form of the sport) is getting too wide, there's no denying its success. In July 2017, *The Guardian* newspaper claimed, 'T20 is evolving so fast it is radically redefining cricket' (Wigmore, 2017).

2007: NFL games in the UK

Over ten years ago, the National Football League (NFL) played its first regular-season game in London. The city now hosts four games per year with attendances of over 80,000 and can boast a fan base of 40,000 individuals who regularly buy tickets. That's more than many EFL teams. But this level of success has not been a fast change. It's the result of a slow and steady presence of NFL teams, staff and management and a dedicated NFL UK office in London.

According to a 2014 article in *Sports Illustrated*, the NFL in London is already an unmitigated success:

> The NFL has jumped from the 16th to the 8th most watched sport during England's football season on Sky Sports, Britain's subscription sports channel. Last season 13.8 million UK viewers watched NFL programming, an increase of 60 percent over the previous year, and the NFL also says more than 12 million people in the UK identify themselves as NFL fans. Amateur football participation has grown an average of 15 percent each year since '07, and there are now 77 university teams playing American football.
>
> (Vrentas, 2014)

However, not everyone is singing the NFL's praises, with *The Guardian* proposing that the selection of teams sent to play represents the NFL 'dumping mediocrity on UK fans', citing that the thirst of their international fan base allows them to treat them in this manner (Caldwell, 2016).

Where you go from here: change literature

Whether there's another BAMTech equivalent out there, waiting to be hatched from another sports rights owner, or whether the rest of the industry just wants to go through its own data-driven and digital transformation, Business Change will be a factor. So, what are your next steps?

In the aforementioned NSU paper, the following statement was of particular interest to me:

> Respondents frequently lamented that while change had to be dealt with, they were uncertain about the best way of dealing with it. In the first instance, it was commonly admitted that a 'tried and tested' approach to change is noticeably absent from the operations manuals of most sporting organizations. This lack of information concerning the best methodology for initiating and sustaining long-term changes is indicative of a general confusion about the two fundamental elements in any change program: what to change and how to change. Thus, not only are sport managers unclear about where to direct their energies in order to initiate change, they are also hesitant when it comes to nominating their preferred tools and techniques for managing, directing, and controlling change.
>
> (Evans, Smith and Westerbeek, 2005)

The change industry has been around for many decades. The first documented reference to the study of change appears to be in Kurt Lewin's 1947 publication 'Frontiers in group dynamics – concept, method and reality in social science; social equilibria and social change', where he refers to the following three-step process:

> A successful change includes therefore three aspects: unfreezing (if necessary) the present level, moving to the new level, and freezing group life on the new level. The 'unfreezing' of the present level may involve quite different problems in different cases. The same holds for the problem of freezing the new level.
>
> (Lewin, 1947)

Fast forward 22 years and psychiatrist Elisabeth Kübler-Ross wrote the book *On Death and Dying*, which outlined the five stages that terminally ill patients experience: denial, anger, bargaining, depression and acceptance (Kübler-Ross, 2003).

This model, later named the Kübler-Ross Change Curve, became widely accepted as valid in many situations that relate to change, including those in a work environment.

When you think this one through, you can actually understand this relationship. Consider the thoughts a stadium gate steward might go through when he hears his employer is purchasing an access control system:

1 **Denial** – It'll never work, they won't get it up and running while I'm still here.
2 **Anger** – I've worked here for 17 years, every match day, rain or shine, I've stood on post and now they want to replace me with a piece of kit.
3 **Bargaining** – If I get here half an hour earlier and don't take a break, would you keep me on instead?
4 **Depression** – Why have I wasted 17 years of my life here when they clearly don't appreciate me?
5 **Acceptance** – OK, so it is a pretty impressive system. Maybe they can train me to use it?

This might seem trite, but when you consider the role of all your stakeholders in making your businesses a success, including the gate steward who's the first to greet your fans as they turn up on a match day, you can understand how and why Change Management is so important.

I personally subscribe to the view shared in a more recent work, John Kotter's 1996 publication *Leading Change*, which features his seminal 8-Step Process, which was updated and expanded in 2014 (Kotter, 2014). I've had permission from Kotter to reproduce his literature here, but have expanded on his words and added some sports industry context. My hope is that you can align his eight steps to your current state, whether you're just tiptoeing around the edge of CRM and data, are at an intermediate level or have progressed to a more mature stage.

John Kotter's 8-Step Process for leading change

Step 1: create a sense of urgency

Kotter suggests that if you can identify and describe an opportunity that will appeal to individuals' heads and hearts, you will have 'a breadth of focused readiness across the workplace that is unprecedented in your organisation'. Let's consider the occurrences that might prompt a sense of urgency:

• For clubs, a new stadium or stadium refurbishment, particularly if the outcomes include increased capacity, more/new corporate hospitality facilities, additional functional areas, etc., would produce that critical focus against a specific timeline.

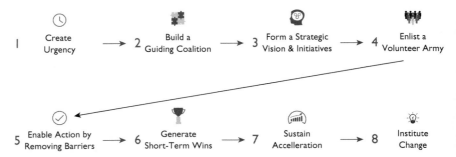

Figure 8.1 Kotter's eight steps for leading change. Adapted from *The 8-Step Process for Accelerating Change* ebook (reproduced with permission).

- For National Governing Bodies (NGBs), qualification for a world championship event would provide the perfect focus, as it would have a finite start point.

But there doesn't have to be a specific event or occurrence on the horizon. Senior management can create a sense of urgency tied to financial goals, a multi-year strategic plan or a set of KPIs.

Step 2: build a guiding coalition

According to Kotter, a guiding coalition would ensure that 'the linchpin of your entire transformation is in place: an accountable, diverse group bound by opportunity, strategy and action'. What's key in the creation of a coalition, or a committee, is that the members are skilled and respected by others in the organisation and have a level of influence. Of equal importance is the need for senior management to support the coalition, providing them with the tools they need to succeed, from resources to power, processes and guidance.

The departments that are represented in your coalition should be cross-organisational and, most importantly, be relevant to Step 1. For example, a focus on increased revenue would dictate the need for commercial staff to be represented. Increased participation would involve your sports development team and, on the basis that data will be integral to your transformation, you would need support from your legal team and technology staff.

Step 3: form a strategic vision and initiatives

The benefits of a strategic vision and initiatives, according to Kotter, is that 'you have a single vision of the future with a credibility and authority that comes from being crafted by a diverse set of employees and validated by senior leaders'. This is something I talk about on many occasions with my colleagues and clients. Working without a vision is like driving a car without a destination. Without destination we just go through the motions; we implement a series of tactics without an end goal.

While senior management might be needed to create a high-level description of the strategic vision, the coalition can complete it using relevant data to inform the past and project the future. The key challenge here is to ensure the vision is simple and that it can be described easily to other colleagues, possibly even sponsors and maybe even fans.

Step 4: enlist a volunteer army

Enlisting a volunteer army will provide you with 'a sizable body of employees excited and able to take action on critically important initiatives linked to your business strategy'. If you can find the colleagues in your team who are excited by what you're trying to achieve; if they buy into the vision and respect the coalition, you'll have a group of people that will change because they want to, not because they have to. They will build on the achievements of the coalition and champion the strategic vision, supporting and perhaps even driving the change initiatives.

Imagine how powerful that could be in your organisation. We already know how passionate people in the sports industry can be. If you can take that passion and combine it with their enthusiasm for your change process, you'll already be *en route* to great success.

Step 5: enable action by removing barriers

Enabling action and removing barriers can be a challenge because it involves empowering your team members. But, as Kotter reminds us, when you do this 'you have tangible evidence of employee innovations stemming from collapsed silos and new ways of working together'.

When I think of some of the natural barriers we have in the sports industry, my mind turns to the following:

- **Gender barriers**: so many of our activities are focused on male participation as opposed to female. This is changing and at quite a pace, but perhaps there is something more that can be achieved in this area.
- **Economic barriers**: money makes the world go round, but can we do something differently, even as a pilot, to support one of the identified initiatives?
- **Knowledge barriers**: within any organisation there are knowledge gaps, so we need a training plan to counter this. We need to equip our volunteer army in the same way we equip the coalition.

Step 6: generate short-term wins

While every one of Kotter's steps is vital to successful Change Management, generating short-term wins is what resonates most. What we need is 'a body of wins data that tells the story of your transformation, that is validated in quantifiable and qualifiable terms'.

When we have those WOW! moments – tangible milestones that have been reached – we must communicate them before we can celebrate. Quick wins keep us motivated and excited; they help ensure momentum is maintained and support a positive attitude across the organisation.

Consider some of the quick wins applicable in the sports industry like surpassing your target attendance for an unattractive fixture, increasing the value of your next sponsorship sales contract or retaining your volunteers from one event to the next. How powerful would these achievements be for ensuring your transformation stays on track?

Step 7: sustain acceleration

At this stage of Kotter's process, 'you have confirmation of organisational threats and stamina that enable the reinvigoration of your mission and help you and your employees stay the course of change over time'. This means you've successfully worked through Steps 1 to 6 and are celebrating your quick wins. The task now is to maintain this momentum, to keep moving forward implementing change after change until the strategic vision of Step 3 looks set to become a reality.

This is where I believe we may encounter a real problem. One of my observations from 30 years working in the sports industry is our natural inclination to focus on the short term. I've even tried to coin a phrase to represent this: 'sport-termism'. It hasn't caught on yet, and I hope it never will because it refers to our quest for the next win we're aiming for, the end-of-season trophy we hope to lift, even the next election we lobby for, when, really, we need to be thinking about and planning for the next three to five years.

When you get to this point in Kotter's plan, when you've started to see the quick wins (increased attendance, more or higher-value sponsors, a squad of volunteers), you risk forgetting about Step 7 and derailing all your achievements so far. You need your senior management, the guiding coalition and the army of volunteers that have driven the change up to this point to ensure you stay on track so you can implement the last step.

Step 8: institute change

You've made it! At this point in Kotter's process, 'you have collective recognition that your organisation has a new way of working with speed, agility and innovation that directly contributes to strategically important business results'.

To institute change and to ensure that it's sustainable and ongoing, you must have the right people, processes and systems in place to support the change vision. This could involve a continual process of training and development, technology upgrades and, in line with Chapter 3 of this book, continuous data collection and analysis. You also need to communicate the changes you've implemented, the successes and behaviours, and the relevance to your business and vision in order to ensure you have continued long-term buy-in.

With a clear strategic plan, Change Management becomes a much less daunting task. Failure is often a consequence of a lack of focus, but Kotter's eight steps provide a fantastic roadmap to successfully instituting change, resulting in a positive outcome for your entire organisation.

(Source: Kotter, 2014.)

But, 70% of change projects fail – or do they?

If you Google it, you can easily discover plenty of repetitions of the common misconception that '60 percent of all CRM implementations fail' (Gould, 2015). If you do the same for Business Change or Change Management, you'll get an even less favourable result at 70%. So, let's start by dispelling that myth.

In 2011, Dr Mark Hughes, a Reader in Organisational Change at Brighton Business School, published an article that unequivocally announced the following:

> Whilst the existence of a popular narrative of 70 per cent organizational-change failure is acknowledged, there is no valid and reliable empirical evidence to support such a narrative.

> (Hughes, 2011)

Hughes' work critically reviewed five separate published instances that proclaimed a 70% organisational-change failure rate and demonstrated that in each instance there was no 'valid and reliable empirical evidence in support of the espoused 70 per cent failure rate' (ibid.).

With that myth dispelled, I can focus on one of Hughes' key points, the absence of empirical evidence. The challenge we have is that the data we generate when setting out our approach to business change tends to be qualitative as opposed to quantitative, generated from a cultural analysis workshop or subsequent root cause analysis. These human behaviour factors can't be quantified in an empirical manner. This is in itself another reason why it can be difficult to justify investment in Change Management and why the sell-in I referred to previously can be more challenging.

With the use of predictive analytics and access to the systems and processes we now have, we can start to transform our approach to Change Management. We've all heard variations of marketing pioneer John Wanamaker's quote 'Half the money I spend on advertising is wasted; the trouble is I don't know which half'. Thankfully, being able to track our Return on Investment (ROI) means we have less money wasted. By applying data-driven approaches to it, we can see what works and what doesn't. This same thinking can, and should, be applied to our Change Management practices.

Until then, you must rely on your management's absolute faith in you or the consistent delivery of Step 6 of John Kotter's process: those invaluable quick wins.

Case study: Mic Conetta

Mic Conetta, Arsenal FC's Head of CRM, is a former Accenture Consultant with a great deal of experience with customer databases and their associated technologies: campaign management, reporting and analysis. Throughout his career, Conetta has encountered change projects on various scales and is acutely aware of the challenges and also the opportunities and benefits that come with getting it right.

I conducted a telephone interview with Conetta on 16 December 2017 and, as a seasoned CRM practitioner, he had an interesting take on where we are in the sports industry:

> CRM is nothing new in sport, there's always been an interaction with a customer or a fan. It's just the automation and the technology to better deliver experiences, customer interactions and services that's new. Ultimately, everyone's always been doing CRM in sport, it's just we're now doing it in a way that helps us leverage a better benefit from that relationship.

In another highly relevant observation, Conetta summarised the uniqueness of our industry.

> Sports properties, unlike many other businesses, are both content generators and product and service providers, which is very different to just being a high street retailer, for example, who is purely focused on selling products. We're doing all three. We're trying to combine those experiences, and CRM helps blend that together.

In this case study Conetta combines his extensive experience from outside the industry with his unique insights from within it to build on the some of the principles discussed in this chapter.

Stakeholder management

Stakeholder management is absolutely critical to the implementation of a CRM platform. Depending on where the transformation is being driven, you effectively need to get stakeholder buy-in. If you're driving an implementation, you're doing that on behalf of a number of business areas, and if those business areas don't fully buy in to what you're doing, that is going to leave you open to failure and make it very, very difficult to do successfully.

In a typical sports club environment, the key stakeholders are anyone who has a customer or fan touch point. Ticketing, hospitality, meeting and events, merchandise, stadium tours and membership schemes are just a few examples of the business areas that can become stakeholders of a CRM project. While some may drive a higher proportion of revenue than others, breaking down those silos and combining data will provide a single view of the customer that benefits everyone. Add to this other elements such as web presence and media channels that combine known individual data with unknown data within CRM, and you have a cross-organisational database that supports multiple business units. But Conetta tells us that knowing this and engineering its delivery can be two very different things.

Everyone knows managing silos in businesses can be challenging: there are lots of stakeholders that are purely driving for their specific area, when you're trying to run a cross-functional service line that meets natural challenges. Your CRM function is providing a service to all of your commercial silos that exist within an organisation. You've got to be prepared to work across that and engage with all of those stakeholders.

Changing the way in which you deal with people based on their abilities and level of understanding is paramount to ensuring the best level of collaboration from stakeholders.

Like any part of the business, dealing with stakeholders is a relationship – a two-way street. The user community needs to be confident in what you're proposing, and be willing to be open with you and your team. The only way you can consistently deliver success is if you truly understand the wants and needs of your stakeholders, and they in turn understand the same from you.

To assist with stakeholder buy-in, Conetta ensures he has one-on-one time with department heads. This not only means that he and his team are providing the services that meet the needs of the stakeholders, but also makes sure that his project team is conforming to some of the requirements set by those stakeholders. This ensures that successful implementation is continuous and open-ended.

Regular meetings allow the project team to see how they're performing with campaigns and if targets are being met. It allows him to take something concrete to his stakeholders to show where they are making gains, and where they might not be making as much progress as they'd like. Ultimately, they can draft creative ways in which they can drive value back into the business.

I asked Conetta how frequently he has these meetings and how much time was actually needed to break down these silos and get the buy-in he needs.

> I engage with the main stakeholders once a month in a one-on-one meeting and my team then runs operational meetings on a bi-weekly basis, but they tend to be popular, or not, dependent on the time of year. As you would expect, people are excited about attending when they've got something in mind that they want to discuss.
>
> We've changed the format so once a month there will be a set agenda, then the other will be more like a drop-in session – 'how can I do this, what's best practice' – that way we know that people will come and bring their challenges.
>
> I don't want my team to do all the talking in these meetings – I've got to try and instil some confidence in our user community to be open with us because the only way we can continue to deliver success is if we truly understand where they're coming from, but also for them to understand where we're coming from. Like anything, it's a two-way street. It's a relationship.

Delivering success

We've already heard Conetta mention success twice so it's clearly an important part of managing a change programme. I asked where he tends to see the biggest success in the smallest amount of time.

> Building personas that represent our fan base, bringing them to life, is one of the greatest areas for growth. You can easily lose people if you get too into the details of data, clustered models, big data and data science, but actually it's the ability to bring data to life and have a consistent way of talking

> about it, be that for Christmas retail campaigns, season ticket renewals, or ticket sales on a per game basis. If you can start bringing that to life a bit and help departments understand a bit more about the make up of our trans-acting fan base or our international fan base, it helps to deliver a stronger creative play into the message that we're trying to get across. It helps them think about the products and services we bring to market to meet those fans' wants and needs when they have different personas to work with.

Note: I introduced personas in Chapter 2 and talk more about them in Chapter 5 but if you're not familiar with them, and to help put Conetta's statement above into context, a simple definition is 'the cosmetic manufacturing of your ideal customers based on the information you have about them'.

An example of how Conetta might put this in action is with something as simple as changing an image in an email for a different persona. For example, a young family is likely to respond to an image of a child's replica kit in the online store more than a persona that doesn't have children. Using a simple example like that makes it much easier for stakeholders to understand how data and personalisation combine to 'get the right message to the right person'.

Knowing where to place your focus when initiating CRM can be a significant challenge and there are many different approaches to this. Some businesses select MVPs – that's *minimum viable product* not *most valuable player*, as some of our trans-Atlantic readers might think (although they could both be used when you think about it). An MVP approach is a development technique that dictates that a new product is developed with just enough features to provide the feedback, learning and data needed to support future development. But this isn't an approach to which Conetta subscribes.

> There isn't a single MVP. What we tend to do is sit down and work out what the objectives are and then try to put some measurable targets against that. Whether it's looking at year-on-year improvement in the success of a campaign, driving more traffic to a site to support a campaign, reducing churn on a seasonal renewal, increased revenue, the number of people entering a competition, brand awareness, all of these things.

But on these success measurements Conetta again has an interesting take – almost calling into question one of the key benefits of using data to enable the tracking of ROI (return on investment).

> It's really hard to say in sport 'you know what, this year we renewed 95% of our season ticket holder base because we invested in CRM'. We know that's unrealistic. You could have the best season, you could have the cup-winning season, you can finish second in the league and win no trophies, or you can finish fourth or fifth. It's really hard to understand, day to day, what the impact is of signing global superstars or how the team are playing versus what you're doing. All you know is that you're working in a way that was different to the way that you were working a few years ago and, with that, it naturally feels that the more sophistication you're putting into your campaigns and your CRM activities the more you're to drive a greater benefit.

You might recognise a not dissimilar school of thought here to that of Amie Becton Ray, the NHL's Director of Database Marketing and Strategy who we heard from earlier in Chapter 3.

However, Conetta does subscribe to the principle of test and learn, an approach credited to financial services company Capital One, that, in 1998, carried out 28,000 individual experiments across advertising and products (Fishman, 1999), and is now the standard approach for data-driven marketers. With that approach naturally comes failure – some new things may not work – so, in that instance, Conetta will try other new things that may work. And those that do are expanded and rolled out.

> All of our campaigns have got test and learn capabilities built in, from data selection, use of personas, subject line testing, dynamic channel mix. All of these things are built in to see what is successful at moving those targets and achieving success.

Corporate governance

I asked Conetta for his top tip for setting out corporate governance when undertaking a change such as the one he implemented and is progressing in his current role. Unsurprisingly, his number one recommendation is not unique to the sports industry.

> Focus on high-level objectives. You've got to create a governance structure that understands and buys into those benefits and is also able to see and monitor how you're progressing against those over time. You want a) to prove that it's working, but b) give your team perspective on how they are performing.

As CRM in any business operates as a cross-functional service provision, it often doesn't bring in any direct revenue, so Conetta has a model for giving his team a sense of worth, providing the performance measurement he refers to above.

> We measure the benefits that we deliver to each of our departments and then we also measure the soft benefits. An example of this is our ability to reduce churn. So the business target might be to hit a certain churn target but then we beat the target and reduce churn further. But because we always knew we could cope with x amount of churn, and churn has never gone above that amount, there's no physical benefit. So, while beating that churn target was never in the business case, it's still a huge benefit – it's our soft benefit.

Building on this sentiment, Conetta comes back to the value of having regular meetings with the stakeholders and regularly asking the following questions:

1 We can see where we're behind. What can we do?
2 Is there something more creative we can do with the offers we're making?
3 Do we need more campaigns?
4 Are our current campaigns working?
5 Is our channel mix right?

This approach introduces the governance that Conetta subscribes to; focusing on objectives, measuring success, and meeting and sharing with his stakeholders.

Business change

I talked about making change easy (and why we choose bananas) at the start of this chapter, and when I asked Conetta to provide his recommendations on how to approach our natural resistance to – and fear of – change, he again focused on communication.

> Education in the right language is essential to business change. Not everyone is going to be at the same level of understanding. It's easy to forget that CRM can be quite a difficult subject for some people, especially if they've not come across it before or haven't worked in marketing or understand some of these principles. Explain it in layman's terms, short and sweet.

This reiterates Conetta's earlier point about personas. Creating a fictional ticket buyer or international fan, summarising their key characteristics and then calling them Jeff or Jack already helps with the challenge of industry-specific language that's unfamiliar to our stakeholders, the very people we need to understand us and buy into the change.

Building on his very first point, that CRM is not new in sport, Conetta goes on to explain that talking about what people are doing in other organisations that your stakeholders may already be familiar with is another way of achieving that necessary level of understanding. This is a tactic we use at Winners. With Amazon, Netflix and Spotify now so ubiquitous, we use them as the standard-bearer for services that make you want to engage or buy more. They make it easy for you.

In reality we're not expecting rights owners to perform at that level. These are pure-play organisations (they only operate in the online world), so operating at the leading edge in CRM is their only option.

> Hardly anyone out there hasn't had an online buying experience, buying off their mobile phone or being advertised to by Google and any sites that they visit. They're all being exposed to CRM on a daily basis they just might not realise it – it's about finding a context that they'll understand.

Conetta's other recommendations include knowledge sharing; ensuring that, whatever your stakeholder's level of understanding, whether beginner or sophisticated, you support them to learn more. Of course the best way of keeping everyone on point, focused in the right direction, prioritising and taking action at the right time is sharing successes, both within your team, with the wider group and with the business as a whole.

In one final fix from Conetta, we share what could be the shortest ever definition of CRM and Business Change.

> Essentially, it's the automation and technology to better deliver fan experiences, customer interactions and the provision of services. The most important thing is to make sure that everyone understands it, to make sure it can be implemented in a way that helps leverage a better return from your relationships.

(Source: Conetta, 2017, 16 December.)

Key chapter ideas

1   Change has to be easy to ensure its success but the industry has been around for many years and there's a lot of documentation for further reading that can guide you through it.

2 Moving from a traditional business to one driven by data and digital technology is too big a shift to be achieved without an informed approach to business change and the implementation of a change management programme.

3 There are established models that you can follow, but the main elements of a change management programme centre on the creation of groups, ongoing communication, documenting of success stories and the sharing of these successes.

4 CRM is not new in sport. It's been around for years and even if you didn't know it, you've been on the receiving end if you've ever bought anything online or on your mobile app. Find the context that your stakeholders will understand and use easy to understand language.

References

BBC (2018). Premier League TV rights: five of seven live packages sold for £4.464bn. BBC. Available at: www.bbc.co.uk/sport/football/43002985.

Brown, M. (2014). The biggest media company you've never heard of [online]. *Forbes*. Available at: www.forbes.com/sites/maurybrown/2014/07/07/the-biggest-media-company-youve-never-heard-of.

Burnes, B. (2011). Introduction: why does change fail, and what can we do about it? *Journal of Change Management*, 11(4), 445–450.

Business Wire (2017). The Walt Disney Company to acquire majority ownership of BAMTech [online]. *Business Wire*. Available at: www.businesswire.com/news/home/20170808006428/en/Walt-Disney-Company-Acquire-Majority-Ownership-BAMTech.

Caldwell, D. (2016). Why the NFL can get away with dumping mediocrity on UK fans [online]. *The Guardian*. Available at: www.theguardian.com/sport/2016/dec/15/nfl-london-games-international-series-wembley-twickenham.

Cleverism (2015). *Understanding the Kubler-Ross Change Curve* [online]. Cleverism. Available at: https://www.cleverism.com/understanding-kubler-ross-change-curve.

Conetta, M. (2017, 16 December). Telephone interview.

Cruickshank, A. and Collins, D. (2012). Change management: the case of the elite sport performance team. *Journal of Change Management*, 12(2), 209–229.

Evans, D. M., Smith, A. C. and Westerbeek, H. M. (2005). The examination of change management using qualitative methods: a case industry approach. *The Qualitative Report*, 10(1), 96–121. Available at: http://nsuworks.nova.edu/tqr/vol10/iss1/6.

Fishman, C. (1999). *This Is a Marketing Revolution* [online]. Fast Company. Available at: www.fastcompany.com/36975/marketing-revolution.

Gould, L. (2015). *Characteristics of a Failing CRM Project* [online]. C5insight.com. Available at: www.c5insight.com/Resources/Blog/tabid/88/entryid/605/characteristics-of-a-failing-crm-project.aspx.

Hagura, N., Haggard, P. and Diedrichsen, J. (2017). Perceptual decisions are biased by the cost to act [online]. *eLife*. Available at: https://elifesciences.org/articles/18422.

Hughes, M. (2011). Do 70 per cent of all organizational change initiatives really fail? *Journal of Change Management*, 11(4), 451–464.

Kotter, J. (1996). *Leading Change*. Boston: Harvard Business Review Press.

Kotter, J. (2014). *Accelerating Change* [online]. Available at: http://go.kotterinc.com/get-the-8steps-ebook.html.

Kübler-Ross, E. (2003). *On Death and Dying*. New York: Scribner.

Lacey, D. (1992). Future sold for pie in the sky. *The Guardian*, 20 May, p. 16.

Lewin, K. (1947). Frontiers in group dynamics. *Human Relations*, 1(1), 5–41.

Luna, T. and Cohen, J. (2017). To get people to change, make change easy [online]. *Harvard Business Review*. Available at: https://hbr.org/2017/12/to-get-people-to-change-make-change-easy.

Nicholson, M. (2015). *Sport and the Media*. London: Routledge, p. 29.

Potter, D. (1992). Premier TV deal under attack. *The Independent*, 22 May, p. 32.

Sweney, M. (2017). Sky faces paying extra £1.8bn for Premier League broadcast rights [online]. *The Guardian*. Available at: www.theguardian.com/media/2017/aug/11/premier-league-broadcast-battle-hots-up-as-sky-face-doling-out-extra-600m.

Vrentas, J. (2014). Why London? And can it work? [online]. *Sports Illustrated*. Available at: www.si.com/2014/10/02/nfl-team-in-london-international-series.

Wigmore, T. (2017). T20 is constantly evolving and is no longer held back by traditionalists [online]. *The Guardian*. Available at: www.theguardian.com/sport/2017/jul/11/t20-twenty-20-tradition-the-spin-cricket.

Williamson, M. (2012). Crash, bang and Pandora's box is opened [online]. *ESPN Cricinfo*. Available at: www.espncricinfo.com/magazine/content/story/579245.

Chapter 9

Data and the law

It's impossible to write a book on the role of data without mentioning the EU General Data Protection Regulation (GDPR). But you might be asking yourself how relevant this chapter will be if you're reading it in December 2020, April 2019 or even August 2018. The reality is that while GDPR compliance is enforceable from 25 May 2018, enforcement is expected to be a gradual process so regulators will be looking to see that you're making progress, showing intent, while also taking care of those issues that can be addressed relatively easily – your 'quick wins'.

In addition to your data compliance being a slow evolution, there are many areas of the GDPR that can be considered 'grey' and solutions will only be discovered through case law. With this in mind, I'm hoping this chapter will stand the test of time and remain relevant. Seminal works such as Mark McCormack's *What They Don't Teach You at Harvard Business School* (1989) or Paul Greenberg's *CRM at the Speed of Light* (2001), now in its 4th edition, are perfect examples of books that, despite the passage of time, remain as relevant now as the day they were published.

According to a late 2017 survey by the World Federation of Advertisers, 70% of brand owners felt their marketers were not fully aware of the implications of the GDPR, and only 65% expected to be ready for May 2018 (WFA, 2017). Within the sports industry, LawInSport's 2018 survey suggested that 43% of sports organisations did not feel their business was supportive in complying with GDPR (Cottrell, 2018).

There's a good chance that some of you reading this will still have a little bit of work to do but, hopefully, you've at least made sure your digital estate (your websites, the websites of third parties you use to provide services such as ticketing, online store, etc.) carries the correct terminology. This is of specific importance when it comes to your Terms and Conditions of Use, Privacy Policy and Cookie/Profiling Policy. Most importantly, you should have by now ensured that your data collection forms all use the appropriate, clear and express opt-in boxes and wording, so the purpose of this chapter is not to explain the GDPR but to highlight some of the questions it raises.

Will this be another Y2K?

The 18 January 1999 edition of *TIME*, a weekly news magazine with the largest circulation in the world for its type, used a cover image that summed up the mind-set surrounding the dominant conversation of that year: Y2K. The evocative image used the words *The End of the World!?!*, pandering to the fear many felt over what Y2K would mean for themselves and their businesses (Rothman, 2014). Despite the accompanying article concluding that the end of the world was not a likely outcome, many people and articles continued to speculate on the impending impact of the two-digit rather than four-digit format used for denoting 'year' that was common in a lot of computer programmes. The speculated consequences of this included everything from complete system breakdowns to global power losses. At that time I was fortunately working in a manner that meant, at worst, there would be an interruption to my workflow, but my husband recalls that rather than joining in the traditional New Year celebrations he was driving from factory to factory; a long cold journey and on a hiding to nothing.

In the end there were a few minor incidents, including a headline-grabbing nuclear power plant in Japan that malfunctioned a few seconds into the year 2000 and a bank of slot machines that stopped working in the US state of Delaware (*BBC News*, 2000), but in the end, life (and business) continued as normal. With no insight into how local enforcement organisations (such as the Information Commissioner's Office in the UK, Datatilsynet in Norway or Informacijski Pooblaščenec in Slovenia) plan to start their day on 26 May 2018, it's impossible to know what might happen next. So, yes, this is very different to Y2K in two respects:

1   The GDPR is a legal regulation that is enforceable without the need for any national government to pass any further legislation.
2   It's not an expectation that every organisation will be GDPR-compliant the day after the regulation comes into force. It *is* expected that you will have started to put in place the right processes and can demonstrate that you're working towards GDPR compliance.

Hence, rather than facing GDPR with fear, I've been advising organisations to face it with enthusiasm for the benefits it will create. For a start, you'll have better systems and processes in place to support your customers and fans – and for those rights owners that cross borders, you'll have a clearer set of guidelines to ensure international ways of working with data. Rights owners such as Manchester United aren't taking any chances. Knowing how high-profile its brand is, how the regulation enforcers may be looking for low-hanging fruit to provide case law and how GDPR-savvy journalists will be looking for headlines, the club went through the whole process of contacting its fans to ask them to opt-in again to receive emails from them (Manchester United, 2018).

Will fines of €20 million really be issued?

The change that ensures the subject gets the attention of the most data-weary management teams is the scope for potential fines. Under the EU Data Protection Directive (the legislation that the GDPR will replace), the maximum possible fine was £500,000. But, after 25 May 2018, it will be €20,000,000 or 4% of turnover, whichever is greater. Will fines of that magnitude ever really be issued or is it simply an amount set to incentivise compliance?

It's impossible to know but, as an indicator of the art of the possible, the Information Commissioner's Office (ICO) had no problem imposing a fine of £400,000 on Carphone Warehouse for breaches that included out-of-date software, lax security controls concerning user access and an absence of anti-virus software on the servers hosting customer databases (ICO, 2018). That's 80% of the maximum possible fine for errors that are easily repeatable by any organisation, including rights owners.

Premiership Rugby team Exeter Chiefs is another UK club not taking any chances, signing a sponsorship deal with a local cyber security firm to provide GDPR-awareness training (Stevens, 2017), while Premier League football club Everton is appointing a Gartner Magic Quadrant leader to undertake a cloud risk assessment. Phil Davies, Everton's ICT Manager, said about this move:

> Data security is a key priority for the club. Information on players and their contracts is a vital asset for us and fans also entrust us with their data, including personally identifiable information. We take this responsibility seriously so we're keen to provide employees with the right tools to boost productivity without compromising on security.
>
> (Murphy, 2017)

I moderated a panel in 2017 at a Sports and Entertainment Alliance in Technology (SEAT) conference that focused on the GDPR. When talking about the fines, one rights owner asked if we could only be fined once a year. It was an interesting question as there aren't many rights owners that could handle a €20 million fine the first time, let alone a second. Even if their insurance covered it, their premiums would become prohibitively expensive when it came to renewal. The question led to a discussion that, regardless of the value of the fine, the reputational damage for rights owners could often be more damaging then any financial loss. When something goes wrong in other industries, the story might be limited to the trade press. In the world of sports, however, we provide fodder for everyone from the world's elite publications to the gutter press. We're not restricted to the sports pages.

Who will be responsible for fines when two parties are involved?

Under the outgoing EU Data Protection Directive, only the data controller was considered liable for data breaches. The data controller is the person or organisation that determines the purposes for and the manner in which any personal data is processed and used. For the purposes of this book, the data controller will generally be the rights owner (with the exception of the use cases when we talk about second-party data).

Under GDPR however, both the controller and the data processor (any person or organisation that processes the data on behalf of the data controller – subject to the specific nature of the commercial and vendor agreements you enter into, this will largely be your service supplier) are jointly liable. Both could receive a fine.

Let's put this into perspective with the Exeter Chiefs and Everton examples above. My interpretation of this is as follows: the Supplier performs a task, for example building a data collection form. The Supplier ensures that everything about it, from the wording used to the data flow into the host system, is GDPR compliant. Great work, Supplier. Then the Club takes the code and embeds it into its website, but accidentally overwrites some of the HTML and the opt-in wording or tick box is corrupted, resulting in the presentation of an opt-out. YIKES! A fan of the Club's biggest competitor spots this and reports it to the authorities, and both the Club and Supplier are hit with a fine.

Is that fair? Would that upset the dynamics of the relationship? I'd say the answer to those questions is both no and yes. There would be a lot of to-ing and fro-ing between the parties to figure it out. But, what if the Supplier is not just a vendor that is supplying services but one of the Club's major sponsors that has a long-standing relationship with the Club that provides both cash and services?

Let's reverse the situation and suggest that the Club gave the correct instructions to the Supplier, which then misinterpreted them, made a mistake or simply didn't pay enough attention: the Club wanted the form to be an opt-in but the form launched with an opt-out instead. Again, both the Club and the Supplier would be issued with the fine but, in this instance, the Club did nothing wrong.

The point I'm making here is that if the breach is serious enough and the Supplier is entirely at fault, the Club would still be deemed liable in the eyes of the enforcement agency and be on the receiving end of a fine of up to €20 million. How many rights owners could handle this? Do you have this level of cover in your insurance policies?

Your supplier agreements will no doubt include a breach clause and will request monetary compensation in the event of termination or non-performance. But there's a good chance the monetary compensation will be limited to the value of the contract with some additional minor multiplier. In reality, you need to take that a lot further and ensure that any GDPR-related fine that is issued as a direct result of a breach by the Supplier should be the full responsibility of the Supplier, regardless of whether the enforcing agency issues the fine directly to the rights owner. If you do that, any Supplier will conversely request that the clause is mutual and the expectation is that you'll have to comply or the Supplier will simply walk away.

The ultimate question here is, how could anyone sign up to a contract of any value that puts them at risk of a €20 million fine if the contracting parties are not prepared to discuss fair liability? As you can imagine, all of the Winners contracts now include clauses with this express intention. Our work will be GDPR-compliant, which will prevent our clients receiving a fine as a result of our actions, but, conversely, we won't be held liable for any fine incurred as a result of our clients' activities as a result of our work.

When a player transfers, how much data has to go with them?

Rights owners' use of data can go beyond their fans, ticket buyers, shop customers and staff. If you're a club, national governing body or even a league, you'll also have participation data to be concerned with that includes players and athletes, referees, coaches, medical personnel and other paid or voluntary support staff.

The key question here is the impact of the right to data portability, one of the few articles in the GDPR that are not updating or refreshing an existing clause of the EU Data Protection Directive. It means that the data subject (any individual whose personal data you hold) has a right to request a copy of all their personal data that is processed electronically to be passed from one data controller to another, in effect allowing them to take their data with them when they move from one environment to another.

Imagine this scenario in the context of a player transfer. Clubs must ensure that *all* personal data they have on a player can smoothly transition from one club's system to another. What's the limitation on the extent of that data? For elite athletes in a professional team, does that mean all their biometric data and the results of the coach or manager's training regime (which is usually proprietary), and for what period of time?

A further question is the right to erasure; the right that all data subjects have for their information to be completely erased from your systems if they request it. What about a player or athlete's performance data that you post on your website as part of your content offering to fans – do you have to erase them entirely from your archived stories?

Would Moneyball be allowed if Billy Beane tried it now?

I talked about the role of data analytics in selecting a winning team in Chapter 3, but, under the GDPR, data subjects have the right to object to any type of processing of their information. While that's clear-cut when it comes to the use of unsubscribes from communication and opt-outs from profiling, another objection right is the use of processing for an automated decision. As an example of this, the financial services industry might use automated decision-making to determine that a customer doesn't qualify for a mortgage but, in the sports world, does that mean a player or athlete could object to their performance data being used to assess whether they're in the squad? If Billy Beane were to apply the same approach, could a player demand the team no longer process his information the first time a player is rejected? In reality, it's not a major issue. If a player objects to this they won't be selected anyway, but it throws up an interesting point. Do we risk this article creating another equivalent of the Bosman Rule, the landmark ruling over 20 years ago that banned any restrictions on EU players moving to another club at the end of a contract without a transfer fee being paid (Brand, 2015)?

What about rights owners outside the EU?

The focus of the GDPR is not just the organisations that operate in the 31 countries that make up the EU (European Union) and EEA (European Economic Area). The GDPR was written with the *residents* of the EU in mind, not the businesses. This means it's not just rights owners that operate in this territory that need to be concerned with these legislation changes; it's any rights owner that provides and offers services to residents of the EEUEA, regardless of where their business is located.

In Chapter 2 you heard Charlie Shin, VP of CRM and Analytics of Major League Soccer, state that MLS doesn't provide an offering for EU residents (it doesn't schedule matches in EU territories or provide a streaming service targeting Europeans). Even so, he will be keeping an eye on the GDPR as he believes it will be the direction the rest of the world will take. Several years ago I had a conversation with a US lawyer who suggested that if the US ever decided to take Europe's approach to data protection, it would put a lot of businesses out of operation. Essentially, this still leaves this question unanswered. In addition to the definition above based on the provision of services (which is irrespective of payment), the GDPR article suggests that any non-EU business with a website using cookies that could be visited by an EU resident not only has to be GDPR-compliant but has to appoint a representative in the EU. Surely that's unsustainable?

What do we do about legacy data?

When you started collecting your opt-ins however many years ago, you were probably asking your fans and customers to opt-in for one thing: to hear from you, either by email, SMS, phone and maybe even direct mail if you've been doing it for a while. Then we started using cookies on websites, so your digital terms and conditions had to be amended to accommodate this, including a cookie opt-in policy. There aren't many of us who would have had the foresight to ask for an opt-in to retarget our fans with digital advertising. But, as I discussed in Chapter 3, now you can use email addresses for remarketing using not just your own websites but networks of websites like Google Ad Networks, Facebook, Instagram and LinkedIn.

So, what do you do about your 'legacy data'; all the email addresses you've collected over the previous years? Can you use them to remarket through a different channel to the ones you've been using thus far? Can the condition of 'legitimate interest' be applied here?

For our purposes, what does 'legitimate interest' mean? The GDPR allows for the processing of data for legitimate reasons not specifically discussed within the legislation itself, so long as it doesn't infringe on the rights and freedoms of your fans or customers as far as their data is concerned. In the case of the sports industry, I would argue that if a rights owner has been using an email list to share news and stories of interest with a fan base, having secured the right to do so through an opt-in, then it would be legitimate for the organisation to continue that relationship through further digital channels. But will that actually be the case, or will the fans have to opt in to every channel individually?

Key points for GDPR awareness

The answer to many of these questions may have to wait for case law before we get real clarification on the implications for rights owners. To avoid being one of the parties referenced in case law, you will need to ensure you have already implemented a pragmatic approach to ensuring GDPR compliance. If you're reading this with the realisation you still haven't done anything about it, don't panic. But do start moving.

The questions I've discussed still need to be answered to have clarity under the GDPR. What follows will be a snapshot of some additional key articles that rights owners need to be aware of. Note that this list is not exhaustive.

The rights of the data subject

Whether a fan, ticket buyer, shop customer, web visitor, player/athlete, coach, referee, volunteer, member of staff, sponsor or any other entity whose data you have in any of your systems, each of these individuals has the following rights:

- **Information disclosure** – such as the way you use data and how you process it, whether for communication, profiling or other decision-making.
- **Access** – giving people access to their own data, including confirmation that their information is being processed and any other supplementary information you may have about them.

- **Correction** – correcting it if the information you have about individuals is wrong or incomplete. In reality, you would want to see this in place regardless of the GDPR, as inaccurate data is no good for your business.
- **Restriction of processing** – the potential to block you from doing any further processing, although you could retain the existing information you have. This is an interesting one for me and aligns with my mantra that 'no data should be thrown away' because it all provides valuable insight. For example, just because a fan unsubscribes from receiving your emails it doesn't mean the information you have about them has no further use. Any profiling you've conducted up to that point can still be used in your BI strategy.

Your obligation to report security breaches

The GDPR places an obligation on you to report any breaches that are likely to result in harm to your data subjects. We've all read stories in the news of laptops being lost or stolen that contain sensitive information, such as the Nationwide Building Society fine reported in February 2007 where a laptop that contained sensitive customer data was stolen from an employee's home (*BBC News*, 2007). You shouldn't be carrying any fan data on your laptop, but, if you do and it's lost or stolen, you have an obligation to report it to your local enforcement agency. This is the same obligation that applies to a major hack in your security systems. With this in mind, while your IT teams will no doubt have processes in place to deal with issues they encounter, your marketing teams should have the same.

Need for a data protection officer (DPO)

It's important to assess whether you need a DPO. According to the GDPR, there are three bases under which this would be the case. Do you fit under any of these?

1   Processing is carried out by a public authority.
2   Your processing operations require regular and systematic processing of data subjects on a large scale (note that there is no definition of 'large scale' here).
3   Your core activities relate to a large quantity of sensitive data or data relating to criminal convictions or offences.

On this last point, rights owners that are responsible for athlete registration may fall into this category if their records include health and medical information. For this reason, many of you may decide it's prudent to appoint a DPO as a precaution.

Looking after children

Unlike the EU Data Protection Directive, the GDPR applies specific provisions that are intended to enhance the protection of children's personal data.

The general ruling is that consent obligations are applicable for a person under the age of 16. In this case, they cannot give consent themselves. Instead, consent much be secured from a person holding parental responsibility. However, it's important to note that each EU member state is permitted to lower that age as long as it's not below 13.

Second party data and third party opt-ins

In Chapter 3 I looked at the difference between first-, second- and third-party data and gave the following definition for second-party: it traditionally comes from customers of your partners (sponsors, ticketing and merchandise agents) who in Europe have ticked the 'third-party opt-in' box. It's your ticketing agents' or your sponsors' first-party data, i.e., their customers who have said their data can be shared with you.

On this point, the GDPR is relevant. While your third parties, specifically your sponsors, ticketing and online store providers, can assist with the growth of your databases, both from a quantity and quality standpoint, it's important they have ensured the relevant opt-ins are in place in their processes before transferring the applicable data to you. This includes an opt-in for the data to be used by you for communication purposes, but also for profiling purposes.

When you work with your third parties to acquire their data (which is classed as second-party data) it's important you do so with full sight of the relevant opt-in. Ensure the processes your partners used are GDPR-compliant, asking for proof if necessary, including the request that when they send you the applicable database, you can see a field that shows a clear opt-in. Without this understanding and proof of provenance, you could leave yourself exposed if your partners have not used the appropriate processes and your data subjects make a complaint.

Case study: AZ Alkmaar

Bas Schnater is the Head of Fan Engagement, CRM and Digital at AZ Alkmaar, a Dutch professional football club from Alkmaar and the Zaanstreek. The club plays in the highest professional league in the Netherlands, the Eredivisie. Schnater shared some insights and strategies on how the club prepared for the GDPR and how he sees it as not just hoops to jump through but also as an opportunity to really get to grips with the team's fan data.

> I started thinking about the GDPR in advance, gathering lots of information that was relevant to each department. I visited some informative events at law firms and asked other companies how they prepared for the GDPR because, in the context of football, we tend to think short-term, and May can seem very far away from now [December]. For me, May is only five months away, and we really need to step up the game.

The Dutch Federation of Professional Football Clubs (FBO) is taking the GDPR very seriously. It set up a pilot audit programme for its member clubs and AZ volunteered to be part of it. Schnater gained a lot of valuable knowledge from it, which the club aims to put into action.

> AZ has been very proactive in this area, starting a task force some time ago that includes a lot of people from the organisation that work with our data, to see what the main problem points are that we need to take action on before the 25th of May.
>
> But it goes way broader than just our marketing data. Of course, we collect a lot of data on the football players, and with the GDPR going into effect on the 25th of May, which is a few weeks before the transfer market opens up again, we have to understand what happens if a player gets transferred to a different club and we have two seasons' worth of data from them.
>
> What do we have to do with that data? Do we have to transfer that or make that available to the player? Do we have to erase that information because they are no longer one of our employees? And what about other employees? If an employer collects information on me, for example, if I pay for lunch on my card every time, then they know exactly what I eat. What do they have to do with that, and what are my rights as an employee regarding that data?
>
> So there are a lot of questions that still need to be answered, and that's why we're forming the task force: first, to create an action list, and later, to collect the information that we need to be able to answer these questions.

Marketing and opt-ins

A significant area of focus for Schnater is marketing data; mainly how to deal with opt-ins in future. As mentioned earlier in the chapter, they will be vastly different under the GDPR. Schnater, however, sees this as a positive change, and one that will help AZ get more from its fan data.

> GDPR gives us a lot of opportunities rather than cramping us up. It gives us the chance to really ask what communications people really want, and what they don't want. In that sense, it will hopefully increase engagement percentages. I see it as a big opportunity to become truly relevant to the right audience.

Opt-ins have been used by AZ since 2015 when it installed its new ticketing platform, but the method of collecting opt-ins is no longer relevant. This has led to the creation of an opt-in management strategy.

We need to outline what we can send the fans, and what we can't. We've been using soft opt-ins, so if someone bought something from the web store we know that they were probably interested in information about the web store, or that they're probably interested in more information on the club. So we use that as an implied opt-in.

But of course we can't do that any more, so to deal with these we decided to run continuous campaigns to collect as many compliant opt-ins as possible from the fans that we already have in our database.

We started this programme in September 2017 and it's working really well – we're letting our fans know we're not being irresponsible with their data.

Naturally, the club wants to secure as many opt-ins as possible, but it's also vital that it doesn't spam its fans with too many requests to that effect. With a new website planned for November 2018, Schnater already has a plan in place to make sure that as many fans as possible are reached for opt-ins in an organic way.

It's going to be relatively easy for us as we'll be renewing our website, both back and front end, and GDPR compliance is actually a considerable part of the process that we're going through. We're also asking potential suppliers for the website how they will handle customer profiling as we will have different fans using our website for different purposes.

GDPR awareness and implications

It's important to make sure that everyone in the organisation is on board with the GDPR changes. Like any business change, it can be challenging to get everyone to work together, but Schnater is doing his best to ensure that everyone at AZ is preparing and changing their processes to be as compliant as possible with the legislation.

We are trying to prepare our staff already and trying to unlearn behaviours that aren't compliant with the GDPR. As an example, it used to be common practice to share lists of people between departments via email because it was the easiest way of working. One of the first things is that we need to unlearn habits like that. We've always had secure servers for internal use, but now on every server we also have a data transfer folder and we've started using

(continued)

(continued)

them. We've already had meetings with the task force to discuss what we can do to make our internal data storage more secure, and that is one of the first aspects that came out of it. It's more inconvenient than emailing it, but it's way more secure.

That's where the task force comes in. Every department has different elements of the business that need attention from a data security perspective. The HR department's needs for employee contracts and for how it deals with sensitive corporate data differ from the needs of the sponsorship team, which will deal with more commercial data. Essentially, the task force is set up to include all parts of the business that will be contributing to things that may be effected by the GDPR and making those decisions and discussions organisation-wide, rather than leaving them as the remit of a single department.

For Schnater it's vital to ask as many questions as possible to make sure that everyone is thinking about their data in the right way, not only for the employees of the club but also for how they deal with fan data. If a fan purchases from the club's web shop, is it right to assume that they would also be interested in ticketing information, allowing them to transfer from the retail to the ticketing silo?

Specifically for Schnater, the right to erasure (or 'right to be forgotten') raises some serious questions.

Is our data supplier going to deliver a platform where fans will be able to check what kind of data we have on them? The other question is, will that actually happen? I mean, we are an emotional business, so fans are more likely to be interested in our product. How do we manage that? Are we going to get a request from a fan once a month for their data, or are you going to get it twice a week or twice a year?

It's very hard to estimate how often we will get those requests, and of course, that will be important for us to decide whether to dedicate resources to that. Do we need to build a platform for fans to check in real time, and how will the internal processes be created for that?

This becomes important not just for fans, but for other aspects of the organisation as well. Players are employees, but clubs have data on them that a lot of other organisations would not have. They have access to health information, medical records and other sensitive data that will need to be navigated and made available to the players on request. Schnater doesn't see any of this as an obstacle. Instead, he sees the opportunities that the GDPR presents.

I asked Schnater his advice for any rights owner who hasn't yet started planning for GDPR or may be in the early stages.

Make use of current connections. Use your sponsor network. I'm not sure that the sports industry will be the first targeted for GDPR. Therefore, a lot of other industries that have wider customer bases will be much better prepared for it. So, for example, if you have a Telco [telecommunications] sponsor, ask them how they've prepared. Ask them how they can help you decide on what steps to take to prepare your own organisation. I think we can get a lot of knowledge and value out of our commercial networks.

The GDPR creates massive opportunities and helps you to get genuine open rates. It will get you closer to genuine click rates and genuine engagement. It will help you to get quality data, not just quantities of it. Less is more, in this case. If that results in you having a smaller database because you have to eliminate inactive records, it will only help, as it will allow other fans to become more visible. It's a great opportunity to cleanse your fan base of old and outdated records that don't show any engagement.

(Source: Schnater, 2018.)

Key chapter ideas

1   While the GDPR is now applicable to the way you manage, collect, transfer and store data, there are many grey areas that will be clarified through case law.
2   The GDPR will be relevant to your organisation if it operates in the EU or is based outside the EU but proactively aims to communicate with individuals who are residents of the EU.
3   Both data controllers (the party that owns the data) and data processors (the party that provides data processing services to the data controller) are liable for a GDPR breach. This is different to the EU Data Protection Directive in which only the data controllers were liable.
4   The maximum fine under the GDPR is €20 million or 4% of turnover, whichever's the greater. Under the previous EU Data Protection Directive this was just £500,000.
5   If you have not yet started to address GDPR compliance in your organisation, don't panic but do start to move.

References

BBC News (2000). Minor bug problems arise [online]. *BBC News*. Available at: http://news.bbc.co.uk/1/hi/sci/tech/586620.stm.

BBC News (2007). Nationwide fine for stolen laptop [online]. *BBC News*. Available at: http://news.bbc.co.uk/1/hi/business/6360715.stm.

Brand, G. (2015). How the Bosman rule changed football – 20 years on [online]. *Sky Sports*. Available at: www.skysports.com/football/news/11095/10100134/how-the-bosman-rule-changed-football-20-years-on.

Cottrell, S. (2018). *Results of Sport Sector GDPR Readiness Survey – Data Protection Report* [online]. LawInSport. Available at: www.lawinsport.com/announcements/item/sport-sector-gdpr-readiness-survey-2018.

Greenberg, P. (2001). *CRM at the Speed of Light*. Berkeley: Osborne.

ICO (2018). *Data Protection Act 1998 Supervisory Powers of the Information Commissioner Monetary Penalty Notice*. London: ICO.

Manchester United (2018). *Stay United Info*. [online]. Available at: www.manutd.com/en/Tickets-And-Hospitality/Stay-united-info [Accessed 1 February 2018].

McCormack, M. (1989). *What They Don't Teach You at Harvard Business School*. Toronto: Bantam Books.

Murphy, I. (2017). Everton FC signs Netskope for cybersecurity [online]. *Enterprise Times*. Available at: www.enterprisetimes.co.uk/2017/08/16/everton-fc-signs-netskope-cybersecurity.

Rothman, L. (2014). Remember Y2K? Here's how we prepped for the non-disaster [online]. *TIME*. Available at: http://time.com/3645828/y2k-look-back.

Schnater, B. (2018, 15 January), Personal interview.

Stevens, M. (2017). *Cybus Global Team Up with the Chiefs* [online]. Exeter Chiefs. Available at: www.exeterchiefs.co.uk/news/cybus-global-team-up-with-the-chiefs.

WFA (2017). *70% of Global Marketers are Not Fully Aware of the Implications of GDPR* [online]. WFA. Available at: www.wfanet.org/news-centre/70-of-global-marketers-are-not-fully-aware-of-the-implications-of-gdpr.

Chapter 10

Where do we go from here?

I thought long and hard about how best to end this book in a way that would give most value to you, the reader. I realised that if I tried to predict the future that wouldn't benefit anyone, as I'm no futurologist. Worse than that, I'm a data geek, so the only prophecy that has any value to me is one that's come out the other end of some predictive analytics process. With the pace of development in the digital world, by the time this book hits the shelves, makes it into your hands, and you get to Chapter 10, anything I say about the future of CRM may well already be the past. As a result, I decided to discuss a few areas of specific interest to me and, more importantly, highlight where, and how, they intertwine with this book's core subject matter.

Networked stadiums

For some years the use of Wi-Fi in sports stadiums has been considered a utility in the US. In the same way electricity and water are considered essential to staging a live event, so too is the use of an Internet connection for fans to share images, videos and emotions. However, this side of the pond, we've had a different situation, where clubs or venues were looking at the cost to install, as opposed to the long-term cost of not installing. But are things changing for European sports fans?

In 2014, fans of PSV Eindhoven famously protested against the use of Wi-Fi in the Philips Stadium (*The Guardian*, 2014), just a week after Manchester United banned fans from taking iPads into Old Trafford (Campbell, 2014). However, a November 2016 report suggested the market for 'smart stadiums' is to grow from $4 billion to $17 billion by 2021, with Europe representing the largest share – 44% (*PRNewswire*, 2017).

The fan-facing reasons for a networked stadium are clear. People expect to have access to the Internet, their social accounts and information on a 24/7 basis, including when they're in a stadium that has to go from a 1% capacity to 99% overnight. However, the upside for rights owners investing in networks can be significant, including increased revenue from the right sales message delivered to fans when a goal or point has been scored. Other direct revenue opportunities include digital signage, managed through stadium Wi-Fi, that advertisers pay so much more for when the ads are personalised, changing in relation to the audience in front of it, or the flow of the game/event. There is also scope for partnerships with online betting companies, of much greater value now that they offer fans in-game betting, as well as the option to get their money back before the end of a match. With more than 50% of purchases now made by card instead of cash, concession stands are able to provide a much better service thanks to their point-of-sale systems connecting to Wi-Fi (Jones, 2017).

But perhaps one of the most valuable opportunities, now that we know the value of data, is the ability to get contact details from those fans that haven't purchased their tickets online. Friends of the pack leader, recipients of gifts or corporate guests, they all tend to end up in a stadium without filling in any sort of form, so if they want to tweet the goal, or Facebook their photo, they have to log in to Wi-Fi first. And that's where we can collect their data.

Another opportunity is understanding fan behaviour when they're in the stadium; from knowing their traffic pattern around the concourse (if you also have beacons and other location identifiers), to watching their digital behaviour on your channels. All this data is unavailable to us unless stadium owners provide Wi-Fi. It may be costly, but it's a simple win that supports everything I've discussed so far.

The TV rights bubble: digital or bust?

For the 30+ years I've been in the sports industry the same topic has come up for discussion every few years (usually via attention-grabbing headlines), that the market for sports TV rights has imploded and the bubble has well and truly burst. But over the last few years that discussion has taken a path. It's not that the bubble has burst, it's just become a virtual bubble; it's gone digital.

The future of the TV rights market has become one of my favourite topics, because there's so much movement, so much speculation, and so much change on a continuous basis. From Amazon, Netflix, Facebook and Twitter buying sports rights, to rightsholders themselves delivering OTT services, the options are plentiful and, of course, there's still the traditional linear deals that have been in play since the 1950s.

Looking at just a few of the many deals made in 2017, we had several different business models where the rightsholder contracted with a third party:

- for live coverage of the 2017 Championship, the PGA combined linear with digital, issuing contracts to the BBC, Twitter and GiveMeSport for streaming on their Facebook page;
- having first secured the linear and digital rights from UEFA, BT Sport broadcast the Champions League and Europa League Finals live on YouTube.

After securing a contract with the NFL for the right to live stream ten games in the US, Amazon signed its first deal outside the US, taking the ATP World Tour rights away from SKY and providing their Prime customers with top-flight men's tennis (Sweney, 2017).

- Formula 1, who many believe were operating in the 'digital dark ages' under the 40-year reign of the deposed Bernie Eccleston, agreed a deal to live stream through Snapchat's 'Our Stories' service (Formula 1, 2017).

We also saw the launch of EFL's iFollow service, providing fans outside the UK with a live stream across their three divisions, hosted on their own website, not through a third party, at a cost of £110 per season. In the words of Drew Barrand, marketing director at EFL, 'In essence, we're becoming a broadcaster' (Connelly, 2017a).

This mirrors the NFL's GamePass, providing Europeans with multiple options for live or on-demand matches, and UFC's (Ultimate Fighting Championship) Fight Pass, which can be personalised by the user to follow a specific fighter. In an August 2017 interview, Chase Carey, Formula 1's CEO, also hinted at a possible launch of their own OTT product as 'one of three or even four potential arenas that [F1 is] engaged with' (Cooper, 2017).

So, while there are many different models involving third parties like digital and linear rights being sold to broadcasters, even non-broadcast media companies getting into the broadcast space, there are also rightsholders doing it for themselves, with major success.

But what's all this got to do with the use of CRM and data? When rights owners move away from linear channels to digital, not only do they give their fans a choice on how, when and for how long they watch, they collect information about them and their viewing habits. According to BT, not only did their YouTube broadcast of the 2017 Champions League Final increase their viewing figures by 1.8 million, they received data about every viewer that streamed the game. This gave them invaluable insight that will assist with future marketing planning (Connelly, 2017b). Amazon echoes this sentiment in support of their deal with the NFL. In an interview with Yahoo! Finance, Saurabh Sharma, Amazon's director of ad platforms, talked about how the data they'll generate from NFL viewers will support their advertising sales model, providing brands with behavioural data previously unavailable about fans of the sport (Roberts, 2017). Most importantly for me, if this is the future of the TV sports rights industry (sports fans having full control of their viewing behaviour via a digital platform), then the more rightsholders know about their fans, the more direct contact they have with them, the more control they'll have over their broadcasting future.

I'm not a sports media specialist (I've never sold a TV deal in my life), but I consume the coverage of this subject in the same way as anyone who wants to stay abreast of this fast-moving industry. When our clients ask me how they should consider their future in this area, my advice is quite clear: even if you, as a rightsholder, think you'll stay with the traditional model of selling, or contracting, your TV rights to a broadcaster, whether linear, digital or a combination of both over multiple channels, then, by having a rich and deep database of your fans, you'll have far more control over your broadcast negotiations. This approach works, regardless of the scale, as it is relevant for any audience. The principle is that if you can go OTT as a rights owner to the fan, and the business model justifies it, broadcasters will want to know about it.

Fans as your affinity marketing partners

One of the underlying themes of this book is the value of data and, more importantly, the data that you've acquired from your fans, participants, customers and other stakeholders. You're not the data owner, but you are the data controller, and you will have received permission from some, or most, of these 'data subjects' to use their data for the purposes you laid out in your opt-in process. I'd like to take that principle one step further and question if there's a business model that can be created from the existing relationship you have with your customers, and your status as holder of their data.

In the same way you might sign a license with a credit card company to use your logo, so for every cardholder they sign up you receive a royalty, could we turn that principle around and, for every fan that opts-in for you to sell their data, could you give them a share of the revenue you make from the sale of that data?

In February 2014 Datacoup launched their service to great fanfare, proposing that individuals 'unlock the value of your personal data' and using their platform to enable Datacoup to sell their personal data and give them a percentage of the proceeds. Early announcements suggested an individual could make $5 per month by signing up to their platform (Datacoup, 2013).

In Chapter 7 I talked about the importance of not handing over your fan data to your sponsors and that the value in your sponsorship was in the association with your brand. But if the monetisation of your fan data provided another revenue stream that could be re-invested in your athletes, stadium development or community programmes there might be a case to answer.

Augmented and virtual reality

Augmented reality (AR) and virtual reality (VR) are no longer new in sports, but do they reinvent the fan experience? There's been a lot of discussion, experimentation, delivery and analysis about the use of these technologies. They're a perfect marriage. They provide delivery of an enhanced or immersive experience in one of the few areas of our lives that we're often absolutely, totally and irrationally passionate about. With the financial prospect being a share of $80 billion by 2025 according to Goldman Sachs, it's no wonder we want a piece of it (Goldman Sachs, 2016).

First things first. I'll just remind us all of the difference between the two. Augmented reality superimposes digital elements onto a 'real world' situation, most commonly through the lens of a camera on a smartphone. Pokémon Go is perhaps the most well known of these, with 100 million downloads in the 13 months since its launch in July 2016 (Dogtiev, 2017).

Virtual reality involves the use of headsets to provide an all-encompassing experience where the user is positioned in an artificial environment that feels entirely realistic. Unlike AR it can't be experienced with just a smartphone but, to help spread its usage, Google has produced a cardboard viewer, and developers are busy making VR apps that can be used to great effect.

Rightsholders are already using AR and VR to bolster their offering.

- In the international world of soccer, Chelsea Football Club went first with the December 2016 launch of Chelsea Kicker. When a user opens the app their favourite player appears as you go on to access unlockable content and challenge friends who are also using the app (Shaw, 2016).
- MLB already have the most successful US Sports app (as measured in minutes consumed), At Bat, which sells for $19.99 and, while I don't know the number of users, it's opened an average 8 million times per day during the season. In 2018 they expect to be adding AR functionality that allows a user to point their phone at the ballpark and images of players, their stats, history of the visiting team, etc., appear for their fans' enjoyment (Ortiz, 2017).
- BT Sport, a relative newcomer to the world of sports broadcasting, placed a stake in the ground with resounding emphasis when they broadcast the 2017 UEFA Champions League Final in 4K, provided it for free via BT Sport's mobile app or YouTube, and produced a VR feed to use with a cardboard Google headset. All at no cost to the viewer! No VR numbers have been published but we know an extra 500,000 viewers watched the 2017 Final via BT Sport over the previous season for a total of 6.5 million (McCaskill, 2017).
- The DFB (German Football Association) is using VR to help their national team prepare for the 2018 FIFA World Cup. Their current focus is on helping goalkeepers with set moves. It's not a fan engagement play, but if they win the tournament as a result of this there will be a lot of very happy fans. And, who knows, at a later date they may release the content as some form of exclusive opportunity to reward loyalty (Katzowitz, 2017).

It's clear that AR and VR are only going to play an ever-increasing role in our world so they do have the potential to reinvent the fan experience, but the point I want to make is that, while we might get carried away with the customer experience and the record-breaking firsts, we need to remember some fundamentals: using data to design and promote the experience (what we know about our fans, their interests, behaviour and needs), then using the application itself to collect more data, has to be a KPI. It can't just be about the number of downloads and minutes of usage. It has to support our cross-organisational objectives. Data has to be key.

Blockchain and sports data

Blockchain technology, invented by an anonymous person or group of people who use the name Satoshi Nakamoto, is a continuously growing list of records, or 'blocks', which are linked together and secured using cryptography, a security method that ensures only those individuals who are supposed to have access to the records can do so. The most well-known use of a blockchain for the transfer of data is Bitcoin, the digital currency system that's currently used by an estimate of between 13 million and 28.5 million users around the world (Lielacher, 2018).

There are other uses of blockchain technology in evidence. For example, British Airways, FedEx, UPS and Walmart use it to track their incredibly complex supply chain (Krauth, 2018). Even in sport, SportyCo is providing a crowdfunding platform that will use Bitcoin to help athletes with funding (Sharpe, 2018), and there's an ice hockey arena in Denmark that will shortly be named the Bitcoin Arena (Redman, 2017).

Blockchain technology is managed directly in a peer-to-peer network that can't be amended retroactively, unless every party in the block is collaborating. To this extent it's considered incorruptible. If this is the case then there's a real opportunity to consider its use for the transfer and storage of data. Consider the range of applications you currently use across the different suppliers that support your business and their role in managing your data for different business units and purposes. With the obligations we're now under with the GDPR, it would make sense that we turn to a technology such as blockchain that can provide us with the security we need, but the ability to involve different parties along the way.

In reality, the growth of blockchain into mainstream usage will be incredibly slow. While the processes currently used by businesses using Bitcoin for currency exchange take just a microsecond (hence the reason for immediate adoption by the finance industry), the actual settlement of the transaction can take as long as a week. The actual technology involved is incredibly complex and so a lot of experimentation will be needed to develop the appropriate use case for an individual business or industry sector. As we discussed in Chapter 8 on Business Change, it takes time for organisations to adapt to new ways of doing things.

With this in mind I can say that, without a doubt, there will be a blockchain for rightsholders dealing with personal data, and it will become a foundational technology for the sports industry. I just don't know when that might be.

Analytics 3.0

In Chapter 4 I refer to Analytics 1.0 as the appropriate era for most rights owners, and 2.0 as the province of Silicon Valley companies such as Google,

Netflix and Spotify. With this in mind, does the sports industry have a need for analytics 3.0, or will that be a stage at which the cost to deliver outweighs the business benefits?

The general definition of analytics 3.0 is the point at which the use of analytics is prevalent across your entire business operation. Data is collected on every device, customer, stakeholder or action. To achieve this, organisations need the right technological infrastructure, which means a level of computing power that can handle complex calculations. But they also need the business requirement and I'm not sure the sports industry has that, or if indeed we ever will.

The possible caveat to that is the depth to which we can push athlete performance data. Will we ever be able to connect a thought process with an emotion and therefore with a physical action? And, more importantly, if we can do that, will the outcome of analysing that data enable us to influence an athlete's response to the extent it will make the difference between winning and losing? When you think about Chelsea FC finishing the 2016/2017 season as Premier League champions, and that it netted them £152 million just in prize money, then it has to be worth looking at (Total Sportek, 2017).

Here's another one: if FC Barcelona's 101 million Facebook followers could actually be converted into records within their own database, with all the rich data that would accompany these fans every time they posted or liked, these fans' actions could be tracked, not just across Barca's digital estate, but across the entire web. In turn, they could be converted into customers of content, merchandise or the club's sponsors. In this case analytics 3.0 is indeed an option.

Sports industry professional Ben Wells has written a lot about the importance of data, particularly for a sports club model. In a phone interview on 12 January 2018 he shared his opinions with me.

> Data on its own is not the answer, but it's a pretty big part of the solution. Sports organisations need to understand that theirs is a model which is atrophying: as they only have a limited number of products to offer (tickets, merchandise), they can only commercialise a tiny constituency, i.e., those interested in those products. To build a greater diversification in their revenue streams they need to behave less like sports organisations and more like lifestyle brands, creating natural brand extensions which appeal to a wider demography. That larger audience will be potentially interesting to a broader suite of commercial partners. This is where data comes in. Investing in building a more dynamic model, which sees matchday as a means to an end (rather than the be all and end all) and which enables the organisation to engage with a varied customer set year round, regardless of location, should be their nirvana.
>
> Sport has an unparalleled ability to connect with people but for too long has relied on 'passion' as a business driver. At the same time the shift of brand spend to digital platforms is effectively a 'who's got the most

efficient algorithm' competition and forgets that ultimately we are all trying to connect with human beings. Harnessing that human emotion and allying it with a smart approach to data should allow the industry to fight back.

(Wells, 2018, 12 January)

Artificial intelligence, machine learning and neural networks

Artificial intelligence (AI) is, at its most basic, the use of computers to simulate human intelligence to enable them to perform tasks. The most popular and well-known examples of this are Siri and Alexa, Apple and Amazon's voice-activated digital assistants. But, did you know that AI has been around for as long as computers themselves? In fact, if you read Pamela McCorduck's 2004 book *Machines Who Think*, you could believe her position that efforts to mechanise human thinking began in ancient history 'with myths, stories and rumours of artificial beings endowed with intelligence or consciousness by master craftsmen' (McCorduck, 2004).

Machine learning is a form of AI that allows computers to learn from data, example and experience, almost like a human. Rather than following pre-programmed rules, applications powered by machine-learning algorithms carry out complex processes by learning from a previous process. Machine learning has also been around far longer than you'd expect, with the term coined by American pioneer Arthur Lee Samuel (Samuel, 1959).

Unlike AI and machine learning, neural networks are a more recent phenomenon, a form of machine learning used for pattern recognition and tasks involving prediction. The algorithms are modelled to reflect the way the human brain processes information and, because of this, they have the potential to identify more of the subtle nuances of human thought that traditional algorithms miss.

We've already seen high-profile examples of AI. Back in July 2016 the NBA launched their chatbot for Facebook Messenger and, while the early version didn't quite live up to the AI hype, they were one of the first movers in sport (McCormick, 2016). Just a year later, in July 2017, this approach to fan engagement using AI had evolved quite significantly. *Bloomberg* reported that IBM's AI agent Watson was used to power a voice-activated customer service bot called Ask Fred (named after tennis great Fred Perry) at Wimbledon, one of the four Grand Slam tennis tournaments. App users could ask Fred for directions to the nearest merchandise store or the nearest place they could find strawberries. In addition to Fred, IBM also used AI to automatically compile highlights videos and use indicators such as the crowd's reaction, analysing the quantity and sentiment of social media posts, the players' facial expressions, and the importance of a particular play on the outcome of a game (Kahn, 2017).

When you consider the incredible power of neural networks to incorporate sentiment analysis, sports and AI it is a match made in heaven – fans have an abundance of passion and aren't afraid to show it. The future for the use of AI in the sports industry is vast and, with the global market expected to reach USD 1.25 billion by 2025 (*Businesswire*, 2017), I expect that whatever rights owners are not currently investigating in this area, they will be soon. However, creating your AI proposition starts with having data in the first place.

Which brings us back in a full circle to the start of this book.

Conclusion

My intention in writing this book was to provide you with a whistle-stop round-the-world-tour of CRM as a business strategy. It can seem quite complex when you're looking at it from the outside, but, by providing some key areas in bite-sized chunks, I hope that you have now had a glimpse of the main areas of consideration for a rights owner operating in the sports industry. We don't have the scale of operation that demands an Amazon-approach to CRM and data, but we do have the same need and intent to service our customers well. We want them to come back for more. If you're a specialist then I'd like to think I've helped tie together some of the missing pieces for you, and helped you understand how your role affects other individuals operating within your businesses. Most of all, I hope I've made the process both interesting and easy.

The key message to take with you is that CRM is not just about software. Even data analysis is not just about data. To implement a data-driven approach you need five key elements to be aligned within your business: strategy, data, technology, process and culture; the Perfect Circle. Without it, your approach will not achieve the same level of success.

I also urge you, if you haven't already done so, to start thinking about how you can achieve your holy grail; a Single Customer View that provides you with a holistic view of all your customers in one database. If you already have an SCV in place then perhaps you're ready to consider upgrading to incorporate unknown and unstructured data into your environment and look at a DMP or CDP.

The data you have in your organisation about your stakeholders and the way you collect, store and use it will be the game changer for the future of your businesses. I can't overstate this. It's unparalleled in its importance to your future. While your number one priority will always be your sport, you need a sustainable infrastructure and business model to ensure its growth and longevity.

Once you have that data, not only will you be empowered to communicate with your fans, customers, participants and other stakeholders with personalised content that maintains their attention, you'll have the tools to make fact-based decisions that will improve your ROI or ROO. You'll also be able to engage with your fans on a highly personalised level, getting the right message, to the right person, at the right time. Your partners will also benefit as you provide your sponsors with enhanced leverage opportunities that add another dimension to their activation plans.

The pace of technological change is constantly increasing and, while you're not expected to be an early adopter (your business needs neither require nor support that), you at least need to swim in the same lane. You can only achieve this by embracing ideas and collaborating with your colleagues to implement the ones that are right for you. In this digital world we can test, fail, test again, learn and, ultimately, improve.

The future for you, and the future for sports rights owners, is exciting. The future is data.

References

Businesswire (2017). Global chatbot market – expected to reach $1.2 billion by 2025 [online]. *Businesswire*. Available at: www.businesswire.com/news/home/20171030 005639/en/Global-Chatbot-Market---Expected-Reach-1.2.

Campbell, P. (2014). As Manchester United ban iPads from Old Trafford, what else should go? [online]. *The Guardian*. Available at: www.theguardian.com/football/blog/2014/aug/12/manchester-united-ban-fans-ipads-tablet-devices-old-trafford.

Connelly, T. (2017a). EFL broadens digital revenue streams with launch of live streaming platform [online]. *The Drum*. Available at: www.thedrum.com/news/2017/05/04/efl-broadens-digital-revenue-streams-with-launch-live-streaming-platform.

Connelly, T. (2017b). BT Sport to show free 360 degree VR live stream of Champions League final on YouTube [online]. *The Drum*. Available at: www.thedrum.com/news/2017/05/16/bt-sport-show-free-360-degree-vr-live-stream-champions-league-final-youtube.

Cooper, A. (2017). Chase Carey says Formula 1's TV options have 'conflicting goals' [online] *Autosport*. Available at: www.autosport.com/f1/news/131265/f1EUR TMs-tv-options-have-EUR~conflicting-goalsEURTM.

Datacoup (2013). *Datacoup – Reclaim Your Personal Data* [online]. Datacoup. Available at: https://datacoup.com [Accessed 16 February 2018].

Dogtiev, A. (2017). Pokémon GO revenue and usage statistics [online]. *Business of Apps*. Available at: www.businessofapps.com/data/pokemon-go-statistics.

Formula 1 (2017). *Formula 1 and Snap Inc. Announce New Global Partnership* [online]. Formula 1. Available at: www.formula1.com/en/latest/headlines/2017/7/formula-1--and-snap-inc--announce-new-global-partnership-.html.

Goldman Sachs (2016). *The Real Deal with Virtual and Augmented Reality* [video]. Goldman Sachs. Available at: www.goldmansachs.com/our-thinking/pages/virtual-and-augmented-reality.html.

Jones, R. (2017). Cash no longer king as contactless payments soar in UK stores [online]. *The Guardian*. Available at: www.theguardian.com/money/2017/jul/12/cash-contactless-payments-uk-stores-cards-british-retail-consortium.

Kahn, J. (2017). Wimbledon to use IBM's Watson AI for highlights, analytics, helping fans [online]. *Bloomberg*. Available at: www.bloomberg.com/news/articles/2017-06-27/wimbledon-to-use-ibm-s-watson-ai-for-highlights-analytics-helping-fans.

Katzowitz, J. (2017). The German national team will use VR to train, and it could change soccer [online] *The Daily Dot*. Available at: www.dailydot.com/debug/virtual-reality-germany-national-soccer-team-strivr.

Krauth, O. (2018). 5 companies using blockchain to drive their supply chain [online]. *Tech Republic*. Available at: www.techrepublic.com/article/5-companies-using-blockchain-to-drive-their-supply-chain/

Lielacher, A. (2018). How many people use Bitcoin? Updated for 2018 [online]. *Bitcoin Market Journal*. Available at: www.bitcoinmarketjournal.com/how-many-people-use-bitcoin.

McCaskill, S. (2017). BT Sport: from young upstart to UK sports broadcasting's top innovator [online]. *Silicon UK*. Available at: www.silicon.co.uk/networks/broadband/bt-sport-tech-220201/2?inf_by=5a2d6423681db89c5e8b48aa.

McCorduck, P. (2004). *Machines Who Think*. Natick: A.K. Peters.

McCormick, R. (2016). NBA rolls out Facebook Messenger chatbot to give you Finals highlights on demand [online]. *The Verge*. Available at: www.theverge.com/2016/6/2/11848874/nba-rolls-out-facebook-messenger-chatbot-to-give-you-finals.

Ortiz, J. (2017). MLB plans to add augmented reality to 'At Bat' app [online]. *USA Today*. Available at: www.usatoday.com/story/sports/mlb/2017/09/25/mlb-at-bat-app-statcast-augmented-reality/699104001.

PRNewswire (2017). Smart stadium market by software, service, platform, deployment model – global forecast to 2021 [online]. *PRNewswire*. Available at: www.prnewswire.com/news-releases/smart-stadium-market-by-software-service-platform-deployment-model---global-forecast-to-2021-300425108.html.

Redman, J. (2017). *Danish Billionaire Renames the Rungsted Capital Ice Rink to 'Bitcoin Arena'* [online]. Bitcoin.com. Available at: https://news.bitcoin.com/danish-billionaire-renames-the-rungsted-capital-ice-rink-to-bitcoin-arena.

Roberts, D. (2017). Amazon's NFL streaming is all about collecting ad data [online]. *Yahoo*. Available at: www.yahoo.com/amphtml/finance/news/amazon-streaming-nfl-games-collecting-ad-data-110006168.html.

Samuel, A. (1959). Some studies in machine learning using the game of checkers. *IBM Journal of Research and Development*, 3(3), 210–229.

Sharpe, K. (2018). Blockchain platform to help promising athletes to jump financial hurdles [online]. *CoinTelegraph*. Available at: https://cointelegraph.com/news/blockchain-platform-to-help-promising-athletes-to-jump-financial-hurdles.

Shaw, S. (2016). *Chelsea FC launches first augmented reality football game* [online]. *SportTechie*. Available at: www.sporttechie.com/chelsea-fc-launches-sporting-worlds-first-ar-game.

Sweney, M. (2017). Amazon outbids Sky to win exclusive ATP tour tennis rights [online]. *The Guardian*. Available at: www.theguardian.com/media/2017/aug/01/amazon-outbids-sky-to-win-exclusive-atp-tour-tennis-rights.

The Guardian (2014). PSV Eindhoven fans protest against introduction of Wi-Fi at stadium [online]. *The Guardian*. Available at: www.theguardian.com/football/2014/aug/18/psv-fans-protest-against-wifi-access.

Total Sportek (2017). *Premier League Prize Money 2017 (Confirmed)* [online]. Total Sportek. Available at: www.totalsportek.com/money/premier-league-prize-money.

Wells, B. (2018, 12 January). Telephone interview.

Index